The Coming British Revolution

by the same author

PAKISTAN: MILITARY RULE OR PEOPLE'S POWER

The Coming
British Revolution

TARIQ ALI

Jonathan Cape Thirty Bedford Square London

FIRST PUBLISHED 1972
FIRST PUBLISHED IN THIS FORMAT 1972
© 1972 BY TARIQ ALI

JONATHAN CAPE LTD, 30 BEDFORD SQUARE, LONDON WCI

ISBN Hardback 0 224 00630 4
Paperback 0 224 00653 3

Condition of Sale

PRINTED IN GREAT BRITAIN
BY EBENEZER BAYLIS AND SON LTD
THE TRINITY PRESS, WORCESTER, AND LONDON
ON PAPER MADE BY JOHN DICKINSON AND CO. LTD
BOUND BY RICHARD CLAY (THE CHAUCER PRESS) LTD
BUNGAY, SUFFOLK

Contents

Preface

This book is not intended as a definitive study of the processes which will make or mar the British revolution. Its purpose is much more modest: simply to open a discussion on some of the problems confronting revolutionaries in Britain. For this reason the book only touches on certain issues which need discussing in much more detail elsewhere. Also it is biased in favour of revolution, a fact which I think will not surprise too many readers.

I would like to thank the following militants of the Spartacus League and the International Marxist Group (the British Section of the Fourth International) who read some of the chapters and suggested certain useful alterations but are in no way responsible for the final product, which is my own responsibility: Patrick Jordan, Julian Atkinson, Peter Gowan, John Ross, David Kendall, Tony Southall, Jane Shallice, Brian Davey, Leonora Lloyd and Bob Purdie.

In addition I would like to thank my comrades on the editorial board of *The Red Mole* for their patience and tolerance while this book was being written, and for their constant harassment, which ensured that the book was completed quickly.

London, April 1971   TARIQ ALI

To the memory of two great revolutionaries
who fought and died in the struggle against
British imperialism :

JAMES CONNOLLY

and

JOHN MACLEAN

Introduction

For large numbers of people in Britain the very idea of a socialist revolution in this country, involving a certain degree of violence, is unthinkable. Decades of bourgeois mystification combined with the very real strength of British imperialism in the past has played a certain role in creating this consciousness. However, the situation is changing, and the realization that capitalism in Britain should have been swept away by a revolution fifty years ago is beginning to dawn in the minds of increasing numbers of people. Two world wars are but part of the price which the British workers have had to pay for the absurd survival of capitalism. How long can it go on? What would destroy it, and what forms will this destruction take? Despite the failings of capitalism, what guarantees are there that the system which replaces it will be any better? These are a few of the questions which are raised whenever revolution is discussed, and because capitalism's problems are so glaringly obvious they are being raised more and more frequently.

Over the last two years the intensity of the class struggle in Britain (and on a world scale, as the two are interrelated) has escalated at a phenomenal pace. In 1970 there were more days lost through strikes—nearly eleven million—than in any year since the 1926 General Strike. The first three months of 1971 saw more days lost than in the whole of the previous year and the largest political demonstration of workers since the last war took place on February 21st, 1971, on a specifically political issue: the Industrial Relations Bill of the Tory government. In Northern Ireland, the struggle has reached a stage where Edward Heath is forced to confront the threat of 'urban guerilla warfare', not in Latin America, but within the confines

of the (so-called) United Kingdom. Rolls-Royce, the very
symbol of the strength and stability of British capitalism,
dramatically collapses, surprising even some groups on the left.
(Thus an anti-Tory-Bill poster showing the front of a Rolls-
Royce with the slogan FINE FOR THEM, FINES FOR US, was
happily dated.) The second largest motor-insurance company
soon followed suit. The dramatic collapse of U.C.S. (Upper
Clyde Shipbuilders) — a historic symbol of Britain's shipbuilding
industry — came soon after and on the revolutionary left bets
are laid as to which big company will be the next to bite the
dust as Britain prepares to enter the Common Market. In
addition, orders for machine tools, a reliable guide to investment
intentions, slumped by about 50 per cent in 1970, and one of
the theoretical journals of British industry, *Management Today*,
claims that a recession is inevitable despite all government
intentions. Unemployment rises rapidly and could well reach
the million mark by the end of 1971, and the Tory government
attempts to keep wage increases down to a level which will
ensure a cut in living standards. In order to make sure that the
working class is really demoralized the Tories institute cuts in
social services and prepare to shackle the unions. The more
oppressed workers — the blacks — are hammered by yet another
racist Immigration Bill, which provides specifically for ways to
keep black workers out of militant politics. Foreign students are
deported (Dutschke and Hoch) in order to prevent any alien
virus from further infecting the British student movement.

But the subjective designs or wishes of British capitalism are
not capable of overcoming its innermost contradictions, which
follow from the mode of production (private property), of distribution (market economy) and of the exigencies of the class
struggle. British capitalism's continued inability to close the gap
between itself and its rivals forces it to consider entry into the
European Economic Community. In doing so it admits that
the era of national capitalism on a European scale is over and
that the only way to face up to the challenge posed by United
States capital is to unite European capitalism by beginning to

unify their trade policies, their capital, their currencies and eventually their state apparatuses, with all that the latter entails. Thus British capital tries to buy a medium-term solution for itself in answer to the crisis knocking at its door. It is prepared to suppress internal rivalries, to combine ancient competitors and even to sacrifice certain sectors of its own class for a 'common cause' which the latter refuse to accept. Entry into the Common Market means entering on terms least harmful to British capitalism and thus the latter attempts to improve its position by attacking the British working class at the cost of sacrificing two aspects of the 'affluent' Britain: the welfare state and full employment. This is not simply a nasty Tory policy (those who think so should compare it to Tory policy in 1951), but reflects the changed circumstances of British capital. The Tories are continuing the policies whose foundation was firmly laid by the Wilson government during its time in office.

However, the Common Market with Britain integrated in it could well increase the scale of the crisis; as the economic integration of capitalist Europe, with all its contradictions, draws nearer, upsurges of mass action will increasingly be linked with each other and will leap from one country to another in a much more synchronized fashion. Far from solving the problems of the British ruling class, the Common Market could well exacerbate them and open the British working class to the influence of its more political and militant counterparts in France and Italy.

It could be argued that British capitalism has been in a crisis before; that it was in a much more precarious situation during the mass workers' upsurges in Scotland, for example, immediately after the First World War. That is certainly true. However, the situation today is in a sense much more optimistic because of the international balance of class forces. It is not necessary to map out the large areas of the world which have liberated themselves from the tyranny of the world capitalist market, or to write about the continuing successes of the Indo-Chinese revolution, or the extension of the struggle in Latin

America. Two events in Western Europe itself have demonstrated to the ruling classes that the spectre of socialist revolution is still there, and their efforts to exorcize it have not been successful. The revolt in France in May 1968 showed the potentiality of both revolutionary intellectuals and the working class — the decisive agency of social change. The following year saw fifteen million workers on strike in Italy (autumn–winter 1969–70), challenging the authority of the bourgeois state. The magnitude and the scope of these upsurges was such as to leave only the blind and deaf in any doubt as to the revolutionary potential of the working class even in the more developed capitalist countries.

There is no general reason to believe that Britain will remain immune to this process. Certainly in many ways Britain is different from the rest of Western Europe, but there is no such thing as British 'exceptionalism'. The present ideas of British workers are not permanent; they are capable of change, depending on the change in the objective conditions. For instance the February 21st demonstration in 1971, in which nearly 150,000 workers participated, was something which could not have been visualized by the 'learned' commentators in the bourgeois press in 1965. The problems faced by British and European workers are different from those that are faced by the ruling class. Whereas the latter, despite its political shrewdness and sophistication, cannot in the long term salvage the decaying social system by which it governs, the workers are burdened with a right-wing leadership, both in their trade unions and in the political parties which they have traditionally supported. This has prevented and sabotaged the growth of political awareness, revolutionary consciousness and revolutionary action. Because it is impossible to deny the fact that the potential of the working class is immense. The trade-union bureaucrats, whether they are tied to social-democratic or Stalinist parties, act to deflect working-class militancy when it seeks to transcend the prescribed limits of seeking higher wages and limited reforms. Thus the last defenders of capitalism, who continue to prop up a decaying social order, appear from within the ranks of the working class itself. In Britain they owe allegiance to the Labour Party; in France and Italy they parade under the stolen banners of communism. These labour lieutenants of capital shit with fear when workers move into big struggles and begin to set up their own democratic organizations. But the workers are hampered by the fact that the very conditions in which they work (division of labour and commodity production) make it difficult for them to have a very clear understanding of what socialism means or of how the grip of the capitalist class can really be broken. Thus it is necessary to prepare them for the struggle by constant propaganda, which becomes meaningful to them in periods of struggle arising from a pre-revolutionary situation.

For the ideas of the mass of workers change only in the concrete process of the struggle itself, but this change is in itself not sufficient unless a revolutionary organization rooted in the working class exists and is capable of utilizing the change to lay the base (dual power) for a revolutionary confrontation with the bourgeois state. Lenin understood this fact better than most of his comrades and wrote in 1905:

> Revolutions are festivals of the oppressed and the exploited ... At such times the people are capable of performing miracles, if judged by the limited, philistine yardstick of gradualist progress. But it is essential that leaders of revolutionary parties, too, should advance their aims more comprehensively and boldly at such a time, so that their slogans shall always be in advance of the revolutionary initiative of the masses ...

Thus the most formidable task facing the revolutionary movement is to aid in the destruction of the reformist and treacherous leaderships of the working-class movement, which have always betrayed the interests of the workers. An excellent example of this was the refusal of the T.U.C. to call a general strike to defend the workers against the capitalist onslaught contained in

2

the Industrial Relations Bill. In fact the General Secretary of the T.U.C., Vic Feather, sought a meeting with the Prime Minister to advise him on the necessity of working out an incomes policy (or in simpler language, wage restraint). What a grotesque proposal from someone who is supposed to represent the interests of the workers! A further example of how even the so-called 'left' trade unions 'struggle' is the way Hugh Scanlon and Jack Jones restrict the fight against the Tory government to the bureaucratic level and tamely accept the T.U.C. decisions, instead of waging a big campaign amongst the rank and file for increased militancy. The task of preparing a new and revolutionary leadership is therefore extremely important, because without it we will have big upsurges, without a doubt, but no victories. The survival of British capitalism, therefore, depends to a certain extent on the inability to develop a revolutionary leadership and challenge existing institutions.

We have to be clear that the only force capable of destroying capitalism is the British working class. It is heavily imbued with bourgeois ideology, and a central theme of this ideology is the example presented by the Soviet Union. It is only too easy to underestimate today the electrifying effect which the Russian Revolution had on the European working class. Even the foremost labour lieutenants of capital in Britain were forced to declare their solidarity with this revolution and mobilize the British workers against any attempt at a major British intervention against the infant Soviet state. The victory of the Stalin faction inside the U.S.S.R. after the death of Lenin and the subsequent degeneration of the Russian Revolution with the establishment of a bureaucratic *caste*, came as a gift from heaven to the British bourgeoisie and particularly to leaders of the British Labour Party. They could quite simply point to the example of the Soviet Union and hold it up as an example of socialism. Huge labour camps, purges, the destruction of all the old Bolshevik leaders and the methods used to destroy the kulaks did not entirely endear the Russian Revolution to the European working class. And when Stalin and his apologists

(i.e. the Communist Parties in Europe and the U.S.A.) presented this as socialism, the workers in capitalist countries were
completely disoriented and became extremely vulnerable to
anti-communist propaganda. While the growing radicalization
of youth has undoubtedly modified the situation somewhat, it
still remains a fact that communism is equated with the Soviet
Union and Eastern Europe and all that this entails. Sometimes
the personality cult of Mao appears on the scene as well, but
in general it is the degeneration of the Russian Revolution
which remains a central theme in the consciousness of the
working class. It is interesting to note that when the Soviet
Armies defeated fascism during the Second World War and
demonstrated the advantages of the socialized base of the
Soviet Union, which despite the bureaucratized superstructure
could sustain a long war, there was an upsurge throughout
Europe. It was successfully deflected in France and Italy by
the Communist Parties of those two countries collaborating
with their bourgeoisies and joining 'national governments'. In
Britain the radicalization of the working class was shown in the
massive victory of the Labour Party. One should remember that
the latter campaigned as the party which could maintain
friendly relations with the Soviet Union. (The British Communist Party was in favour of Churchill continuing in power
as the head of a National Government, but British social-
democracy proved to be slightly to the left in this instance and
demanded a general election!) The defeat of the European
working class, thanks to the class-collaborationist policies
of the Stalinists after the Second World War which allowed
capitalism to stabilize itself, further delayed the advent of the
revolution. An understanding of the processes which led to the
degeneration of the Russian Revolution is therefore extremely
important, as in periods of upsurge the workers will demand all
the answers. There are, of course, easy ways out of this (like
arguing, for instance, that Soviet society is a new form of
capitalism). However, these demoralize the working class and
restrict the development of political consciousness, as the only

future seems to be between different forms of capitalism, and the nature of our epoch is therefore no longer admitted to be revolutionary. But equally important is the fact that unless one understands the degeneration of the Russian Revolution one cannot explain to the working class why such a degeneration is ruled out today (cf. Trotsky, *The Revolution Betrayed* [Merit, 1937]).

It is ludicrous to imagine that British workers who made a revolution today would be presented with the same situation as faced Soviet Russia in 1917. The very fact that we have constantly to explain this demonstrates the tragedy of the defeat of the German Revolution in the years following the First World War. A revolution in an industrialized country would have shown the rest of industrialized Europe an image of its future and at the same time prevented the degeneration of the Russian Revolution. Britain is an advanced industrial country where the workers constitute the largest and rapidly expanding social class (cf. Chapter 2). The young workers, in particular, have known comparatively full employment, 'affluence' and strong trade-union practices, and have not experienced any really big defeat (for example the 1926 General Strike, two world wars, Stalinism). Virtually everyone can read and write: thus the cultural level is today very different from that of Czarist Russia. It is not possible that workers who have enjoyed bourgeois democratic rights would make a revolution which left them even fewer rights than they enjoyed before. The exact opposite would be the case, even if a counter-revolutionary intervention took place. Workers who have seen through the charade of Parliament and the manipulative aspects of the mass media are not going to replace these institutions with others more restrictive or manipulative. In fact the British Revolution would improve the quality of life as a whole and give rise to new institutions and new cultural forms which it is even difficult to conceive of at the moment. One could even say that a revolution in Britain or any part of Western Europe would be able to give a tremendous impetus to workers in the Soviet Union and the rest of Eastern Europe and present them with a revolutionary alternative which would enable them to overthrow the bureaucracy and restore workers' democracy, with the free interplay of all working-class parties and tendencies. Thus, far from degenerating, a British revolution would lead to the end of degeneration in the Soviet Union itself, as well as act as a powerful boost to the revolutionary movements in Asia, Africa and, to a lesser extent, Latin America.

Many people still seem to doubt that Britain is in a crisis and feel that the situation will be stabilized once again as it was after the Second World War. Certainly this is a short-term possibility (particularly if Britain enters the Common Market), but the structural problems of British capitalism could only begin to be sorted out if the working-class organizations in Britain were viciously smashed. The attempt to solve the chronic problems of British imperialism through a Labour government pledged to 'put Britain back on its feet again' by integrating the trade unions into neo-capitalist planning ended in complete failure. Far from taming the trade unions, the Labour government stimulated a huge wave of wage-militancy and was compelled to withdraw its anti-trade-union proposals. The Tories, who have picked up where Labour left off, might be able to inflict temporary setbacks on the workers' movement, but they are no more capable than their predecessors of solving all the accumulated problems of British imperialism. An excellent indication of their decline on the political-military plane is their total inability to rescue a British ambassador kidnapped by the Tupamaros in Uruguay. In the old days a firm display of strength would have sorted out 'the natives'. Even when the Industrial Relations Bill becomes law and the Tories are able to limit severely the rise in the standard of living by inflicting defeats on the trade unions, they will not solve their problems. Apart from everything else, the scabs' charter they want to make law has a certain logic of its own: by intervening frequently in wage negotiations they undermine bourgeois democracy itself by making it obvious that the state is not 'neutral'.

This in turn begins to politicize vanguard layers inside the working class and thus prepare for new forms of action and struggle, which will tend to bypass the bureaucratized trade-union structures. In that sense Harold Wilson was correct when he referred to the Tory Bill as a 'Trots charter'. (We are pleased to note that Mr Wilson knows who the real enemies of capitalism are!) But a simple increase of political consciousness will not be sufficient unless it develops into a realization that to seize power the working class needs its own political organization—a party of revolution. That's why the construction of a revolutionary party and a revolutionary International is the key task for an overthrow of capitalism in Britain and in Western Europe. The objective conditions will occur time and time again, but unless a new revolutionary leadership rises and is accepted by the vanguard layers of the working class, the result will be defeat.

That is why we don't make sensational forecasts or prepare a time schedule for revolution and a draft blueprint for the future socialist society. The time for forecasts has not yet arrived and will only arrive when a revolutionary party begins to take shape and command the allegiance of vanguard layers inside the British working class. This party will develop not arithmetically, by the odd recruit here or a group of students there, but will grow organically out of the mass struggles which take place. A revolutionary party cannot come into being simply by a thousand or so people getting together, proclaiming its existence and de-claring themselves the vanguard simply on the strength of a political programme. The latter is indeed vital, but its possession does not necessarily imply its fruition. History is littered with examples of dedicated revolutionaries, who have sown dragon's teeth only to harvest flies, and we must learn from these experiences. Therefore one can say categorically that no revolutionary party can exist outside the working class. At best there can exist the nucleus of such a party or the fragments of such a nucleus; and that is what all the extreme left groups constitute today, despite pretensions to the contrary by some of them.

The question of a revolutionary party becomes all the more important as many workers begin to see through the Labour Party. The latter is still recovering from the haemorrhage of its six years in office. Nearly one-third of the constituencies did not send delegates to the 1970 Labour Party conference. The Wilson leadership is so deeply committed to British capitalism, and the task of helping it solve its problems, that the Labour Party has been unable to make a demagogic 'shift to the left' as it was able to do after 1951. Small wonder then that up till now no significant section of the working class has called for the return of a Labour government. Even the trade-union bureaucrats prefer to rely on their own strength and deal directly with the Tories rather than mediate their intervention through the Labour Party. Of course, this situation could change rapidly: for instance a defeat of the working class at the hands of the Tories could result in a return to Labourism and be reflected in an electoral campaign designed to return Labour to power. However, the precise nature of capitalism's crisis necessitates certain nasty decisions, and if the Labour Party were back in power it would very soon expose itself completely to the mass of workers for what it is—a thoroughly bourgeois prop of British capitalism. Once this was out of the way, the task of building a revolutionary party would become that much easier.

Revolutions are always unpredictable. They have their own laws, their own methods of leaping from one part of the world to another. Thus the effect of the 1968 Tet Offensive of the Vietnamese resounded in the streets of Paris in May 1968, and the May Revolt in its turn decisively affected the social and political explosions in Italy in 1969–70. The struggle in the Six Counties of Ireland, occupied at the moment by British imperialism and its puppets, could well overflow into Southern Ireland and expose the Green Tories (all varieties) in Dublin, paving the way for the first socialist workers' republic in Western Europe. This could have dynamic consequences in Britain. But without entering into the field of speculation, we can say that even the behaviour of British troops in Ireland is a good indication that they could easily be used against the workers in Britain itself, provided the workers' struggle showed signs of seriously damaging the bourgeoisie. Thus if a whole series of factories, or even some small cities (for instance Port Talbot, St Helens or Stafford), are occupied by the workers and the latter set up their own elected councils to run them, a show of force could become necessary to prevent the example from spreading to the large industrial centres. The whole question of an insurrection is thus posed, and once again we return to the nub of the matter: who will prepare the insurrection (for this is an art, and needs careful preparation)? Who will preach its necessity? Who will provide experienced cadres to direct military operations? The answers lie in the existence of a revolutionary party. What will happen if such a party does not exist? Will there be a complete disaster if there is a revolutionary upsurge without the existence of a revolutionary party? Only a hardened and dogmatic sectarian could reply in the negative to the latter question.

Even when a revolutionary upsurge ends in defeat, it is an undoubted step forward. It gives the workers an idea of the problems they face. It gives them an entirely new experience, totally different from their alienated everyday existence, and advances their consciousness tenfold. Even when there is a return to 'business as usual' the workers retain the memory and absorb the lessons of the defeat, and when the next upsurge takes place they are more prepared.

The success of a revolutionary upsurge in Britain requires the existence of an organized revolutionary party. There can be limited periods of dual power *without* a revolutionary party, when the spontaneous thrust of the workers leads them to a conclusion which completely transcends their initial aim and in the process radicalizes them enough to make possible factory occupations, seizure of towns, battles with the repressive apparatus of the state and a temporary hold over certain areas. However, the seizure of state power, even when the balance of forces is most favourable, requires a revolutionary proletarian party. The task of this party is precisely to prepare the insurrection and articulate in practice the demands for which the mass of workers is striving. Thus this party would have to thoroughly infiltrate and control certain key unions (not necessarily big unions: in late capitalist society a few well-planned actions by small groups of workers in vital industries could affect capitalism quite severely!). In addition a strategy has to be prepared for the struggle in an advanced capitalist country, which will take place largely in the cities. For we may be certain that the capitalist class will not surrender power automatically when threatened with a revolutionary mass movement. They will fight viciously to preserve their privileges. And they will use all the means at their disposal. It is, therefore, vital that the revolutionary movement, as well, begins to understand that it is essential to discuss these questions and formulate a strategy for the future even though the situation we are in *today* is totally different. The sharpness of the present crisis is such that things could change very rapidly and the revolutionary left in Britain, almost obsessed with legalism and working within the framework of bourgeois democracy, would find itself totally unprepared to work underground. There is bound to be an increase in repression of the left as the condition deteriorates: increasing unemployment, anti-working-class laws, anti-blacks measures and victimization of student militants.

At present there exists no alternative to the Tories which the revolutionary movement could support. To build up the Labour Party would merely create illusions as to its nature in the working class. For the Labour Party is a bourgeois party dedicated to defending the capitalist order and preserving its heritage. The traditional role which the ruling class expects this party to play is of appeasing and containing the working class during times of crisis. If the crisis worsens considerably, we should not rule out a triple alliance between the Conservative government, the Labour Party and the Trades Union Congress leadership to bolster the capitalist system and to smash any real resistance. It is completely mechanistic to imagine that once workers are disillusioned with the Labour Party they will automatically move to a revolutionary position. Of course, the destruction of trade-union support for the Labour Party, based though it is on an alliance of the trade-union bureaucracy with the Labour Party leadership, will help in winning over layers of the working class to revolutionary positions. But that is different from presenting the entire development of working-class consciousness in certain prescribed stages. The logic behind this leads to the following methodology: Because Lenin said so-and-so in 1919 or 1920 in completely different circumstances, therefore as followers of Lenin we say exactly the same today. This anti-dialectical method leads to diversions from the struggle against capitalism. Therefore the Labour Party has to be attacked constantly and vigorously. To raise the slogan of 'Labour to Power on a Socialist Programme', as some left groups do, is to create the impression that this is possible—that the Labour Party could transform itself (or be transformed by the formulators of this absurd slogan) into a party capable of a socialist programme. It is to say that the House of Commons could be transformed into a Soviet and the House of Lords flooded with 'Soviet peers'. Hence any attempts to strengthen the existing illusions of sections of the working class in the Labour Party must be strongly resisted.

The only real alternative to capitalist policies is provided by the revolutionary left groups as a whole. Despite their smallness and despite their many failings, they represent the only way forward. What is crucial today, however, is to organize *internationally* from the very start: because the repercussions of every struggle today are international; because capitalism is an international system; because the development of political consciousness is uneven globally. Therefore the task facing revolutionaries is to help build a mass revolutionary International. Today this is more necessary than ever. The French C.P. betrays the revolutionary struggle in France in May 1968;

the Bolivian C.P. actively sabotages the struggle of Che; the Chinese government supports the Pakistani fascist dictator Yahya Khan against the Bengali masses; the Soviet Union sends helicopters and arms to help Mrs Bandaranaike, the Ceylon Prime Minister, confront a revolutionary movement which threatens her government's existence. Thus the Fourth International, founded by Trotsky in 1938, today takes on an important task on behalf of the world revolution. Despite its limited resources and the fact that it doesn't have state power, its militants fight guns in hand in its name in Bolivia and Argentina. They struggle against capitalism all over Western Europe, they fight against bureaucracy in Czechoslovakia and Poland. Thus we see the modest beginnings of a new mass International which will take shape in the heat of the struggle and continue to wage war against capitalism and bureaucracy. The world is in a state of flux. The future of mankind is being decided on several battlefield. The struggle for socialist revolutions in Britain could play a vital part in ensuring that this future is free from the fear of war and destruction, free from the poverty and alienation suffered by the peasant and the worker and the student. A future in which the words of an old revolutionary can be fulfilled: 'To each according to his needs. From each according to his ability.'

1   The Problems of British Capitalism

> The growing realization that existing social institutions are irrational and unjust, that reason has become nonsense and good deeds a scourge, is only a sign that changes have been taking place quietly in the methods of production and the forms of exchange with which the social order, adapted to previous economic conditions, is no longer in accord.
>
> F. ENGELS, *Anti-Dühring* (1885)

Several decades ago the undeniable might of British imperialism was aptly summed up in the proud boast of one of its leading ideologues in a phrase which proclaimed that the sun never set on the parts of the world dominated by British capital.[1] To grasp the extent of the decline and decay of this same capital one has only to invert the old phrase; few would deny that today the sun hardly rises on the territory under the rule of British capitalism. This decline has naturally been accompanied by a change in the social, economic and political conditions within Britain itself which in turn has resulted in a changing consciousness amongst different social layers in British society. Unless we understand the changed nature of British capitalism it will not be easy to understand the optimism of many British revolutionaries.

The decline of British capitalism is not a new process. It did not suddenly begin in 1947 when India was granted political independence, or slightly later when the 'winds of change' swept through Africa in the shape of a Tory Prime Minister. These

---

[1] Though the actual phrase was slightly different, this was what in fact it meant.

events were a somewhat belated recognition of the decline which had taken place during the last decades of the nineteenth century. This was the period when the United States, Germany and other Continental countries were undergoing a process of rapid industrialization. During this period a new technical revolution was taking place which, in essence, changed the source of power. Petrol and electricity were coming alongside coal and steam and were gradually beginning to replace the latter in key sectors of industry.[2]

In Britain, however, there already existed a pattern of production and markets that had been constructed in the early part of the nineteenth century. This had been accomplished as a result of Britain's position as the pioneer of the first industrial revolution and to transform this pattern would have been both difficult and extremely expensive. Britain was heavily dependent on exports of textiles and of capital goods to the various developing areas of the world. For a period before the First World War, Britain's exports continued to grow, but at a slower rate. The newly industrialized countries were producing goods for their own markets and were erecting tariff barriers against Britain. It was precisely the inability of British capitalism to participate in the 'second industrial revolution' which undermined its competitive position on the world market.[3] The balance of payments was increasingly dependent on invisible earnings, and in particular on the tribute exacted from the colonies, where Britain had vast investments. The annual income from imperialist exploitation, or what is known in polite economists' language as overseas investments, was approximately between £20 and £30 million in the period 1850–55, £60 million in the early 1880s, £100 million in the years following 1890 and £200 million in 1913.

The inter-war years saw much of the Victorian economy in

[2] Ernest Mandel, *Marxist Economic Theory*, 2 vols (Merlin Press, London, 1968), vol. 2, pp. 393–437.

[3] Between 1876 and 1910, world exports expanded at 2·55 per cent per annum, whereas Britain's exports expanded by only 2·1 per cent per annum.

virtual ruin.[4] Between 1912 and 1928 exports fell brutally, and the cotton manufacturing, coal and ship-building industries suffered a severe decline. The table below provides a telescopic view of the failure of British exports to stand up to competition:

per cent shares of trade in manufactures (1899–1937)

COUNTRY	1899	1929	1937	CHANGE (1899–1937)
U.S.A.	11·2	20·7	19·6	+ 8·4
Japan	1·5	3·9	7·2	+ 5·7
Canada	0·3	3·5	5·0	+ 4·7
Sweden	1·0	1·7	2·5	+ 1·5
Belgium	5·6	5·5	5·9	+ 0·3
Germany	22·2	21·0	22·4	+ 0·2
Italy	3·7	3·7	3·6	− 0·1
India	2·3	2·4	2·1	− 0·2
Switzerland	3·9	2·8	2·9	− 1·0
France	15·8	11·2	6·4	− 9·4
Britain	32·5	23·6	22·4	−10·1
	100	100	100	

The figures represent exports of manufactures from the countries listed which accounted for 80–85 per cent of world trade in manufactures from 1901–38.
Source: H. Tyzenski, cited in S. J. Wells, *British Export Performance* (Cambridge University Press, 1964), p. 15.

Only the City of London part of the old Victorian export economy resisted collapse, and by the mid-1920s Britain was earning more from her 'overseas investments', financial and insurance services than ever before. Even in this field the supremacy of the City was gradually being shaken, and Wall Street in New York was taking over as the capitalist world's leading financial centre. But despite these severe setbacks, the inter-war years did see the laying down of the foundations of

[4] E. J. Hobsbawm, *Industry and Empire* (Weidenfeld and Nicolson, London, 1968), p. 207.

new growth industries, such as electrical goods and cars, which relied mainly on the domestic market.[5]

The Second World War, like the First, had an important impact on the British economy. The most urgent and pressing problem which confronted British capitalism at the end of the war was the balance of payments position.[6] Overseas investments had diminished and as a result the 'invisible' earnings of the British bourgeoisie had dropped considerably. A quarter of overseas investments totalling £1,118 million had been sold off, while overseas debts had increased.[7] In order to try and fill this widening gap it was calculated that exports would have to be increased by at least 50 per cent in volume above pre-war levels, 'to meet at the same time the need to repay sterling debt, of building up a shrunken gold and dollar reserve and of investments in the more backward parts of the Empire, the volume of exports would have to be raised by 75 per cent at least.'[8] The export drive was successful and exports increased dramatically by 77 per cent between 1946 and 1950.

Post-war capitalist reconstruction, carried out firmly and fairly efficiently by the Labour government (a government which would be regarded by many in the Labour Party today as a bit 'pinkish' in political complexion), ended in the early 1950s as did indeed the Labour government which had done so much to put Britain back on capitalist rails. The next decade of Toryism was the period cynically labelled by Tory politicians as the 'you-never-had-it-so-good' phase. This was the message so loyally and euphorically carried to the masses by the Tory press and 'independent' television. The pathetic claim by Labour 'theoreticians' that the Tories were only reaping the benefits of the regenerated capitalist seeds so ably sown by Labour government was true but totally irrelevant. And even this truth was limited. The economic boom, which enabled the

[5] Op. cit., p. 220.
[6] Sidney Pollard, *The Development of the British Economy 1914–1967* (Edward Arnold, London, 1969), p. 354.
[7] Ibid.
[8] Ibid.

Tory leaders to coin advertising phrases and sell the capitalist system to the people, resulted from certain exceptional factors. Once the effect of these factors began to wear off, it was obvious that the boom would begin to tail off.[9] The healthy balance-of-payments situation could not conceal the much slower growth-rate in Britain as compared to the rest of Europe. Michael Barratt-Brown listed five specific factors which contributed to this surplus but these had played themselves out by the beginning of the 1960s:

1. The slow economic recovery of Britain's key competitors, Germany, Italy and Japan, after the Second World War.
2. The flow of capital into both Britain and the sterling area from the United States: first in the shape of State-Department sponsored capital (i.e. aid), and secondly and increasingly in the shape of private investment.
3. A steady fall in the price of imports. For instance in the period 1951 to 1959 import prices fell by 13 per cent and export prices rose by 9 per cent so that there was a 25 per cent net improvement in the terms of trade.
4. Steady spending by the 'underdeveloped' countries of their foreign exchange accumulated during the Korean War boom to buy capital equipment for their economic development, mainly from Britain.
5. The fact that an important part in the sterling area's overall balance of payments was financed by the gold sales of South Africa and by the dollar earnings of Ghana, Malaya and the oil states in the Middle East.[10]

By the early 'sixties these factors had lost their importance; the prices of imported goods began to rise again and the newly 'independent' colonies began to purchase their imports from countries other than Britain (in particular the United States and Japan). The economic recovery of Germany, Japan and Italy made British exports increasingly uncompetitive in world

[9] Ibid.
[10] Michael Barratt-Brown, 'Labour's Economic Policy 1964–67', *International Socialist Journal*, year 4, no. 21, pp. 444–65.

markets. This marked the beginnings of the balance-of-payments crisis and the slow rate of growth which have haunted British economists ever since and have severely curtailed the reformist options open to either Labour or Tory governments. The recurrent balance-of-payments crisis coupled with the 'stop-go' cycle tended to inhibit investment, and hence growth. British capitalists and politicians were wont to admire the 'virtuous circle' at work in West Germany, where a high growth-rate produced a high expectation of continued growth and thus led to increasing investments. The ill-fated 'National Plan' was designed to produce high expectations in Britain regarding possibilities of growth and encourage British capitalists to invest, but the latter refused to fall for this particular trick and the plan had to be completely scrapped.

Basically the real reason for the slow rate of growth was the low rate of capital accumulation in Britain as compared with other capitalist countries. In other words the rate of exploitation is lower in Britain than in her competitor countries. The low rate of productivity means that the capitalists must deal with the rise in wages by either higher prices or cuts in profits. This only tends to reinforce the structural problems which confront British capitalism. Even to begin to solve these in the medium term requires cutting the living standards of the working class, which means tackling the trade unions and defeating them. Hence Barbara Castle's and Harold Wilson's pathetic attempts to thrust their proposals, contained in *In Place of Strife*, down the throats of the trade unions. Hence Robert Carr's and Edward Heath's decision to open wide the door unlocked by the Labour government, by a frontal attack on the trade unions and the social services.

By the early 'fifties Britain was concentrating on the growing sector of world trade and was moving away from her dependence on the old empire—the remnants of the latter are now embodied in the sterling area as a source of markets.[11] Most of Britain's trade is now with Western Europe. This is one reason

[11] Ernest Mandel, *Europe versus America* (New Left Books, London, 1970), p. 61.

for the increased eagerness of the most advanced sectors of British capital to enter the Common Market as 'The danger that British exports may stagnate or even fall casts a shadow over the whole of Great Britain's industrial future'.[12]

The response of big business to the situation confronting British capitalism — stagnant growth-rates and declining ability to compete in the world market — was not original. It was the classic response of accelerating the process of concentration and centralization on the one hand and trying to increase the rate of exploitation on the other. This process was not new by any means. The post-war development of British capitalism revealed an increasing trend towards the interpenetration and mono-polization of capital on a large scale. Thus in the first two years of the 1950s, ' ... the nine directors of the Midland Bank sat on the board of 38 companies, including Imperial Chemical Industries, Dunlop Rubber, J. & P. Coates, International Nickel, etc. The nineteen directors of Lloyds Bank sat on the board of 75 companies, including Royal Dutch Shell, Vickers, Rolls-Royce, English Electric, etc. The thirteen directors of the National Provincial Bank sat on the boards of 60 companies, including British Petroleum (formerly Anglo-Iranian), Imperial Tobacco, Burmah Oil, Tube Investments, Prudential Insurance, Ford Motors, and a number of tea firms.'[13]

The 1960s saw an accelerating merger boom. After the electoral victory of the Labour Party in 1964, it received government blessing in the shape of handouts from the newly formed Industrial Reorganization Corporation. Expenditure on takeovers of quoted companies ran at £275 million per annum in 1960–63, £400 million per annum in 1964–66 and by 1967–68 was as high as £1,000 million per annum. Despite the fact that there was a fall in the *number* of acquisitions in 1964–68, the total amount spent rose sharply.[14] The merger boom has been increasingly confined to the bigger firms. As

[12] Ibid.

[13] Ernest Mandel, *Marxist Economic Theory*, op. cit., vol. 2, p. 413.

[14] Monopolies Commission Report, *General Observations on Mergers*.

far as the size of the firms is concerned, British firms do not
compare so very unfavourably with Continental companies.
Nevertheless, when faced with the might and size of the giant
American corporations British firms suffer big disadvantages.
This is also true of the companies in Western Europe. One of
the chief reasons for the merger boom is the growing power of
American penetration via investments which today dominate
certain key sectors in the British economy. But mergers between
even the largest British firms are only a temporary solution;
the most advanced sectors of British capital recognize this fact
perfectly well, as does the organ which outspokenly defends
them, *The Economist*. The long-term prospects for British
capitalism are bleak indeed if it cannot get into the Common
Market and align itself with the process of capital interpenetration which is taking place on a European scale. Here lies
the only hope of both European and British capital of stemming
the tide of advancing American capital. In addition, 'British
capital realized that the appearance of "European" firms ...
capable of reaching the size of the American corporations
would ultimately no longer leave British industry any room for
an independent place in the world market. It would be ruth-
lessly squeezed between these giants.'[15]

Thus in facing the American challenge the British firm is
faced with the same disadvantages as its counterparts in the
European Economic Community. Neither can really overcome
this handicap alone: the Common Market countries need the
influx of British capital as much as British capital needs their
resources. The problem of increased American domination
confronts precisely the most economically advanced sectors of
British capitalism. Harold Wilson, like every other Prime
Minister, appreciated this danger and in his Strasbourg speech
of January 23rd, 1967, he said:

> Let no one doubt Britain's loyalty to NATO and the
> Atlantic Alliance. But I have also always said that loyalty

[15] Mandel, *Europe versus America*, op. cit., pp. 61–2.

must never mean subservience. Still less must it mean an industrial helotry under which we in Europe produce only the conventional apparatus of a modern economy while becoming increasingly dependent on American business for the sophisticated apparatus which would call the industrial tune in the 70s and 80s.[16]

That this remains the intention of United States capital is beyond doubt and is admitted quite openly and fully by its ideologists. A leading bourgeois apologist for an international company has stated that

The peculiar features of much American foreign investment in high technology industries, however, are that the size of most domestic markets outside the United States does not permit more than one or two firms to derive the fullest advantage from economies of scale and, because of the economies of large scale research, larger firms often have the edge over their smaller competitors. This means that, to maintain effective competition against the American challenge, some host countries may need to encourage the merger of enterprises not only within their boundaries, but across boundaries.[17]

Thus the merger boom of the 1960s and the move towards entering the Common Market are different parts of the same economic process.

The structural crisis which confronted British capitalism could only be solved in the medium term by hammering the workers' movement. In the view of the most intelligent sections of the bourgeoisie this task could be handled better by a Labour than a Tory government. That is why *The Economist* called for the return of a Labour government in the 1964 general elections.

[16] Quoted in Uwe Kitzinger, *The European Common Market and Community* (Routledge & Kegan Paul, London, 1967), p. 196.

[17] John H. Dunning, 'The Multinational Enterprise', *Lloyds Bank Review* (July 1970), p. 30.

Thus at the level of government policy it fell to the Labour Party to attempt to rationalize British capitalism. The ideology that accompanied this process for a time confused and disarmed the Labour movement. Socialism meant planning. Incomes policy was the planning of incomes. Incomes policy therefore meant socialism. This was the crude logic employed by the social-democratic apologists and even 'left' social-democracy found itself whining that while it was in favour of an incomes policy it wanted one of a different sort.[18] (We will discuss the utopian cretinism of the latter in later chapters.) Apart from the incomes policy lark, the other favourite ploy of the Wilsonites was to refer constantly to the 'white heat of the technological revolution' which would burn away all the problems of the class society and would usher in a new Jerusalem and, more important, a sound balance of payments.[19]

Incomes policy was designed to slow down the rate of increasing wages and this together with the National Plan—an exercise in neo-capitalist programming that fell flat—was designed to increase the rate of exploitation and thereby capital accumulation. The National Plan was quite clear in its perspective of devoting the incremental resources from growth towards capital accumulation. While the incomes policy of the Labour government succeeded in imposing a wage freeze for a certain period, it was inevitable that it would soon break down. In the first place sections of the bourgeoisie were not prepared to lose the flexibility they enjoyed at the level of enterprises. In a situation where there is low unemployment and rising output the employers themselves will wish to get hold of scarce supplies of labour power and will therefore be prepared to pay more and

[18] Michael Barratt-Brown and Royden Harrison, *Tribune*, January 8th, February 5th, 1965. Similar views were expressed by Ken Alexander, John Hughes and Henry Collins. What was both amusing and somewhat sick was that these left-reformists were throwing quotes from Marx and Lenin at the revolutionary left for opposing the idea of an incomes policy in a capitalist society, on principle!

[19] A useful critique of this ideology was provided by the May Day Manifesto Group in *May Day Manifesto 1968* (Penguin, Harmondsworth, 1968). While the book remains, the group itself has disintegrated.

thus defy the incomes policy. Secondly the Labour Party itself found it more and more difficult to maintain the policy in the face of massive opposition from the workers on whom they depended for their electoral victories. The large-scale abstention from voting at successive by-elections between 1966 and 1969 was only one of the indications of working-class dissent.

As an essential component of the incomes policy the employers and the government began an offensive to weaken the power of the workers' movement at shop-floor, plant and enterprise level. Here the bosses were confronted with the reality of the two-tier system of industrial relations: 'The autonomy of shop stewards is one of the most remarkable characteristics of British unionism; it is so pronounced that collective bargaining in post-war Britain has frequently been described as a "two-tier system" and ... its impact on conditions affecting plant productivity has been adverse ... '[20] The chief finding of the Donovan Commission on industrial relations was precisely this: namely the existence of two systems of industrial relations. (The existence of such a system had been known long before the Donovan Commission Report.) Frequent bargaining about piece rates had enhanced the power of the shop stewards and their ability to push earnings upward. Moreover, the 'adverse' impact on conditions affecting plant productivity (what bourgeois commentators call 'restrictive practices') has occurred where shop stewards have been able to win a very limited degree of control over working conditions. Hemmed in by the pressure of increasing international competition, the employers' offensive has been two pronged. On the one hand there has been a growing trend towards the introduction of productivity bargaining, which has as its main purpose the aim of weakening decisively the power of the shop stewards by eliminating bargaining over piece rates and beginning to restore 'management prerogatives'. The introduction of such systems as Measured Day work, by the setting of performance

[20] Lloyd Ullman, 'Collective Bargaining and Industrial Efficiency', in *Britain's Economic Prospects*, R. E. Caves, ed. (Allen and Unwin, London, 1968), p. 349.

standards and the use of the stopwatch, is designed to give the
employer control of every minute of the worker's working life.[21]
On the other hand a direct legal attack on the power of the
workers in this 'tier' was contained in the Labour government's
In Place of Strife proposals. The Tory proposals on industrial
relations are a logical step forward from *In Place of Strife*. We
shall discuss what these proposals mean for the trade-union
movement in some detail in the next chapter, but the type of
thinking behind these proposals is best typified by the editorial
comment on the Donovan Commission Report which appeared
in *The Economist* on June 15th, 1968:

> Unofficial strikes that are unknown in some other
> countries account for 95 per cent of the strikes in this
> country ... One of the few useful features of this report is
> that it demolishes the old argument that many 'foreigners''
> industrial relations are worse than ours, by pointing out
> the unpredictability of Britain's lightning unofficial stop-
> pages makes them far more damaging ... because British
> managements must lack confidence that the plans they
> make and the decisions they reach can be implemented
> rapidly and effectively or, in extreme cases, at all. In other
> countries a breach of contract, such as is involved in most
> unconstitutional lightning strikes, is met by legal sanctions
> under contract law; while in Britain the law has been
> twisted into a shape that gives deliberate and exceptional
> protection to any stoppage whatever.

Thus it is very clear that all the different proposals have
essentially been directed against the powerful backbone of shop

[21] A good description of the danger of productivity bargaining is contained in
Tony Cliff, *The Employer's Offensive* (Pluto Press, London, 1970). At a meeting
organized by *The Red Mole* in solidarity with the postal workers' strike in January
1971, the postal workers had the entire meeting rocking with laughter at their
description of the supervisors walking round in circles and bumping into each other
in a bid to increase productivity. The fact that there were too many supervisors
who had nothing much to do did not induce the postal workers to increase
productivity.

stewards, who have done more to maintain the strong position of the trade unions than most of the highly paid bureaucrats that fill the union offices. It is shop-floor militancy that worries both the Tories and Harold Wilson.[22]

Both the ill-fated incomes policy and the 'national plan' were envisaged as long-term cures of the ailments of declining British capitalism. They were regarded as an alternative to another strategy suggested by the economic 'technicians', namely a permanently higher level of unemployment. The critical state of British capitalism enabled the foreign bankers to dictate the terms of Labour budgets. First deflation and subsequently devaluation were forced down the Labour government's throat. Both were an attack on the living standards of the workers : devaluation raised the price of imported foodstuffs and deflation raised the level of unemployment. Deflation has three main objectives : to reduce imports, to slow down the rate of increase of wages (the classic solution to rising wages has, of course, always been to reconstitute the industrial reserve army of unemployed) and also to provide the resources for exports and import substitution provided for by the devaluation. While this Labour 'strategy' did succeed in improving the balance-of-payments position, the high level of unemployment still remained. Despite this there was a phenomenal upsurge of working-class militancy for higher wages and this undoubtedly reflected the collapse of the wage freeze (or incomes policy) and the stagnation of living standards under the Labour government. At the time of writing employers and the government are still trying to control wages. The foreign balance has only been protected by the existence of inflation in the other imperialist countries which have also been beset by crises.

Caught in a web of inter-imperialist competition, the British ruling class needs to increase the rate of capital accumulation

[22] In a Panorama interview on BBC television on January 25th, 1971, Wilson bemoaned the increase of shop-floor militancy which, he said, was being 'misused and exploited'. He suggested that the government should sit down with the trade-union bureaucrats and 'devise a policy of dealing with strikes'.

and to rationalize its economic structure. In order to do this it needs to increase the rate of exploitation and at the same time requires a disciplined and quiescent labour force that will not rock the capitalist boat. If the merger boom is to lead to a genuine reorganization of industry then the power of the shop stewards ('restrictive practices' in both Labour and Tory jargon) has to be smashed. This becomes even more important if Britain enters the Common Market and there is an intensification of competition.

However, history never develops in a straight line. It is marked and shaped by its uneven development. As noted above, certain factors in the 1950s combined to protect Britain from the worst effects of foreign competition. We cannot therefore predict mechanistically in the fashion of a computer how protracted the crisis of British capitalism will be. There are even certain indications that in the short term there might be tendencies in operation which are favourable to this country's economy.[23]

But it would be stupid to see the problems of British capitalism in isolation. The new upsurge of revolutionary and pre-revolutionary situations which started in 1968 is the result of certain objective and subjective factors which Britain cannot avoid. The objective basis for a revolutionary upheaval in Britain should therefore not only be seen as the result of factors that are peculiar to Britain.[24] The problems which confront capitalism in this country are not unique. Similar problems

[23] 'Other countries, especially the large continental countries, gained more than the United Kingdom from the shift of labour out of agriculture and non-farm self-employment in 1950–62, mainly because such employment was more important in these countries in 1950. They will continue to secure much larger contributions to growth from these sources than the U.K. However, the differences are likely to be considerably less than in the past because international differences in the importance of such employment have narrowed.' Edward F. Denison, 'Economic Growth', in Caves, ed., op. cit., p. 268.

[24] 'The End of the Long Imperialist Boom', printed as Appendix 1 and extracted from the document The New Rise of World Revolution, which was adopted by the Fourth International at its Ninth World Congress in 1969. It is available from Red Books, 182 Pentonville Road, London N1.

face virtually every single late-capitalist country in the world, and they have produced two explosions which have shattered the complacency of the European bourgeoisie: the May revolution in France in 1968 and the crisis which confronted Italy in the last half of 1969. These were the two most spectacular manifestations of the fact that capitalist Europe was not immune to social upheavals. Today we see that even the social-democratic paradise, Sweden, is beset by 'problems' of working-class militancy, despite the fact that the trade-union leaderships are completely integrated with the state and there are penalties against 'illegal' industrial action!

Capitalist development is always very uneven. There are many cases of advances in one sector being accompanied by sharp declines in the 'backward' regions. To try and overcome this unevenness special projects have been designed to alleviate the sufferings of the 'declining areas', but these have only had a very marginal effect and have, for example, provided the objective basis for the upheaval in Northern Ireland. In this region unemployment is several times above the national average. Scottish nationalism is a partial reflection of the same tendency in various parts of Scotland. Britain's entry into the Common Market will in all probability considerably extend the uneven character of capitalist growth. Certain sectors will lose out in face of tough competition. These will probably be shoes, cotton, clothing, metallurgy and machine tools. The industries that are likely to gain are computers, electrical industry, textile machinery, woollens and rubber.

In addition it is necessary to remember the effect of the giant 'multinational' corporations which will tend to dominate the major imperialist economies in the future. For instance, even today, ' ... foreign multinational firms in the U.K. account for about 25 per cent of the manufacturing exports and, on present trends, are likely to supply the same proportion of manufacturing output by 1980.'[25] At the moment there is no evidence that the foreign firms have engaged in a large-scale closure of

[25] Dunning, op. cit., p. 22.

industries in Europe as a result of *international* rationalization plans, but the experience of some areas is a pointer as to the direction in which this could develop in the future.[26]

The increased power of the multinational companies (which are of course dominated by U.S. capital) is just one part of the increased interdependence of the imperialist economies. For instance, in the foreign exchange market, 'The size of their current capital to hand is often very large compared to that present in many national money markets, and they are able to shift significant sums of capital from one country to another at very short notice.'[27] Another sign of interdependence is the increased trade between the major imperialist nations. This interdependence is moving towards a synchronization of recession in the capitalist world which, coupled with other factors — the perennial problem of inflation, the problem of growing excess capacity and the fall in the average rate of profit — is tending to undermine the relative prosperity of the post-war period and to slow down the rate of growth in the major imperialist countries. The combination of the competitive crisis, peculiar to British capital, with the problems which confront the entire imperialist world will provide the economic basis for social explosions in Britain. Is this situation alone a sufficient cause for revolution? Certainly not. But in combination with other factors, which we will discuss in the chapters that follow, the ground can be prepared for an overthrow of the capitalist state in Britain.

[26] Mandel, *Europe versus America*, op. cit., p. 64.
[27] Ibid., p. 93.

2 The Labour Movement: The Trade Unions and the Labour Party

> Throughout the whole history of the British Labour Movement is to be found the pressure of the bourgeoisie on the proletariat by means of radicals, intelligentsia, drawing-room and church socialists, Owenites, who reject the class struggle, put forward the principle of social solidarity, preach co-operation with the bourgeoisie, curb, enfeeble and politically debase the proletariat.
>
> LEON TROTSKY, *Where is Britain Going?* (1925)

I

Marxism maintains that consciousness determines history. In that respect it does not differ from other theories of history. What Marxism demands is that consciousness itself must be explained; that not only must it be examined as it exists at the moment, but the factors which determine its future development must also be constantly subjected to analysis. In late capitalist society the sole agency of social change is the working class. It is therefore essential to put into perspective the historical features which have shaped the present level of consciousness of the working class and attempt to analyse how this consciousness could develop and change in the future.

In no state is it possible for the bourgeoisie to rule simply by virtue of its own strength as a class. It is too weak numerically for this. In order to safeguard its position it must gain political hegemony over some other, numerically stronger section of

45

society. In the nineteenth century and in many colonial and semi-colonial societies today, the power of the bourgeoisie rests on the support it receives from large sections of the urban or rural petty-bourgeoisie. It is the latter social layer which provides the bulk of the support which the bourgeoisie needs by servicing its repressive apparatus. Even in twentieth-century France the petty-bourgeoisie is an important source of strength to the ruling class and forms a backbone of support to Gaullism. In Britain, however, the numbers of the petty-bourgeoisie have diminished and it has virtually ceased to exist as a class, as Jeremy Thorpe and his friends in the Liberal Party are finding out to their cost. The only mass class is the working class. The existing social structure, therefore, necessitates bourgeois dominance over a section of the working class itself.

The degree of proletarianization of British society can be seen quite clearly: out of a total work force of approximately 26 million, over 22 million are wage earners and only a little over 3 million are self-employed or dependent on the labour of others. Some of the 22 million are not proletarians as defined by their relation to the means of production, and many others would not consider themselves as members of the working class. Nonetheless, if these figures are considered together with the estimate that 81 per cent of all industrial shares are controlled by 1 per cent of the population, it becomes obvious that the working class is the only numerically significant class. The British bourgeoisie could not survive for long unless it dominated a significant section of that class ideologically. And it is precisely the necessity of maintaining that hegemony which determines the political expression of bourgeois rule.

The greatest single asset to this ideological domination by the ruling class in Britain is undoubtedly its own imperial past. Every school student is 'educated' in the knowledge that large areas of the world were once coloured red and were 'ours'. Every school student is told about national 'heroes' such as the plunderer and financial swindler 'Clive of India', or the openly racist Cecil Rhodes. In these nurseries of bourgeois ideology a whole section of youth is raised in the boy-scout and girl-guide movement on the ideology of the Boer War and the mythology of the 'thin red line' of British troops, always armed to the teeth versus the 'savages'. People are taught idiocies such as that Britain conquered India in order to convert the population to Christianity or in order to build railways and fight disease! Much is made of the 'barbarity' of the Indian forces which revolted against the British occupation in 1857. The three hundred years of British imperialist bestiality and exploitation are conveniently forgotten.

Imperialist ideology was once used to raise armies to go out and fight the 'wogs'. Today British imperialism has been forced to abandon these aims, though occasionally it still reminisces nostalgically about the good old days.[1] Despite the fact that imperialist conquest is not on the agenda any longer for British capitalism, imperialist ideology still serves a certain purpose. By emphasizing the old hoary myth of 'plucky little Britain versus the rest' it hopes to maintain a condition whereby the ideas of a large section of workers are dominated by national rather than class consciousness. It is on this fertile ground that both Powellism and fascism feed and attempt to extend their tentacles deep into the working class itself.

But the necessity to maintain a grip over a section of the working class has impelled the direct ideological representatives of the bourgeoisie, the Conservative Party, to make concessions to the working class. It was out of both this and the specific needs of neo-capitalism that the phenomenon of 'Butskellism' developed. But today the situation is considerably changed and the contradiction which confronts all defenders of British capitalism, whether they be Labour or Tory, is that economically they can no longer afford to make any concessions to the working class. Reforms are no longer the order of the day.

---

[1] A good example of this was an editorial in *The Economist* during the February 1971 oil crisis; the journal mournfully recalled the days of departed glory when the whole wretched business could have been sorted out by the dispatch of a gunboat or two!

They are therefore forced to attack the working class, but because of their ideological influence over a section of it, the attack cannot be too direct. The form of this attack is therefore dictated by the political requirements of ruling a country which is almost completely proletarianized.

The main requirement for such an attack is to split the working class from within; hence a key role is played by ideological weapons such as racialism. In addition, sections of the bourgeoisie pin their hopes on the Labour Party and the role it plays within the working-class movement. They rely on social-democracy to demoralize the class thoroughly. To understand how the ruling class can be defeated and swept off the stage of history involves understanding of the historical role of the trade-union movement and its inter-relationship with the Labour Party and, to a lesser extent, the Communist Party of Great Britain (C.P.G.B.).

There seems to be a belief, even amongst certain revolutionaries, that the domination of working-class consciousness by the Labour Party was somehow the inevitable result of the non-conformist conscience, Methodism, or that the British empiricist tradition coupled with the might of British imperialism, the creation of a labour aristocracy, etc., conspired together to deprive us of a good, healthy Stalinist tradition and instead left us holding the most reformist social-democracy in Europe. Obviously there is a lot to this argument, but things aren't all that simple. Of course, it was inevitable that a large reformist party should develop in Britain, but the extent and the length of the domination by social-democracy was *not* inevitable. It arose from the mistakes of the revolutionaries themselves, and provides us with yet another example of the damage that can be done by a lack of theoretical clarity.

Revolutionaries cannot decisively alter the consciousness of the working class at will. Only in periods of acute social unrest does a mass of the class experience the fact that reality is somewhat at variance with the 'conventional wisdom' with which it has been imbued since birth. It is only through the direct experiences of the class, which create a contradiction in its consciousness, that revolutionaries can intervene decisively and influence the course of the struggle. One such period was 1888–91. It was in this period that the core of the modern trade-union movement was established. The late 1880s and early '90s were periods of tremendous growth in the working-class movement, which reached a political climax on a European scale with the founding of the Second International in 1891. In Britain, however, a bigger impact than the Second International was made by the 1889 dock strike and the beginning of mass unionization of unskilled workers.

During this period the leading force in socialist agitation and propaganda was the Marxist Social Democratic Federation (S.D.F.). As early as 1883 it had been agitating for the eight-hour day. Tom Mann was only one of the great working-class leaders of his day who graduated through the S.D.F. The heroic Irish working-class leaders James Connolly and James Larkin were also connected with the S.D.F. The driving force behind the latter's agitation was the realization, taken from Marx, that the existing class antagonisms were irreconcilable. It was this realization that led to a fundamental break with the old ideas of trade unionism.

The trade unionism of the early nineteenth century had been concerned largely with preserving the privileges and positions of skilled workers. This policy involved schemes of apprenticeship which, apart from dividing workers against each other, could only be enforced with the agreement of the management. This led inevitably to class-collaboration. The policy was based on a view of society which did not accept the irreconcilable nature of the contradiction between capital and labour, and therefore projected the possibility of existing groups of craft workers maintaining their privileged positions within the framework of capitalism. This concept was fundamentally opposed to the idea of combining all workers in order to collect the maximum strength against the bourgeoisie. As a result the mass of workers were to be vigorously excluded from the unions, and

4

agreements and coexistence were sought with the employers against the unorganized rabble. This policy was of course utopian, and therefore, even within its own terms of reference, unsuccessful. Any Marxist could have foretold this, and their belief in scientific socialism gave agitators like Tom Mann an enormous advantage over other organizers. Mann wrote:

> To trade unionists, I desire to make a special appeal. How long, *how long* will you be content with the present half-hearted policy of your unions? I readily grant that good work has been done in the past by the unions, but, in heaven's name, what good purpose are they serving now? All of them have large numbers out of employment even when their particular trade is busy. None of the important societies have any other policy other than of endeavouring to keep wages from falling. The true unionist policy of aggression seems entirely lost sight of; in fact the average unionist of today is a man with a fossilised intellect, either hopelessly apathetic, or supporting a policy that plays directly into the hands of the capitalist exploiter.[2]

Partly as a result of Marxist agitation, and partly as a result of a general economic boom leading to unusually high levels of employment, trade unionism was spreading rapidly by 1889. What was needed was a victory which would fix trade-union consciousness in the minds of the workers. This victory was not long in coming. It arrived in the shape of the 1889 dock strike. The key figure in the events leading up to this strike was yet another S.D.F. member, Will Thorne. He had formed a gas-workers' union in the East End which had won the battle for an eight-hour day against the South Metropolitan Gas Company. This success inspired Ben Tillett, leader of a small union of warehouse men, to commence an agitation for a wage of sixpence an hour for dock workers (the famous 'docker's tanner'). A strike commenced under the leadership of Tillett,

[2] H. Pelling, *A History of British Trade Unionism* (Macmillan, London, 1954), p. 74.

stevedore leader Tom McCarthy and the S.D.F. in the person of Tom Mann and John Burns.[3]

After a five-week strike, and largely by means of the magnificent financial support from Australian trade unionists, the tanner was won. As a result the Dock, Wharf, Riverside and General Labourers Union was established. From now on the unionization of semi-skilled and unskilled workers proceeded at a tremendous rate. By the beginning of the twentieth century, just over two million workers were organized and the base of the modern trade-union movement had been firmly established. The Trades Council system was also off to a firm start and sixty Trades Councils were set up in the years 1889–91 alone.

In many of these cases of unionization and the founding of new trade unions the S.D.F. members were in the vanguard. Having grasped the basic essentials of Marxism they were more fully aware of the importance of the new unions than were the old craftsmen. Thus the worker militants of the S.D.F., despite the fact that they were skilled workers, were seen to be giving the lead for the creation of unions for the non-skilled. There was no doubt that Marxists were playing a key role at the very inception of the trade-union movement. If they had followed a correct strategy they would have been able to gain a massive base in the organized ranks of the working class. This would not have prevented the birth of a mass reformist party, but it would have provided a revolutionary challenge to that party from the very beginning. This could well have been decisive in the stormy period of 1910–19 and could have changed the whole course of British history. But this opportunity was missed; the politics of the S.D.F. became a trifle insane and it turned away from trade unionism completely. Instead of seeking to build a base inside the trade-union movement the Federation paralysed itself, thanks to the policies of its leader, Hyndman, whose attitude towards trade unionism

[3] Burns was another industrial leader of the S.D.F. who had gained a reputation as a working-class leader for his part in the 1886 riots of the unemployed in London.

was summed up in his declaration that 'I never knew a strike which gained anything', and whose contempt for mass action became clear when he declared his hostility to 'uneducated and undisciplined democracy'.

As a result of these mistakes the Labour Party was not faced, in the critical and early years of its development, with a revolutionary rival with whom it would be forced to contend for the loyalty of the working class. It could develop undisturbed, and it was not until the founding of the C.P.G.B. that it was faced with a political challenge, but by then its hegemony had been fairly well established. The domination of the working class by a social-democratic party which did not even pay lip-service to Marxism brought about a very particular relationship between the working-class party and the mass of the class itself. Their relationship was not based on the Labour Party organizing the working class directly in struggle, but instead was mediated through the trade-union bureaucracy. We will discuss this in some detail later, but the reasons for this approach can be seen in the historical and theoretical differences between social-democracy and Leninism.

One of the fundamental features separating social-democracy from Bolshevism was that the latter saw no difference between the economic and political struggles. It drew a very sharp distinction indeed between trade-union and political *consciousness*, but saw all forms of struggle as political. The following passage from Krupskaya drives this point home:

Vladmir Ilyich was interested in the minutest detail describing the conditions and life of the workers. Taking the features separately he endeavoured to grasp the life of the workers as a whole—he tried to find what one could seize upon in order better to approach the workers with revolutionary propaganda. Most of the intellectuals of those days badly understood the workers. An intellectual would come to a circle and read the workers a kind of lecture ... Vladmir Ilyich read with the workers from

Marx's *Capital*, and explained it to them. The second half of the studies was devoted to the workers' questions about their work and labour conditions. He showed them how their life was linked up with the entire structure of society, and told them in what manner the existing order could be transformed. The combination of theory with practice was the particular feature of Vladmir Ilyich's work in the circles ...

When the Vilna pamphlet *On Agitation* appeared the following year, the ground was already fully prepared for the conducting of agitation by leaflets. It was only necessary to start work. The method of agitation on the basis of the workers' everyday needs became deeply rooted in our party work. I only came fully to understand how fruitful this method of work was some years later when, living as an émigré in France, I observed how, during the tremendous postal strike in Paris ... the French Socialist Party stood completely aside and did not intervene in the strike. It was the business of the trade unions, they said. They thought the work of the party was simply the political struggle. They had not the remotest notion as to the necessity for connecting up the economic and political struggles.[4]

The Labour Party has never seen the complete connection between economic and other forms of struggle. This is seen most clearly in its organizational forms. It has never been based on the systematic and co-ordinated organization of cells inside factories. The Communist Parties, on the other hand, were always rooted in the working class at the point of production; they were organized directly inside the class rather than through the trade-union bureaucracy. Although these parties have long since degenerated into Stalinist and revisionist parties, their definite relation to their sociological base makes them qualitatively different to social-democracy, though the differences are narrowing in many countries.

[4] N. Krupskaya, *Memories of Lenin* (Panther, London, 1970), p. 21.

The belief that unites all social-democrats is that class differences can be removed by reforms. Accompanying this, in fact inevitably concomitant with it, is the desire of good social-democrats to confine all struggle within Parliament. Nothing frightens them more than a display of independence by the working class. This is not a new characteristic. During the 1926 General Strike that veritable Virgin Mary of British social-democracy, Beatrice Webb, wrote:

> The failure of the General Strike of 1926 will be one of the most significant landmarks in the history of the British working class. Future historians will, I think, regard it as the death gasp of that pernicious doctrine of 'workers control' of public affairs through the trade unions, and by the method of direct action. This absurd doctrine was introduced into British working class life by Tom Mann ... On the whole I think it was a proletarian distemper which had to run its course and like other distempers it is as well to have it over and done with at the cost of a lengthy convalescence ... [5]

If we want to understand further the difference between social-democrats and revolutionaries let us contrast the above passage with the following text by Lenin, extracted from *A Contribution to the History of the Question of Dictatorship*:

> What was the main difference between the period of 'revolutionary whirlwind' and the present 'Cadet' period, from the point of view of the various methods of the people's historical creativeness. The first and principal difference was the fact that in the period of the 'whirlwind' several special methods of creativeness were employed which are alien to other periods of political life. The most essential of these methods were: 1) *Seizure of political liberty by the people* — the exercise of this liberty without any restriction (freedom of assembly, even in universities, freedom of the

[5] K. Coates and T. Topham (eds.), *Workers' Control* (Panther, London, 1970), p. 138.

press, freedom of association, freedom to convene congresses, etc.) ; 2) the creation of new organs of *revolutionary government* — Soviets of Workers', Soldiers', Railway Workers' and peasants' deputies, new village and town authorities, etc. These organs were created exclusively by the revolutionary strata of the population, without laws or norms, in an entirely revolutionary manner, as the product of the inborn creativeness of the people, which had freed itself or was freeing itself from the old police shackles. These were precisely organs of *power*, notwithstanding their embryonic, spontaneous, informal and diffusive character as regards composition and method of functioning ... You are a working man? You wish to fight to liberate Russia from a handful of police thugs? Then you are our comrade. Choose your delegate at once, immediately. Choose as you think best. We shall willingly and gladly accept him as a full member of our Soviet of Soldiers' Deputies, of our Peasant Committees, of Workers' Deputies, etc. It is a power that is open to all, that does everything in sight of the masses, that is accessible to the masses, that springs directly from the masses and of their will.[6]

This was a far cry from the Stalinist degeneration which followed Lenin's death. Here in a nutshell is the difference in psychology between a social-democrat and a revolutionary. Small wonder that the Webbs preferred Stalin's Russia to that of Lenin and Trotsky, which seemed to them nothing but anarchy!

II

By the 1930s it was obvious, for reasons we discussed in the last chapter, that British imperialism was in a bad way. It was completely out-produced by German and American imperialism. Yet it continued to cling to its old possessions. The

[6] V. I. Lenin, *Collected Works*, 45 vols (Progress Publishers, Moscow, 1963–70), vol. 32, p. 340.

outcome of this, in particular because of the disproportionately difficult position in which it placed German imperialism, could only be war. Brilliantly prophetic, Trotsky warned:

> The flagrant and ever-growing disproportion between the specific weight of France and England ... in world economy and the colossal dimension of their colonial possessions are as much the source of world conflicts and of new wars as the insatiable greed of the 'fascist' aggressors ... *A new partition of the world is on the order of the day.*[7]

Trotsky went further and forecast who would benefit the most from the new holocaust: ' ... the United States is heading towards an imperialist explosion such as the world has never seen.'[8]

The war completed the decline of British imperialism, but it did so in a somewhat distorted form. Two victors emerged from the Second World War: The United States *and* the Soviet Union. If no capitalist power presented any threat to the United States, the U.S.S.R. certainly did, but not in the military sense. Stalin kept to all his promises and used the C.P.s to preserve the status quo in Greece, France and Italy. The threat from the Soviet Union was economic and political. This meant that instead of wiping out all rival imperialisms in the economic sense, the United States was forced to revive them against a more dangerous enemy. In addition the rearmament boom directed against the Soviet Union created a similar situation in Western Europe which was intensified by the increased use of technological innovations. This process succeeded in shielding some of the glaring weaknesses of British capital, and indeed bred the illusion among sections of British capitalism that it could exist as an independent economic unit, and avoid the Common Market. The period of the boom of the

[7] Leon Trotsky, 'A Fresh Lesson on the Character of the Coming War', *Writings 1938–9* (Pathfinder, New York, 1970).
[8] Ibid.

'fifties and early 'sixties created a situation where it was politically more expedient for the Tory Party to stay out of Europe than to go in. This meant, of course, that as the facts of capitalist life caught up, the price of entry went up. To enter the E.E.C. now, British capitalism has to streamline itself and this is where the trade-union movement comes in.

In the economic conditions of relative boom which have existed since 1945, it has been possible for the trade unions to use their bargaining position to push up wage rates. However, some qualifications must be made before discussing this in detail. We have to be clear about the fact that the benefits of the boom have only extended to sections of the organized working class. Other sections, such as pensioners, black workers, women workers, low-paid sectors, students, etc., have not benefited to anything like the same extent. This was made inevitable by the precise nature of the conditions created by the boom: one in which rises in living standards were not automatic, but could be won only by determined action. Moreover, the rise in living standards was confined almost entirely to 'luxury' consumer goods cars, refrigerators and the like. The problem of social expenditure—roads, schools, hospitals, housing—was far from solved. If anything, the post-war period demonstrates vividly the inability of capitalism, even in the most favourable conditions, to solve these problems.

However, within these limitations there is no doubt that the standard of living of large sections of the working class did rise during the 1950s and 1960s. The rise was, as we have suggested, the result of the complex process of struggle.

During most of the 1950s the leadership of the main unions was in the hands of the right wing, and in the case of the crucial Engineering Union, the A.E.U., the extreme right wing. The president of the A.E.U. was Lord Carron (or Carrion, as the rank-and-file militants referred to him). 'Carron's law' was thus enforced by a man who held several directorships in open defiance of his union's rule book. He was notable for his red-baiting and was more often than not attacking A.E.U. shop stewards engaged in militant action. During a struggle at Briggs Motors which involved his union, Carron declared: 'For a long time now subversive elements have been at work at Briggs. Last year alone there were 200 stoppages at the plant. In my view these subversive elements were responsible for most, if not all of them' (*Sunday Dispatch*, February 24th, 1957).

Until 1956 the Transport and General Workers Union (T. and G.W.U.) was in the hands of Deakin, who was as right-wing as Carron, though a bit more subtle in his approach. There was a slight change when Frank Cousins replaced Deakin, but until the accession of Jack Jones and Hugh Scanlon, the trade-union leadership remained in the hands of right-wingers. Today, while Scanlon and Jones divert the struggle they also partially express it. They will not support the most militant actions by their members, but they will not take disciplinary action against them, and this is a development of great significance for revolutionaries inside the trade unions.

During the right-wing leadership of the two most powerful unions, there was an increase in the number of unofficial actions by militants on the shop floor. Strikes became more frequent and smaller, reflecting an increasing proportion of strikes led by shop stewards. Wage gains made in this way became a central part of the income and way of life of many workers. The Donovan Commission Report gave the following example of the breakdown of the pay packet of a skilled engineering time-rated fitter in a factory in north-east England in a week in December 1967:

£	s	d	
11	1	8	Time rate for the industry negotiated nationally
4	8	8	Overtime – rate negotiated nationally
3	13	11	Night shift premium – negotiated nationally
11	14	11	Lieu bonus – negotiated by the stewards in the factory
30	19	2	Total

The ability to make these kinds of gains was, however, dependent on the conditions of economic boom, and by the late 'sixties and early 'seventies this trend was beginning to be reversed. Although all kinds of strikes were increasing, the most marked increase was in mass national strikes of municipal workers, dockers, Post Office workers, power workers, etc. Nevertheless, a vital part of the strategy of the ruling class will be that of trying to eliminate the power of the shop stewards which have been the backbone of the trade-union movement. The key element in this attack is introducing methods of wage payment which do not involve frequent negotiations with shop stewards. This can prove to be a very expensive exercise.[9]

The employers are fully conscious when they introduce productivity deals involving new methods of payment that this reduces the power and authority of shop stewards. G. R. Burn, who is in charge of courses for shop stewards in Bristol, said in a speech to the Coventry Employers' Association: ' ... with the introduction of Work Study, by which I mean methods and measurement, we are going to reduce the power of the shop stewards ... This is something which we are careful not to say to any shop steward, but it will in fact reduce his power and his apparent authority.' A Blue Book, published by the Coventry Engineering Employers' Federation, also points out that the end of negotiations involving the shop steward will mean a greater possibility of keeping down wages: 'The complete elimination of bargaining about money or payment between the operator and the rate-fixer ... means that higher management is in a much better position to control its labour costs than at present.'

This carrying of the economic struggle right into the workplace instead of at nationally negotiated levels has led some left-wing organizations to believe that the workplace struggle is the key to changing the consciousness of the working class. Nothing could be more dangerous. Although the Labour Party

---

[9] In Pressed Steel at Cowley in Oxford the management has been forced to pay £1·05 an hour in order to replace the piecework system with a Measured Day Work system.

as an organization is dying, its ideological influence is not dead. That influence extends to many more fields than that of the struggle in the workplace. It involves racism, attitudes to British imperialism, attitudes to women, to the Irish struggle, to the police and to Parliament. It is madness to think that these accumulated pressures can be defeated simply by leafletting factories on economic issues. All that this produces in the long term is a depoliticization of the members of the organization engaged in such activity and a rightward drift of the organization itself. More important, it still leaves the working class under the domination of bourgeois ideology. The key question for revolutionaries is how we destroy the ideological domination of social-democracy over the British working class. In the course of the economic struggle the working class is being forced to act like a class, but purely workplace agitation will never lead it to think like a class.

III

What then is the strategy of British capitalism today? As we mentioned earlier, the price the bourgeoisie paid for creating the conditions under which the working class remained under the domination of the Labour Party was the creation of a working class with an immensely strong trade-union consciousness. To break the trade unions the bourgeoisie must destroy that consciousness, either by inflicting a massive defeat which will lead to a severe demoralization, or by racialism, fascism or some similar means. This cannot be achieved by a confidence trick; no details of a productivity deal, no matter how subtle, will achieve this. It can only be done by changing the modes of thought of an enormous mass of people. It is this aspect of the Tory attack that we must study instead of the minutiae of how the Tories are going to increase the rate of surplus value.

One fact is abundantly clear. The Labour Party at present is not seen by the most advanced workers as a force for social change. At a time when the class struggle is intensifying, the

Labour Party's membership is in decline, and what membership is active is increasingly middle-class. The class struggle is not reflected inside the party and the 'left-wing' around *Tribune* is powerless, having been effectively co-opted and outmanœuvred by Wilson, Castle and their cohorts. The clearest indication of this was the T.U.C. demonstration of February 21st, 1971, where there were less than a dozen Labour Party banners. At probably the largest workers' demonstration since the 1920s *none* of the slogans put forward even by the trade-union bureaucracy were related to the Labour Party; there was no spontaneous call from the trade unionists which made a reference to the Labour Party and there were fewer people selling and buying *Tribune* than the papers of the revolutionary left. Even the *New Statesman* was forced to draw attention to the disillusionment with the Labour Party:

> But it was a political protest without politicians. It was no accident that no parliamentarians were included in the list of speakers. Indeed, Labour's leaders were politely, but firmly told that there would be no room for them on the plinth in Trafalgar Square ... The harsh truth is that a speech from any leading member of the last Labour government—and the whole atmosphere of harmony, unity and amity would have vanished in an instant.[10]

One can even discern a change in the ideological dominance of Labour over the working class. The great upsurge of class struggle around the anti-union laws saw no turning of the class towards the Labour Party with an expectation of action. This change has not of course occurred overnight. It has been determined by the conditions in which the Labour Party has existed since 1945. The post-war Labour government represented the *end* of an epoch. It was the last government which was able to give significant reforms to the working class after it had been swept to power on a wave of anti-capitalist feeling which, of

[10] *New Statesman*, February 26th, 1971.

course, it diverted. Despite the fact that it clashed sharply with the dockers and other sections of the working class, it did introduce a few reforms (such as the Health Service) which benefited the workers.[11] These reforms were only possible because of huge loans from American capital, and since the 1945–51 government no government has been able to grant even the most basic reforms to the working class. How far any capitalist government is now from being able to grant reforms can be judged from the record of the last Labour government. We will deal with other aspects of Wilson's policies in a later chapter, but it is necessary to discuss here the balance sheet of the Labour government as far as social services and social inequality is concerned. It is necessary to do this because pro-Labour writers tend either to ignore this side of Wilson's policies or distort them beyond recognition.[12]

1. *Housing.* The Labour government's record on housing is in practice no better than that of the Tories. During the 1964 election campaign the Labour leaders made great play of the Tories' 'Rachmanite' Rent Act. However, the 'constructive alternative' put in its place by the Labour government was virtually meaningless. By failing to extend protection of tenure to furnished property, they created a situation where all a landlord had to do was to stick a few chairs in a room, claim the property was furnished and leave the tenant with practically no security at all. The effect of the Rent Tribunals was at best marginal.

In 1968 it was calculated that an additional three million houses were needed simply to replace slums which it was not worth while repairing. These facts on the housing situation were not hidden from the Labour government. An official report in 1967 admitted that 1,700,000 houses were unfit for

[11] The Conservatives, if elected, would have done exactly the same. Quintin Hogg admitted that if the reforms had not been carried out by whichever government was in power, there would have been a real danger of a repetition of the massive social upheavals which followed the First World War. He was correct.

[12] For a typical apologist's account *see* Brian Lapping, *The Labour Government, 1964–70* (Penguin, Harmondsworth, 1970).

human habitation.[13] The report stated that of these houses, 79 out of every 100 lacked a hand-washbasin, 77 out of every 100 lacked an inside lavatory, and 72 out of every 100 had no proper bathing facilities. When it came to cuts in the economy after devaluation, absurd contracts like the Concorde went ahead, but the number of council houses to be built was cut by 15,000. The general effect of the Labour government's policies can be seen in the housing records of the following boroughs. A fine record for the last full year of Labour government:

	No. of houses built in:	
	1968	1969
Tower Hamlets	952	669
Barking	720	641
Newham	1,393	496
Southwark	3,345	430
Gateshead	1,317	688
Wallsend	298	18
Jarrow	406	87
Worksop	181	6

2. *Unemployment*. Clearly, terrible shortages existed in housing as indeed they did, and still do, in every other social service. Such is the economic system of capitalism that instead of utilizing every available person to remedy these shortages, the government is systematically involved in putting people out of work. When the January 1971 unemployment figures were announced (690,000) the Labour Party spokesmen in Parliament chirped that unemployment was unacceptable as a

---

[13] R. Holman, *Socially Deprived Families in Britain* (Bedford Square Press, London, 1970). It is also important to realize that despite the large number of people living in council houses, almost the entire profit from housing goes into the hands of the capitalists. For the G.L.C. in 1969–70 it was estimated that out of every £1 income from rents, 92p (18s 3d) would go to the moneylenders. Under the Labour administration the proportion going this way went up steadily from 79 per cent of all income from rents to 89 per cent of all such income. The biggest money-making racket of all is privately rented housing. An official survey in 1967 found that 33 per cent of all privately rented housing was unfit.

method of economic control. Few, however, took these objections seriously as the Labour government itself accepted the dictates of the capitalist economic system and had created unemployment as a way of controlling the economy when in office.

In the first five years of Labour government alone, and as a direct result of the government's policies, the number of unemployed rose from 340,000 to 551,000. The increase in unemployment of over 200,000 represented a loss of production of over 45 million working days a year. Did we hear Harold Wilson or Barbara Castle denouncing the lost production which resulted from this unemployment? No. Instead he was busy with McCarthyite red-baiting against the seamen for daring to go on strike for a better wage and for better working conditions. Or else he was denouncing the 'wreckers' in the car industry. Never in the entire period Labour were in office did the number of days of production lost through strikes reach even one-tenth of that lost through unemployment. Not even the 'left' M.P.s could bring themselves to attack the capitalist 'wreckers' in the government. The situation deteriorated considerably not only because there was a general increase in unemployment but because the duration of unemployment for men out of work for over a year went up by nearly a half, and the number of men out of work for over eight weeks doubled.

Particularly disturbing was the concentration of unemployment in certain areas. For example in Northern Ireland unemployment had reached 8·6 per cent in October 1968 and in Northern England it had reached 6·2 per cent.

3. *Low pay and inequality of wealth.* Before the Labour government came to power there were constant references to how the Labour Party would eliminate low pay and poverty. The familiar voice of Wilson was heard intoning more than once: 'In the part of the world where I come from, men are very ruggedly equal. The Yorkshire Socialist [*sic*] reacts from poverty not so much because it is a product of inefficiency and a badly run social system, but because it is a crime against God

and man.'[14] How God reacted to this speech is not yet known, but the men and women living on low pay are not amused when reminded of Wilson's brave words, because it was probably in the field of low pay that Labour's record was the worst and most dishonest.

It is calculated that over one in six children now lives below the poverty line.[15] The Labour government did little to alter this situation except mumble pious phrases about the general economic situation and the national interest. They tried to conceal these facts by announcing that the aim of the incomes policy was to help the lower-paid worker, but this pretence was dropped as Labour's Joint Parliamentary Under-Secretary of State at the Department of Employment and Productivity, Harold Walker, was forced to admit that 'It is not a primary function of the government's prices and incomes policy to redistribute wealth'. Even this was dishonest, as the incomes policy *was* an attempt to redistribute wealth, but in the direction of the employers. After their bluff with the incomes policy the Labour government did not even pretend to help the low-paid. It would have been a bit difficult for even Wilson or Castle to do this, as even a pathological liar would have been hard put to explain away the statistics which showed that in the last four years of Labour government the figure of those at or below the Supplementary Benefit level doubled.[16] The increase in poverty is inevitable when you have a situation where prices have been going up at 6–8 per cent a year, but in at least ninety industries wages have only been going up by 4 per cent a year.[17] When Harold Walker admitted the failure of the incomes policy he stated that the elimination of inequality was being carried out by Labour's taxation policy. It is worth laying this little myth to rest as well in order to disperse completely the smokescreen which Labour will begin to

[14] P. Foot, *The Politics of Harold Wilson* (Penguin, London, 1968).
[15] Child Poverty Action Group Press Release, January 21st, 1971.
[16] Ibid., and *D.E.P. Gazette*, December 1970, pp. 1114–16.
[17] Incomes DATA report on 126 industrial groups.

spread around itself as the Tories try to run British capitalism.

During the first three years of Labour government, taxation went up fastest on those who were the worst off. On a wage of £16 a week, the proportion of total income paid in all forms of taxation went up by over 15 per cent, whereas for incomes of over £60 a week, it went up by less than 3 per cent.[18] Even for old-age pensioners, the Labour government did nothing about the fact that over 20 per cent of their miserable pension income goes in tax. The situation is worse if children are taken into account.[19] Nothing was done about the retrogressive rates system, either. A family with an income of £22 a week paid in rates over 50 per cent more, as a proportion of its income, than did a family with an income of over £58 a week.

In addition to all this the Wilson government overstepped the mark as far as a large section of conscious workers were concerned with the attempt to muscle through the notorious *In Place of Strife* proposals. Coming at the end of a long wage-freeze this produced a revulsion against the Labour Party and certainly cost it the 1970 general election, as large numbers of its supporters voted with their arses and stayed at home. A sign that the resentment had not died down was the fact that Wilson was viciously heckled by at least half of a hand-picked audience of six thousand at a T.U.C. meeting on January 12th, 1971, held at the Royal Albert Hall.[20]

Despite the fact that the Labour Party succeeded in alienating itself from the trade-union movement, its economic policy was singularly unsuccessful even in its own capitalist terms. Despite an enormous number of turgid speeches from turgid politicians (nothing is more obscene than Labour social-patriotic politicians sounding self-righteous), calls for the 'Dunkirk spirit', wage-freezes, guiding lights, National Plans, etc., its incomes

[18] *Economic Trends* (February 1969).

[19] In the case of families with one child, the proportion of income paid in taxes during the first three years of the Labour government went up as follows: for a family with an income of £11, taxation went up by nearly 30 per cent whereas for a family with an income of over £35, it went down slightly.

[20] *The Red Mole*, vol. II, no. 2, carries an amusing report of the great occasion.

policy, for example, succeeded in shifting the distribution of national income by only 1 per cent in favour of the capitalist class, and even this was temporary. For if the truth be told even in the period of harsh and anti-working class policies of the Labour government the workers succeeded in shifting national income in their favour. This process which still continues and now begins to dog the footsteps of the Tory government shows the real crisis which confronts British capital.[21] The fall in distributed profits led to a catastrophic decline of investment, and, to quote but one example, the orders for machine tools fell by 42 per cent in 1970. It is this economic situation which determines the policy of any capitalist government, be it Tory or Labour. Any such government will have to carry out an attack on the living standards of the working class and the organizations which try and defend these standards. It is extremely important to understand this fact if one is serious about adopting a certain strategy towards the Labour Party.

Did the last government carry out reactionary policies because capitalism left it no other option or because, like the 'left' Labour M.P.s and the C.P., it had betrayed 'socialism'? In his more lucid moments even Harold Wilson admitted that there was no choice for Labour. In a speech to the T.U.C. in 1964 he said: 'If you borrow from some of the world bankers you will quickly find that you lose ... independence, because of the deflationary policies and the cuts in the social services that will be imposed on a government that has got itself into that position.' Wilson was only partially correct. He should have looked closer to home, for not only the 'gnomes of Zurich' wanted cuts, but the gnomes of the City of London as well. That lesson was rammed home in the first few weeks of the Labour government, when hundreds of millions of pounds-worth of capitalist assets were transferred out of the country simply because the bourgeoisie had a misguided fear that Labour might do something to improve the situation of pensioners.

[21] A. Glyn and B. Sutcliffe, 'The Critical Condition of British Capital', *New Left Review*, no. 66 (March–April 1971), provides an interesting analysis of the situation.

The country's financiers and capitalists were carrying out a capitalist political strike. The lesson to Wilson was clear, and he understood it. It didn't need a Marxist to tell Wilson that this sort of action by the bourgeoisie was inevitable. Even Sir Stafford Cripps had pointed out that the 'idea that the wielders of economic power will co-operate with a Labour government is quite fantastic'. What he meant of course was a Labour government which attacked capitalism, but there was no risk of that at all. Because the working class has illusions about the Labour Party, the bourgeoisie frequently prefers that attacks on the working class should be carried out by the Labour Party. Thus as far back as 1931, a prominent representative of the bourgeoisie offered the following piece of advice to George V: 'In view of the fact that the necessary economies would prove most unpalatable to the working classes it would be in the general interest if they were imposed by a Labour government.'[22] Before the 1964 election, *The Economist* was for similar reasons in favour of a Labour government and, as we've seen, Labour's 'economies' were 'most unpalatable to the working classes'.

The 'left' of the Labour Party refuses to understand that the power of the ruling class lies in its ownership and control of the means of production. It does not depend on its ability to win or lose elections. But the entire Parliamentary Labour Party, from Harold Wilson upwards, is united in fostering this myth. Thus we see that *Tribune* and its parliamentary supporters try desperately to confine the struggle entirely to parliament. Thus for example when one of *Tribune*'s columnists implied that an M.P. was demanding industrial action, that M.P. sent in a hurried letter explaining: 'I should hate Francis Flavius to give anyone the idea that I am now calling for mass action from the trade-union movement against it [the incomes policy].'[23]

While *Tribune*, and for that matter the *Morning Star*, place a great deal of emphasis on the electoral farce, the bourgeoisie

[22] R. Miliband, *Parliamentary Socialism* (Merlin Press, London, 1970), p. 176.
[23] Foot, op. cit., p. 337.

does not. It knows that its power to bend any government to carry out policies in the interests of British capitalism will last as long as the bourgeoisie controls the economy. In a sense even the Tribunites realize this fact. That is why even their most 'extreme' leader does not demand that a Labour government should take ownership out of the hands of the capitalist class *immediately* after being returned to office. The reason for this is not difficult to fathom: no social class in history has given up its position, power and privileges without a struggle. The British ruling class is no exception.[24] The Labour 'left' cannot point this out; if it did, it would be forced by its own logic to argue that the workers should prepare to meet force with force and the very idea would create severe strains on the heart conditions of many good Tribunites. The C.P. tries to have it both ways *on paper*. It states that violence is not inevitable but then also states that of course it cannot be ruled out. This is meaningless. The working class will not use violence, even defensive violence, if it has been told for decades that everything is obtainable by peaceful means. It will only use violence if it has been hearing the arguments which show that violence is inevitable. Communist Party members and left social-democrats all agree that it would have been correct for the German working class to resist Hitler by force. But how can you expect the working class to respond to such appeals against fascism if you have been telling it for decades that violence is unnecessary? If violence is necessary, and we think it is, then the case for it must be prepared from now. The *Morning Star* and *Tribune*, by glossing over the long period needed to educate the working class in the need to use force, prepare the way for

[24] Anyone who still believes in the uniquely 'peaceful and democratic' nature of the British bourgeoisie should consider the example of Belfast. Here we see the might of the British army employed in the defence of a regime that refuses to grant even the most elementary rights on housing, jobs, etc., and which is openly 'racist' as regards the Catholic minority. The lesson is quite obvious: if the British bourgeoisie is prepared to use force in this situation, it would not hesitate to use it against its own working class, if that class was trying to deprive the bourgeoisie of its power. Of course, in that case some of the soldiers would join the workers, but there would still be a struggle.

terrible working-class defeats. It is not the revolutionaries who are 'unrealistic', but those who believe that the capitalist class will co-operate in actions against its own interests, or will even peacefully accept its own defeat.

IV

Because we can't expect realism from the C.P. or the Tribunites, the task which confronts the revolutionary movement in relation to the class struggle is immense. As the struggle commences against the Tory Industrial Bill the conditions are being created for a large-scale revival of *politics* within the workers' movement.

The clauses contained in Mr Carr's Industrial Relations Bill would greatly hamper the activities of trade unionists. Among the most important provisions are those which declare unlawful strikes called by shop stewards; which ban the blacking of goods; restrict peaceful picketing; which establish machinery for legally enforceable procedure agreements; legal actions against newspapers supporting unlawful strikes and which facilitate victimization by employers.[25]

Although these specific provisions are important in themselves, they do not represent the nub of the Tory attack. The main aim of the British ruling class is to change the attitude of workers towards trade-unionism; by discrediting the unions they will make them ineffective in the eyes of large numbers of workers. Any opposition then must be to the laws as a whole and not to this or that particular provision. While the T.U.C. leadership has accepted this in theory and can call a massive demonstration outside working hours to 'Kill the Bill', some of its other actions play into the hands of the bourgeoisie. For example the T.U.C. spent a great deal of money on advertising in the national press to argue that shop stewards were not

[25] For a detailed analysis of the Tory proposals see the pamphlet *The Industrial Relations Bill: A Declaration of War*, produced by the International Marxist Group (I.M.G., London, 1971), which is available from Red Books, 182 Pentonville Road, London N1.

'subversive troublemakers', but were reasonable men. By this sort of propaganda the T.U.C. are agreeing with the bourgeois press that militant action in defence of workers' interests, which the bourgeoisie and its agents characterize as 'troublemaking', is wrong. This is precisely what the Tories want to get across and the T.U.C. makes this task easier and panders to the most backward elements of the working class.

The ruling class is aware that in any factory there is a section of workers who will always oppose the machinations of the management. These workers have a certain political conscious-ness, and not merely trade-union consciousness. The bourgeoisie has no chance at all of influencing this section of the working class and if a fascist solution is decided upon this is the section that they will try to liquidate physically. On the other hand all sections of the class contain workers who are totally under the control of bourgeois ideology and suffer from a completely false consciousness. They are the scabs who vote against any strike, who joined the trade union because of the closed shop. If they were not gutless they would openly blackleg during every strike. They are the basis of fascist street squads in periods of severe economic problems for the bourgeoisie. No action by the advanced sections of the working class will ever influence them. Between these two extremes are the great mass of workers. They are also affected by bourgeois ideology and hold racialist views, but the grip of this ideology on them is not so great that they cannot see the contradiction between these ideas and their own living reality. They are fully aware that there is a sharp distinction within the factory between workers and manage-ment. The question of whether or not they will support strike action depends on and is decided by the continual battle between the backward workers and the bourgeois press and television on the one hand and the ability of the conscious workers to combat this on the other. What the Tories want to do is to help the backward sections of workers by intimidating or sharply changing the ideas of the middle group of workers. During the struggle for a one-day strike on December 8th, 1970, the T.U.C.'s attacks on the militant leaders of the action helped the Tories. A hysterical 'red scare' campaign was used in relation to Kevin Halpin and other C.P. militants who were working for the strike. The fact that the T.U.C. worthies joined in this campaign undoubtedly aided the most backward sections of the workers. Of course the T.U.C. is also forced to respond to some of the pressures from its rank and file. Hence the meetings and demonstrations, which despite the T.U.C.'s bid to restrict them have a certain logic of their own. That most strident defender of British capitalism, *The Economist*, was quite clear on what it thought of all this. In an editorial entitled 'On the Road to Ruin' it commented:

> It is not difficult now to visualise a situation in which the moderate T.U.C. leadership was as damaging to the national interest [it is to me — T.A.] as the militants would be if they were in control at Congress House. If it comes to that ... the Government would have no choice but to fight the unions to some finish or other. And if that happened it might not even be too much of a tragedy if the moderates were smashed in the process, for the only point in supporting the moderates is if they continue to exercise a moderating influence.[26]

The other strategy which is condemned to failure from the very start is the policy of pressure politics, and it is the favourite ploy of the C.P. The latter believes that if we put sufficient pressure on Jack Jones, Vic Feather, Harold Wilson or even the Tories they will be forced to give in. Hence there are signature campaigns, lobbies of Parliament, etc. This view is profoundly mistaken because it refuses to accept that it is the objective political and economic conditions which determine governmental policy. Any capitalist government would like to buy off shop-floor militancy by reforms, concessions and other similar devices. They don't because they can't. The laws of motion of capitalism at the present time do not permit it. Hence the C.P.

[26] *The Economist* (February 27th, 1971).

leadership even views the extra-parliamentary action as a pressure on the government instead of the beginning of a situation which makes it impossible for the Tories to stay in office. This policy of the C.P. flows out of its projection of a pact with the Tribunites and in the near future a 'left' Labour government peddling reforms. As we have seen this is merely utopian defeatism and can only lead to a demoralization of even the most advanced sections of workers.

In Chapters 5 and 8 we will discuss a concrete strategy for the revolutionary left which takes into account the death agony of the Labour Party today. This party is becoming more and more 'bourgeoisified' as its links with the trade unions become more and more strained. This process was greatly helped by the period of Labour government we have recently experienced. Another spell in office would result in the total disillusionment of the mass of workers with the Labour Party. The next few years might see a growing break between the T.U.C. and the Labour Party which might result in the trade unions stopping the subsidy which they give to the Labour Party, and which forms the party's only—and somewhat tenuous—link with the working class. The destruction of the Labour Party by the revolutionary left is an event which the revolutionary movement has long been waiting for and which will be greeted with much rejoicing. Lenin once advised the British revolutionary movement to support the Labour Party like the rope supports the hanging man. The revolutionary movement missed many chances to do this and thus prolonged the death agony of Labourism, but it seems that the situation of British capitalism today will be sufficient to perform this task with the aid of the trade unions.

3 The British Communist Party's Road to Socialism: Half a Step Forward, Four Steps Backward

The opportunists have long been preparing the ground for their collapse by denying the socialist revolution and substituting bourgeois reformism in its stead; by rejecting the class struggle with its inevitable conversion at certain moments into civil war, and by preaching class collaboration ... ignoring or rejecting the fundamental truth of socialism, that workingmen have no country ... by making a fetish of the necessary utilization of bourgeois parliamentarism and bourgeois legality ...

V. I. LENIN,
The War and Russian Social-Democracy (1914)

The British Communist Party was formed in July 1920,[1] directly under the impact of the October Socialist Revolution in Russia in 1917 and the Third International.[2] As Britain

[1] See J. Klugmann, *History of the British Communist Party* (Lawrence and Wishart, London, 1968), vol 1. This account suffers from the fact that it was 'official'. L. J. M. MacFarlane, *The British Communist Party* (MacGibbon and Kee, London, 1966), gives a more balanced account.

[2] Usually referred to as the Comintern. Once the degeneration of the Second International had been established by its total capitulation to chauvinism at the outbreak of the First World War, Lenin worked unceasingly for the creation of a new revolutionary International, in the tradition of Marx and Engels. He worked in the Zimmerwald Group, forming its left wing, which brought together socialists who opposed support for their governments in the First World War. After the February 1917 Revolution in Russia, Lenin fought for the Bolshevik Party to leave the Zimmerwald Group and start a new International. At first he did not succeed, but in 1919 a call signed by Lenin and Trotsky was issued for the launching of the

was a leading imperialist power, Bolshevik leaders, and in particular Lenin himself, took a great deal of interest in the formation of the British C.P.[3] Lenin used his personal influence and prestige to accelerate the unity negotiations between the various revolutionary left groups which were in favour of setting up a British Section of the Third International, and at the same time he vigorously combated the sectarianism which was rampant in many of these groups.

The main characteristic which distinguished the British Communist Party from its equivalents in other parts of Europe[4] was that it did not develop organically out of an existing mass movement. It was essentially the result of the fusion of several small propaganda groups:[5] the British Socialist Party, elements of the Socialist Labour Party,[6] the Workers Socialist Federation,

---

Third International, The founding conference was held in 1920. See E. H. Carr, *The Bolshevik Revolution 1917–23,* 2 vols (Penguin, Harmondsworth, 1966), and Jane Degras, ed., *Documents of the Comintern* (Oxford University Press, 1956), for an understanding of the reasons which led to the establishment of the Comintern.

[3] V. I. Lenin, *Left-Wing Communism, an Infantile Disorder* (Progress Publishers, Moscow, 1966). See also V. I. Lenin, *The British Labour and British Imperialism* (Lawrence and Wishart, London, 1969).

[4] Julius Braunthal, *History of the International 1914–1943* (Nelson, London, 1967). Despite the fact that the author is a social-democrat, the book is extremely well documented. In France and Italy a large proportion of the socialist parties were won over to the Third International. In Germany the Communist Party came into existence as a result of a series of splits from the huge German Social Democratic Party.

[5] This fact has often been used to argue that it was a mistake, under these circumstances, to launch the C.P.G.B. Walter Kendall uses this argument to justify his own social-democratic views in his book, *Revolutionary Movement in Britain, 1900–1920* (Weidenfeld and Nicolson, London, 1969). While splendidly documented, the book completely misunderstands the role played by German Social Democracy in strangling the German Revolution. The failure of the 1919 German Revolution was the main factor enabling Western capitalism to survive the post-First-World-War revolutionary wave. Under these circumstances, the Third International was entirely correct in using all possible means to build revolutionary parties rapidly. Hindsight tells us that they may have overestimated the potential of the situation in some instances; however, had they not carried out this policy perhaps even the Russian Revolution itself would have been strangled.

[6] The C.P.G.B. has always claimed that the majority of this party came in, but there is considerable doubt about this. See Macfarlane, op. cit., Kendall, op cit.

the South Wales Socialist Society, together with sections of the shop-stewards movement which had sprung up during the First World War, and small tendencies within the Independent Labour Party and the Guild movement.[7] One of the main reasons for this difference was the lack of a Marxist tradition and a Marxist culture in the British labour movement, a factor which has also shaped the development of many left intellectuals, and which we will discuss in detail in Chapter 7. Unlike the Second International[8] parties in most European countries, the British Labour Party never had even a formal commitment to Marxism or the class struggle. Its creed was much more a Fabian Methodism and in fact there was considerable opposition to the Labour Party being allowed to join the Second International. Another important factor coloured the development of British social-democracy. The immense resources of British imperialism coupled with its total ideological hegemony allowed it to bribe sections of the working class, in particular trade-union officials and highly skilled operatives, thus creating what Lenin correctly described as a 'labour aristocracy'.[9] This aristocracy in turn became an instrument for keeping the labour movement committed to bourgeois ideology, and as the class struggle in Britain today begins to intensify we see once

[7] Cf. Klugmann, op. cit., Macfarlane, op. cit., Kendall, op. cit. One of the smaller groups which came in was the Socialist Prohibition Fellowship. This resulted in the founding conference of the C.P. passing a resolution calling for the prohibition of the production, distribution and sale of all alcohol!

[8] Formed in 1889, when the French and German supporters of Marx and Engels (together with others) gathered at a conference in Paris. However, the Second International was not a centralized international party: the International Socialist Bureau, its only central organ, was not established until 1900 and it held only nine congresses (eight regular, one special) in its twenty-five-year history. Its revolutionary high-point was the Amsterdam Congress in 1904, when the revisionism of Bernstein and the entry into bourgeois governments of Millerand and Jaurès were soundly condemned. However, parliamentarianism gradually gained ground and in 1914 at the outbreak of the war nearly all the sections of the International forgot their internationalism and acted as recruiting organizations for their own bourgeois class to lead them to slaughter.

[9] V. I. Lenin, *Imperialism, the Highest Stage of Capitalism* (Progress Publishers, Moscow, 1968), p. 11.

again how the trade-union bureaucrats, even the supposedly 'left' ones, reveal clearly how keen they are to preserve the existing social structures despite the 'unreasonableness' of the bosses and the government in power.

The fact that the Communist Party was created outside the mainstream of the working-class movement has had important consequences for both the party and the development of the revolutionary left as a whole. For instance the party has never been able to develop as a serious political force and has never been able to present itself as an alternative pole of attraction inside the working-class movement to the Labour Party. Nor has it been able to dent the electoral support of the same party. Even in the few places where the C.P., for specific local reasons, did manage to gain electoral support (Fife, some valleys in South Wales, Stepney) and actually managed to get two Members of Parliament, Willie Gallacher and Phil Piratin, it could not retain that support. In both West Fife and Stepney, C.P. support has dwindled to little more than the national average and Labour has a firm grip. Also the C.P. has never been able to clarify in a satisfactory and effective fashion its relations and its position regarding the Labour Party. Because of the lack of a thorough-going political split with social-democracy, the C.P. even in its best days and with the valuable tactical advice of Lenin has never had a strategy for breaking the Labour Party's grip over the mass of the working class. Depending on the requirements of the Russian bureaucracy, the C.P. could with comparative ease turn from the wildest ultra-leftism[10] to the most craven opportunism[11] as far as the Labour

[10] For instance, at its Eleventh Congress, held towards the end of 1929, the party passed a series of resolutions describing the newly elected Labour government as 'social-fascist'.

[11] Under the 1945 Labour government, the C.P. called for higher production and the establishment of production committees. This was outlined in a C.P. pamphlet published in 1947, *Britain's Plan for Prosperity*. A small extract from this has been reproduced in K. Coates and T. Topham, *Workers' Control* (Panther, London, 1970). Another extract in the same collection is from a pamphlet by Reg Birch (now the leader of the only Maoist group in Britain to be recognized

Party was concerned. Apart from disorienting its own members the twists and turns created a serious credibility gap as far as many sympathetic rank-and-file Labour Party members were concerned. This inability to develop a local political base was not totally unconnected with the fact that the British C.P. became even more dependent on its links with Moscow and thus one of the more pliant sections of the Third International after the degeneration of the latter organization.[12] The British section was one of the few Communist Parties which did not experience an important echo of the struggle which Trotsky and the left opposition were waging against the increasing

---

by Peking) in which he argues that engineering workers would be 'willing to co-operate' in increasing productivity so as to assist the Labour government 'to carry out the will of the people'. This same Labour government was engaged in massacring communists in Malaya, Vietnam, and Greece, though admittedly the British C.P. did not stoop to the same level as the French C.P. and did pro-pagandize against some of the 'atrocities'.

[12] The isolation of the Russian Revolution (especially after the defeat of the German Revolution) and the terrible blows inflicted on the new workers' state by the imperialist armies of intervention, created suitable conditions for the rise of a privileged bureaucratic caste. (This is not to imply that the victory of this caste was inevitable, as some revisionist writers maintained and as Deutscher argued in his writings.) The bureaucracy found in Stalin an effective weapon for gaining power and lent him its support. Lenin was only too well aware of this danger and spent his remaining years (by 1922 he was very ill) trying to combat the process. During the course of this he formed a bloc with Trotsky, cf. V. I. Lenin, *Collected Works*, 45 vols (Progress Publishers, Moscow, 1963–70), vol. 45; Moshe Lewin, *Lenin's Last Struggle* (Faber, London, 1969).

After Lenin's death it fell to Trotsky to continue the struggle. Together with other Bolsheviks he formed the Left Opposition, but, for reasons it is not necessary to discuss here, by 1929 the fight had been lost and Trotsky was exiled. Outside the Soviet Union, Trotsky first formed the International Left Opposition and then the Fourth International to continue the fight against Stalinist degeneration and for a new revolutionary leadership. As Stalin and the bureaucracy gained the upper hand, they gradually converted the Third International into an instrument of Soviet state policy. From organizations committed to revolution, most sections of the Comintern were converted into pressure groups designed to support the international manœuvrings of the Soviet bureaucracy (cf. Leon Trotsky, *The Third International After Lenin* [Pioneer, New York, 1957]). Those sections that did make the revolution clashed in every instance with the Soviet bureaucracy and made their revolutions despite the Soviet leadership as in China, Vietnam and Yugoslavia.

bureaucratization of the Russian party itself. A party branch in Balham in South London did raise the question of Stalinism inside the party, but did not meet with much success. However, the Balham group were the originators of British Trotskyism and in the first issue of their newspaper *The Red Flag*, which was described as the 'monthly organ of the British Section, International Left Opposition' and was published in May 1933, they described the regime which prevailed inside the British party:

In the Communist Party of Great Britain the reign of the bureaucrats has been so far uninterrupted and complete. Discussion, of any real character, has been prevented by the simple method of expulsion and by keeping from the Party all the essential documents. Let those who still believe that there is intelligent and revolutionary discussion within the Communist Party examine the events which led up to the expulsion of ourselves. Or let them ponder over a decision of the recent party congress at Battersea where all the delegates condemned Zinoviev, Kamenev, and other Russian Bolsheviks without discussion as 'counter-revolutionaries'. The delegates knew no more about the viewpoint of the people they so condemned than they know about the man in the moon. But they voted, because, you see, they were told that these old Bolsheviks were 'counter-revolutionary'. And so in a thousand cases. There is no discussion save that prompted and controlled from above.'

Thus right from its earliest years the C.P. had the reputation of being the most docile of parties as far as accommodating to the policies of the Soviet bureaucracy was concerned. The cumulative effects of this docility were felt with a vengeance in the post-1956 period when Khrushchev's speech at the Twentieth Party Congress, together with the brutal suppression of the Hungarian Revolution, resulted in some ten thousand members, including some of its leading intellectuals, leaving the Party. There were a few exceptions to this blind obedience, such as Harry Pollitt's failure to recognize the 'imperialist nature' of the Second World War when it first broke out, but he was soon back in line. The rest of the party accepted the Hitler-Stalin pact faithfully, as they did the Stalin-Churchill-Roosevelt agreements. It is important to understand the total dependence of the C.P. on the Soviet bureaucracy if we are to grasp exactly why the C.P. is in a shambles today, and what political and psychological effects even the slightest criticism of the Russians has on the old and loyal rank and file. Thus it is useful to study how the line of the C.P. changed overnight during the years leading up to the Second World War, and what role the C.P. played during the war and immediately after its conclusion.

In a C.P. pamphlet published in 1934 and entitled *The Labour Party and the War*, the important question is raised: 'But supposing Fascist Germany attacks the U.S.S.R.: are you now in favour of the workers supporting the British and French governments in an attack on Germany?' The reply is equally clear: '*Under no circumstances*. Such action would help the German capitalists to represent the war as one of self-defence; it would immensely strengthen the British capitalists, and weaken the British workers; it would put British imperialism in the event of victory in a favourable position for attacking the U.S.S.R., it would mean suppressing the inevitable revolt in India and the Empire.'[13]

Only a few years later the C.P. had come out in support of Churchill and were only bemoaning the fact that Churchill did not have 'better men' around him. The leading Stalinist hack in the party, R. P. Dutt, was talking in terms of 'strengthening national unity'; in other words he was advocating class-collaboration. No criticism of Churchill was to be tolerated, and the C.P. openly boasted: 'Events ... have proved the correctness

---

[13] Cf. Robert Black, *Stalinism in Britain* (New Park Publications, London, 1970). While this book contains some well-researched information, the author does not see the contradiction between exposing Stalinism and using Stalinist methods himself in describing other revolutionary currents on the left.

of the general line of the Communist Party, particularly their refusal to countenance attacks on Churchill, urged by "leftist" elements in the labour movement ... ' (*The Communist Party and the National Front*, April 1942).

Of course, the 'leftists' in the labour movement on whom the entire wrath of British Stalinism was soon to descend consisted of Trotskyists and other revolutionary Marxists, who refused to accept the subordination of the class struggle in the interests of British capitalism.

The C.P. became an ally of the bosses and of Churchill. It was opposed to strikes. It was constantly exhorting the workers to increase productivity and openly encouraging strike-breaking. At the 1942 Conference of the C.P.G.B. its veteran leader Harry Pollitt boasted:

> I salute our comrade, a docker from Hull, who was on a job unloading a ship with a cargo urgently wanted ... When the rest of the dockers struck work, he fought against it because he believed that the course of action he recommended would get what was wanted without a strike. What courage, what a sacred spirit of real class consciousness, to walk on the ship's gangway and resume his job ... The Trotskyists and the I.L.P. charge the Party and me in particular with being strike-breakers. We can face that from people whose political line is consciously helping the development of fascism.

This was the leader of the British C.P. laying down the line: strike-breaking was now to be regarded as the highest form of class consciousness and all those who opposed it were agents of Hitler. Today, because of the changed balance of forces between Stalinism and the revolutionary left, this rubbish would be treated with the contempt it deserves.

It was partly a sign of the times that these Stalinist slanders were accepted without question. Today when the C.P. writes a pamphlet attacking the revolutionary groups, it has to tread more carefully and the old slanders are discarded and replaced

6

with new and more sophisticated ones. Readers interested in studying the changing face of British Stalinism should compare the recent pamphlet by Mrs Betty Reid, *Ultraleftism in Britain*,[14] with a pamphlet of a much older vintage by William Wainwright, the present Assistant Editor of the *Morning Star*. Wainwright's literary masterpiece of the 'forties is touchingly entitled *Clear Out Hitler's Agents*, and in case one is in any doubt, our Churchill-fearing Stalinist makes himself even more explicit:

> There is a group of people in Britain masquerading as socialists in order to cover up their fascist activities ... They are called Trotskyists. You've heard of the fifth column. The Trotskyists are their allies and agents in the rank of the working-class ... The Home Guard has been taught a quick way to deal with enemy paratroops and spies. You must train yourself to round up these other, more cunning enemies on whom Hitler depends to do his work for him in Britain. This book is a simple training manual. It will explain to you the tactics of the strange war Hitler is waging in your factory ...

This policy of sabotaging the class struggle during the war itself was followed by a programme after the war which argued the case for a continuation of a National Government. The C.P. was in this instance well to the right of the British Labour Party. The April 1945 issue of the C.P.'s theoretical journal, *Labour Monthly*, argued:

> All these tasks will require national unity of a strong and united Britain led by a strong and united Government whose mandate and representative character will be recognized by the entire country and not only by a section. Hence it would be dangerously unrealistic for the labour movement and progressive opinion to dismiss idly and without consideration the need for a National Government in the transition years following victory in Europe.

[14] Communist Party, 1969.

Fortunately the working-class movement was not interested in such drivel and both Churchill and His Majesty's Communist Party were a bit taken aback at the extent of the Labour landslide in the July 1945 general election. The C.P. soon adjusted to the new victory and R. P. Dutt now described the Tories as the 'half-brothers of fascism' and claimed that the work of the C.P. during the preceding ten years had now obviously borne fruit in helping to build up the Labour majority. Forgotten was Dutt's patriotic rhetoric of April 1945. Reality had not conformed to the requirements of British Stalinism and therefore history had to be slightly distorted to bring the party back in line. A political organization which cannot explain its own past has a bleak future, and unless the C.P. leadership makes a thorough-going critique of its past it will disintegrate.

As far as organization was concerned, the C.P. right from the moment of its foundation functioned largely as a federated propaganda group until it was 'reorganized' as a result of Comintern influence in 1922. Even its own historian, Klugmann, noted: 'The old socialist groups were above all propagandist bodies; membership of one of their branches was often a loose token of general political support. It did not necessarily carry with it an obligation to activity in the locality or still less to pay the official party dues.' The C.P. only adopted the cell-type structure to bring itself in line with the decisions taken by the Third Congress of the Comintern,[15] and this remained in force till the late 1930s. Then a gradual shift began to accelerate towards election-oriented area branches, as the party became more and more committed to the parliamentary road. This position was virtually formalized by the adoption of the 'mass party' concept. Thus the full circle has been turned and today the average C.P. branch is very much like the propaganda group one described by Klugmann: a typical branch would have thirty or forty paper members (paper in the sense that they are registered on paper and read the *Morning Star*). Of

[15] Cf. Degras, op. cit., Klugmann, op. cit.

these perhaps seven or eight could be regarded as active, and one of their main activities is the regular collection of dues from the 'members' who don't attend branch meetings. Every year the party has a drive to re-register its membership, and in some of the weaker areas this is the only time that a reasonable percentage of the members are seen.[16]

Apart from being a cynical mockery of the organizational principles of Leninism, this situation also leads to a bureaucratic dualism. In reality there are two 'Communist' Parties: one comprises the entire registered membership and turns up on select occasions (like *Morning Star* birthday rallies) and the other, the 'real' one, consists of the party activists around the central core of full-timers. The latter have a political life and existence of their own; they have their own discussions and their own perspectives. For example, when the party's present programme, *The British Road To Socialism*, was first adopted, the inner core often explained that its adoption was merely a tactic devised by J. Stalin, who had also corrected the original draft and added some material of his own. Thus at official party meetings they vigorously defended this appalling document against 'ultra-left' critics within the party. This organizational structure creates confusions even within the narrow political limits of the C.P. itself, and even when the party decides on certain actions which demand a certain degree of mobilization and militancy, many of its members, used as they are to a reformist inactivity, find themselves incapable of participating.[17]

Despite all its weaknesses of both ideology and organization, in one field of activity the C.P. has the edge over all its critics on the revolutionary left—in the vital industrial field where the

[16] It is a common joke amongst cynical C.P. members that the revolution could not possibly take place in January because the party would be busy re-registering its membership.

[17] For instance on the December 8th, 1970, strike against the Tories, an action industrially sponsored by the C.P., the C.P. teachers in the National Union of Teachers were opposed to the Inner London Teachers' Association participating in the strike and joined hands with right-wingers to oppose the action, but were defeated (cf. *The Red Mole*, vol. 2, no. 2).

C.P. has the overwhelming allegiance of industrial militants who consider themselves Marxists. To admit this fact is not to accept its permanence, but precisely to see how revolutionaries should act in order to change the balance of forces between them and the C.P. in industry. In the last chapter a certain strategy in this regard is outlined. Despite traumatic shocks such as the mass exodus in 1956–7, the E.T.U. scandal[18] and the Sino-Soviet split, its industrial base has remained fairly solid.[19] Indeed the industrial militants have, in general, been amongst the most loyal supporters of both the party leadership and of Moscow.[20] Their loyalty to Moscow prevailed during the invasion of Czechoslovakia, when a significant number of militants correctly saw the leadership's mealy-mouthed opposition to the Czech invasion as a move to the liberal right and as part of a more generalized effort to appease what remained of 'left' social-democracy; hence they supported the invasion. Many of them also couldn't understand why the party had suddenly decided to stop supporting Moscow, nor could they see the difference between Budapest 1956 and Prague 1968. The sad truth was that no one in the C.P. leadership was capable of explaining it to them. The disparity between the industrial and political influence of the C.P. is best illustrated by the fact that in certain areas well-known members of the party will be returned time after time with handsome majorities in trade-union elections, not only as shop stewards,

[18] The Electrical Trades Union (E.T.U.) was controlled by the C.P. till a 'ballot-rigging' scandal erupted and was used as a general exercise in red-baiting by the mass media. The fact that the C.P. was only following the customary practice in the E.T.U. was totally ignored and the C.P.'s leading militant, Les Cannon, capitulated to the bourgeoisie and later became one of the most right-wing of right-wing social-democrats in the labour movement. His death was mourned by all bourgeois commentators.

[19] A small section of its industrial base was, however, lost to Maoist formations, especially in North London A.E.F. and D.A.T.A.

[20] This does not mean that there has been no conflict between the industrial militants and the party apparatus. On the contrary there has always been friction between the aspirations of the militants and the desires of the C.P.'s industrial department to win as many trade-union positions as possible.

but also when standing for important union posts. The same men will contest elections in the same area for both Parliament and local councils and will get derisory votes.

Although anti-communist propaganda undoubtedly plays a role in this, the real explanation is to be found elsewhere as it is, after all, the militants who tend to vote for Communist Party candidates in union elections and they are less influenced by capitalist ideology. Two complementary factors are at work here: one we have already indicated, namely that the C.P. is incapable of projecting itself as a viable alternative to Labour; the second is the fact that sections of left-inclined workers do not trust the C.P. They hold the view that the C.P. is a 'Russian' party; that whilst it is all right to elect Communist Party candidates to union positions ('because they are good fighters against the boss'), it is dangerous to elect them to Parliament (a common comment is 'Once the buggers got in you'd never get them out'). Of course, there is a right-wing element here, but this is by no means the whole story. Many militants hold these views because years of experience with the C.P. have taught them that the party will make 180 degree turns at the behest of the Russian leadership. These people remember the C.P.'s defence of the crimes of Stalinism,[21] its

[21] The Communist Party used all the propaganda means at its disposal to justify the Moscow Trials in the mid 'thirties, when nearly the whole of Lenin's Central Committee were tried and shot as 'imperialist agents'. Countless articles and pamphlets were issued 'proving' how fair the trials were. The C.P. used its influence to publish a Left Book Club edition along these lines (Dudley Collard, *Soviet Justice and the Trial of Radek* [Gollancz, London, 1937]), and a 'theoretical' gloss was given to the butchery in J. R. Campbell, *Soviet Policy and its Critics* (Gollancz, London, 1939), also a Left Book Club edition. Could it be mere coincidence that the doughty warrior against 'Trotskyism', Mrs Betty Reid, was employed by the Left Book Club at that time?

This policy did not end with the Moscow Trials. J. Klugmann wrote *From Trotsky to Tito* (Lawrence and Wishart, London, 1951), shortly after the break between Stalin and Yugoslavia, to prove that Tito, like Trotsky, had been an important imperialist agent all along and that his leadership of the Yugoslav Revolution was part of an imperialist plot. After the reconciliation between Khrushchev and Tito, the book was withdrawn. It will be interesting to see how the C.P.'s official historian deals with that particular piece of history!

somersaults during the Second World War and its thuggish attitude towards other political tendencies.[22] If revolutionary politics are discredited inside the working-class movement, the British Communist Party has a large share of the responsibility.

How then do we explain the C.P.'s influence in the industrial field? Again, the origins of the party provide the answer. Although the active membership of the groups which came together to form the C.P.G.B. in 1920 was probably not much greater than those of the revolutionary left groups which exist today,[23] it included a fair proportion of shop stewards and other union militants (especially in Scotland and South Wales). This provided the C.P. with an industrial base from its very inception.

Also, despite the fact that the C.P. has been guilty of many ultra-left and opportunist errors,[24] in the trade-union field it has at the level of wages militancy appeared to many militants as the only credible alternative to the right-wing trade-union bureaucrats. Even in its most opportunist phase the C.P. was slightly to the left of the trade-union bureaucrats. Where other important 'left' tendencies have developed inside the labour movement they have usually either accepted the hegemony of the C.P. within an industrial united front (e.g. the Independent Labour Party) or relied upon its grass-roots organization (the Jones/Scanlon/Daly tendency today).

Another factor which explains the C.P.'s effectiveness inside the trade-union movement is that its work in this field has always been of a higher order. It applied the Third International's policy of creating trade-union cells much more

[22] In the mid and late 'thirties it was a common occurrence for Trotskyist militants to be beaten up if they attempted to sell papers outside C.P. meetings. While the C.P. has abandoned this practice it has left its mark on the revolutionary movement.

[23] Macfarlane, op. cit., Kendall, op. cit. Even Klugmann admits as much.

[24] It failed to criticize certain 'left' T.U.C. members because they were members of the Anglo-Russian Trade Union Committee (formed in 1925). This led to the C.P.G.B. abdicating an independent role in the period prior to the 1926 General Strike and contributed to the T.U.C.'s betrayal of that strike. During the ultra-left 'Third Period' the C.P. set up small revolutionary unions which damaged trade unionism in important areas.

effectively than it applied the line of the united front. In certain activities such as the Minority Movement,[25] the struggle to break the grip of company unions (Spencerism) and the unemployed workers' movement, it managed to strike deep roots in the working-class movement.

Also the industrial base of the C.P. has proved more durable than its political fronts. At its height the political influence of the C.P. did extend to left social-democracy in the last half of the 'thirties. This was during the Left Book Club upsurge (the form the Popular Front took in Britain) when it was possible for Harry Pollitt to speak with Strachey, Stafford Cripps and Lloyd George to audiences of tens of thousands and be greeted with rapturous applause. C.P. influence was extremely strong in the network established by the Club—some 57,000 members organized in some 1,200 discussion groups. Most of these were local, but they also included clubs whose members were scientists, architects, teachers, poets, musicians, lawyers, actors, accountants, commercial travellers and even cyclists! Books were published in editions of 50,000,[26] and it seemed as though the British C.P. was on the verge of a big breakthrough. But all this was virtually destroyed in one blow with the signing of the Hitler-Stalin Pact in the autumn of 1939. This disaster did not seriously affect the C.P.'s industrial work, which was harmed but far from destroyed. It is also worth noting that no similar disaster—not even the 'ballot-rigging' case in the E.T.U.—has struck its trade-union work.

The C.P. has made good use of its industrial base and has succeeded, by careful attention to union elections, use of its daily paper, organization of industrial caucuses based upon union and industry, in appearing relevant and sometimes even necessary in the left/right struggle in the unions. Its industrial department has always been one of its most important and carefully nurtured sections. It has been manned by its most high-

[25] Cf. Chapter 2.

[26] Cf. J. Lewis, *The Left Book Club; an Historical Record* (Gollancz, London, 1970), for a pro-C.P. account.

powered and able officials. The overwhelming majority of the C.P.'s industrial militants are good class-conscious workers who genuinely believe that the C.P. is the most effective instrument for fighting capitalism. It is precisely this fact which makes C.P. influence in the trade-union movement extremely dangerous. Because the C.P. is regarded as left wing by the rank and file its reformist practice can cause a great deal of damage to the revolutionary movement by deflecting the struggles which are taking place. In recent years, for instance, as an integral part of its 'parliamentary road to socialism' strategy, the C.P. has pursued what it describes as a 'unity of the left' policy. This means, in essence, unity with those on its immediate right — the *Tribune* supporters in the Labour Party and 'left' trade-union leaders such as Jones and Scanlon. The latter in their turn advocate what they call the 'unity of the labour move-ment', which means making verbal criticism of the right but drawing back from a real struggle on some inane pretext. The C.P. is thus useful in providing 'left' social-democrats and the like with a left cover so that they can try to obscure the fact that they are engaged in dampening down important class struggles. But the relationship is two-sided. In order to preserve friendly relations with the social-democrats with whom they are trying to form an alliance, the C.P. has capitulated to 'friendly pressures' fairly regularly. A prime example of this was in the struggle against the Labour government's anti-union proposals outlined in *In Place of Strife*: once the Labour cabinet had made a concession, the C.P. played a major role in divert-ing the movement into harmless channels and succeeded in containing the first political strike movement for forty-three years by restricting it to the level of making purely defensive demands.[27] A similar danger will arise as the campaign against the Tory government gains momentum. During the mammoth, 140,000-strong demonstration against the Tory Industrial Rela-tions Bill on February 21st, 1971, the C.P. made no effort to

[27] For a detailed critique of this policy see Pat Jordan, 'Revolutionaries and the Trade Unions', *The Red Mole*, vol. 1, no. 9.

provide a lead; it tamely tail-ended the official leadership of the demonstration (i.e. Vic Feather & Co.) instead of raising the question of a generalized struggle to defeat the Tory Bill via a mass general strike. That task was left to the smaller groups of the revolutionary left.

In fact the Communist Party of Great Britain is a considerable hindrance to the cause of revolutionary socialism in Britain in two important ways. First, the very fact that the C.P. equated Stalinism with socialism politically damaged the whole idea of socialism and revolutionary politics. The bourgeoisie, too, quite deliberately fostered the image of the bureaucratically degenerated Soviet state as socialism in practice, in order to discredit socialist ideas inside the working-class movement; and one has to concede that it has been partially successful. Secondly, because of its industrial base the C.P. tends to defuse and mystify the class struggle. This is related to its belief that bourgeois democracy is in danger from monopoly capitalism and that a multi-class coalition is necessary to defeat the monopolies and *extend* bourgeois democracy. At a time when Parliament is increasingly losing its credibility, and large numbers of people are seeing through the sham of the House of Commons, the C.P. is concerned with strengthening this very same Parliament. A quick read of the *British Road to Socialism* makes the party's reformist perspectives crystal clear, and this was a programme adopted well before the Twentieth Party Congress and the *official* sanctification of peaceful coexistence between classes within the limits of the bourgeois state.[28] The party's Stalinist heritage has created confusion in other fields: it was totally incapable of organizing a solidarity campaign with the struggle of the Vietnamese revolutionaries—a task

[28] For a well-argued, sympathetic but forceful critique of the *British Road to Socialism* see Bill Warren, 'The Programme of the C.P.G.B.—A Critique', *New Left Review*, no. 63 (September–October 1970). This was originally written as a discussion document inside the C.P. The fact that Bill Warren was not expelled for publishing it publicly also gives us an insight into the present regime. In the old days Warren would have been expelled and denounced as a Trotskyite saboteur!

which was taken up by the revolutionary left; it refused to make a stand against the use of troops in Ireland by the Labour government. The list could be extended to include a whole variety of crimes. Even its well-publicized condemnation of the invasion of Czechoslovakia was a rightwards move, and when the Czech government brought up twenty-six revolutionary militants of the Revolutionary Socialist Party for trial there was not a murmur of protest from the *Morning Star*.

The mild criticisms of the Soviet leadership are a necessary feature of its alliance with the Tribunites and 'left' trade-union bureaucrats. However, they have a logic of their own. Once having trodden this path it is a trifle difficult to pull back. But despite these criticisms the C.P. is still committed to the interests of the Soviet bureaucracy. Because the ruling bureaucracy in the Soviet Union still draws its power from the nationalized property relations created by the October Revolution and has to defend those relations, albeit in its own distorted fashion, the C.P.G.B. retains a link with the Russian Revolution. While this subservience to the Soviet bureaucracy leads the C.P. to act against the interests of world revolution, the very same subservience prevents it from degenerating into a straightforward social-democratic party. In the event of the interests of the Soviet bureaucracy clashing with British capitalism, the C.P. will be quite strong in its opposition to capital. But these links are weakening. The general crisis of Stalinism which led to the Sino-Soviet split, polycentrism in Western Europe and open revolt in Eastern Europe has not left the C.P. unmarked. One of the C.P.'s nightmares is to discover that Moscow itself is in flames and that the workers are storming the Kremlin. These facts and possibilities put a constant pressure on the C.P. to become more and more critical of the Soviet leadership. One can therefore say that the party is at the crossroads: either it continues to be a Stalinist party reflecting the interests of the Soviet bureaucracy, or it evolves into a small social-democratic party. In either case it is in severe trouble. If it continues to defend the Soviet bureaucracy it will continue to pay a heavy price and on the other hand there is no place in Britain for a *small* social-democratic party.

The C.P.G.B. is in a pretty sorry state. It has set itself a parliamentary perspective and yet is farther away from the House of Commons than it ever was. The existence of a radicalized layer of youth in the late 'sixties virtually by-passed the C.P. Between 1967 and 1969 it lost 6 per cent of its members and the circulation of the *Morning Star* went down by over five thousand.[29] The Young Communist League suffered a disastrous 34 per cent loss of membership.[29] The growth of revolutionary forces on the left of the C.P. makes the outlook for the party even more bleak. Every new blow struck for world revolution anywhere in the world undermines the theoretical base of the C.P. and provides it with new problems. Within the next decade or so it will try to grapple with the problems which confront it.[30] In this process it will die; its death is long overdue.

[29] More recent figures are not at hand at the time of writing.

[30] Most of the key leaders of the C.P.G.B. now in office were trained in the period of the Pollitt-Dutt clique. Gollan was groomed for leadership from a very early period. He was a leader of the Y.C.L. (Young Communist League) during the Moscow Trials! There is no record of any of these leaders examining their own past. One gets the impression that they say as little as possible, hoping that the crisis of Stalinism will go away. It won't, and the present leaders of the C.P.G.B. stand condemned as minor accomplices in one of the most monstrous crimes in the history of the world workers' movement: the physical liquidation of practically the entire leadership of the world's first successful proletarian revolution. History is making its own judgment.

4 The Politics of Protest: C.N.D. and the Beginnings of Youth Radicalization

The Kautskyite advocacy of 'disarmament', which is addressed to the present governments of the imperialist Great Powers, is the most vulgar opportunism, it is bourgeois pacifism ... The main defect of the disarmament demand is its evasion of all the concrete questions of revolution. Or do the advocates of disarmament stand for an altogether new kind of revolution, unarmed revolution?

v. i. LENIN, *The 'Disarmament' Slogan* (1916)

The Cold War was brought about by the irreconcilable differences 'between capitalism and the gains of the October Socialist Revolution. As the Stalinist bureaucracy felt the immense power of American capital, and its military consequences, they abandoned their policy of collaboration with the Eastern European bourgeoisies and brought the social structure in those countries into line with that of the Soviet Union. Whilst this meant Stalinization, it also meant a complete and total break with the capitalist world market. At the same time, as we have discussed earlier, U.S. capital for this very reason was forced to sponsor an economic boom in Western Europe and revive British, French, Italian and German capital. The boom which seemed to many social-democrats to be an old dream come true thus also provided the ideological basis for defending capitalism and democracy. The logical corollary of this was to rearm the German bourgeoisie and integrate it ideologically with the rest of capitalist Europe, thus avoiding the mistakes of the post-World-War-One period. German rearmament, needless to say, became an extremely live issue in Britain and precipitated a 'controversy' within the Labour Party where the Labour left again revealed its lack of clarity. (The C.P. fellow-travellers quite openly used an anti-German chauvinism.) However, the fight in the Labour Party did reflect a general horror of even the idea of another global confrontation so soon after the conclusion of the Second World War, this time with the Soviet Union as the enemy. With the development of the hydrogen bomb and the rapidity with which the Soviet Union acquired nuclear arms it appeared as though the entire existence of the human race was in question.

This was the background to the dramatic development of the Campaign for Nuclear Disarmament (C.N.D.) in Britain. While the activities of the Tribunites and the Communist Party represented the development of left tendencies inside the labour movement, the support for C.N.D. and the spectacular growth of its annual Easter marches developed outside the traditional structures. The same period of the late 'fifties and early 'sixties saw the Committee of A Hundred with its direct-action techniques and its rejuvenated Gandhism, and to a lesser extent the Young Socialists and the National Association of Labour Student Organizations (N.A.L.S.O.). All these movements were characterized by diversity, complete theoretical confusion and, on the whole, a total failure to understand the importance of the international class struggle and its various manifestations. Nevertheless, the radicalization was of extreme importance: it was a precursor of the large-scale youth radicalization which the whole of Europe was to witness a decade later, but because of the confused political leadership and the strength of social-democracy no real headway could be made and the first real strivings of a post-war generation of youth towards revolutionary political ideas and extra-parliamentary activism ended in a blind alley.

It was no accident that the Bomb shaped the political consciousness of large numbers of young people and became their main preoccupation. The production by capitalist society at enormous cost of weapons capable of destroying the entire world provided a very clear indication of the barbaric nature of the system. The total lack of control which people felt in relation to thermonuclear weapons also in fact symbolized their general impotence in the face of capitalist society as a whole:

> In this sense, the hydrogen bomb became the central myth of the society itself. In refusing it, the campaigners necessarily refused the forms of organization of which it was the ultimate logic. Thus C.N.D. became a movement of protest, not only in its aims, but in its methods and organization. Confronted with the atrophy of political parties and the bureaucratisation of public life, it was a pure affirmation of spontaneity, a living refusal of the petrified society around it.[1]

At the same time on a small island just off the shores of the United States a historic drama was beginning to unfold. On January 1st, 1959, the forces of the July 26th Movement led by Fidel Castro and Che Guevara marched triumphantly into Havana, sealing the fate of the imperialist puppet dictator, Batista, and signalling the victory of the Cuban Revolution. By the end of the year the Cuban leadership was in conflict with the United States government. Within the next two years diplomatic relations were severed and a trade embargo imposed by U.S. imperialism: a socialist transformation was beginning to take place in Cuba. For many young people identification with the Cuban revolution also brought an awareness of the possibilities which were opening up. This factor was enhanced by the youthfulness of the Cuban leadership, by its intense revolutionary vitality and most important by the fact that they were not linked to the Stalinist movement either nationally or

[1] Perry Anderson, 'The Left in the Fifties', *New Left Review*, no. 29 (January–February 1965).

internationally. This was of key importance in radicalizing many young C.N.D. members and extending their consciousness beyond British waters.

The other area which excited the sympathy of large numbers of young people was South Africa. The massacre at Sharpeville was a traumatic event for a movement pledged to non-violence. Nevertheless, Sharpeville together with the civil-rights struggle in the United States helped to imbue the movement with a sharp anti-racist spirit, though in many cases this remained at a level simply of a liberal awareness. This interest in 'outside' struggles was a step forward, but when compared to the actual power of the advancing colonial revolution appeared practically insignificant. This reflected the general lack of an overall perspective: there was no realization or understanding of the phenomenal importance of the overthrow of capital in China in 1949, nor of the political and psychological impact of the historic victory of Dienbienphu in 1954. If a firm and solid base had been laid at that time how much more easily and effectively solidarity actions with the Vietnamese Revolution could have been launched.

The great boast of capitalist politicians in the 'fifties was that the 'affluent' society had been ushered into existence; that the future was going to be one of unparalleled prosperity, the like of which had never been known by mankind. While the economic horizon in Britain was a bit spotted by the oscillations of the trade cycles and Selwyn Lloyd's famous 'pay pause' of 1960, the general atmosphere remained one of an ostrich-like euphoria. In the Labour Party the ideas of Crosland and Strachey predominated and there was no rigorous Marxist critique of their presentation that the fundamental contradictions of capitalism had been resolved. Crosland could actually write in terms of humanity (i.e. British and European humanity) being poised on the 'threshold of abundance'.

The initial reaction to this complacency stemmed from two sources. First, from an increasing realization that the so-called affluent society had brought with it no reduction of social inequality or change in the distribution of wealth. On the contrary: there still existed a substantial minority of low wage earners and old-age pensioners who in no way shared in its benefits; there was still a general and increasing shortage of housing; educational privilege was still rampant and large areas of the country, for example the North East, Scotland and Northern Ireland, were stagnating economically.

The second source of reaction against the values of a society which measured all in terms of wealth and its accumulation was vague and idealistic. One could in fact discern the beginnings of a hippie, drop-out culture on the one hand and a certain vogue for voluntary social work at home and abroad on the other. These were the confused but easily explicable manifestations of young people groping towards an understanding of the contradictions of late capitalist society.

C.N.D. was the first movement which expressed some of the preoccupations of this new youth milieu. The Easter 1959 Aldermaston demonstration was the first sign of the real significance of this movement and of its capacity to mobilize large numbers of people. However, the weaknesses and the ultimate causes of its failure were discernible from the very beginning. The original inspiration for the Aldermaston protests came from the Direct Action Committee against Nuclear War, a dedicated group of Gandhian pacifists which included Quakers, anarchists and other pacifists of varying descriptions. They were advocates of individual martyrdom and many of them put their beliefs into practice, but the theme underlying this was the lame half-hope, half-belief that pressure of this sort could have an effect on the conscience of the ruling class: in other words, the 'revolution of the heart and mind'. Idealists that they were in their conceptions, many of them recoiled and refused to participate when their tactics were taken up on a larger scale by the Committee of A Hundred. They claimed that the large numbers who took part in the latter's demonstrations were not imbued with the ideals of pacifism, but merely used its methods for opportunist reasons.

7

With the growth of C.N.D. there was also a growing disparity between the bulk of its supporters, who were largely
working-class and lower-middle-class youth, and the bulk of
the leadership and those close to the leadership, who were
firmly rooted in the liberal tradition of England—middle-class
humanitarians, whose whole outlook was coloured by the
politics of manœuvre and who were symbolized by Canon John
Collins, Ritchie Calder and the Rev. Michael Scott. They
moved in the same circles as certain sections of the ruling class
and shared a similar outlook. This provided them with the
semi-divine knowledge that it was only necessary to convince
those in power of the absurdity of nuclear warfare and policies
based on it for things to work out right. Their sense of moral
outrage and their self-induced superiority found a response in
the heart of liberal England:

> Its [C.N.D.'s] lineage was that of the Campaigns against
> the Slave Trade, Governor Eyre, the Bulgarian Atrocities,
> the Boer War. Authentic English liberalism was fighting
> its last, and most critical battle. The moral consciousness
> of that section of the middle-class which has traditionally
> been the sanctuary of liberal values in Britain, was seized,
> like no other, by images of infinite destruction, the abolition
> of man. It responded with its finest energies, maintaining
> a passionate pressure for change under the most adverse
> historical circumstances. The campaign which resulted
> surpassed in its earlier history.[2]

In a sense the very success of the campaign scared most of the
liberals. Because they saw politics, and certainly liberal politics
of protest, as pressure politics they were obsessed by the desire
to appear responsible and restrained. Thus the final days of the
Aldermaston marches became notorious for the frantic attempts
of a worried leadership to restrain the potential militancy of the
demonstrators. As far as the Committee of A Hundred was

[2] Ibid.

concerned, the liberals were viciously hostile from the very outset to the very idea of civil disobedience.[3]

Besides the liberal humanitarians the other current which gained predominance in C.N.D. was left social-democracy. They saw C.N.D. as the vehicle for promoting their politics within the Labour Party. They too believed in pressure, but their pressure had less ambitious aims than that of liberals of the Collins variety: the Labour left simply wanted to bring pressure to bear on the leadership. They were also fully aware of the danger of allowing a movement to develop which could outflank them from the left and expose the charade of their assumed and unchallenged positions as leaders of dissent. Their attitude towards C.N.D., however, was largely dictated and determined by the needs of the struggle inside the party. Thus when a debate opened up inside C.N.D. as to whether the campaign should, in addition to unilateral nuclear disarmament, call for British withdrawal from NATO, the Labour left opposed this logical extension of C.N.D. policy because it would make the task of persuading Labour Party conferences more difficult: they were not too worried at revealing the unprincipled nature of their political positions as they knew that what they regarded as the 'real' C.N.D. (i.e. the leadership) would sympathize with the dilemma they faced.

During the heyday of C.N.D. the Labour Party was very different from what it is at the moment. The fact that it had been out of office for several years meant that there were countless inquests into electoral defeats. Also the reforms initiated by the 1945 Labour government had given the party a certain credibility, and most of the struggles which took place in British society were reflected albeit in a distorted way inside the Labour

[3] Bertrand Russell broke with the majority of the C.N.D. leadership on this question and backed civil disobedience. Relations between him and Canon Collins became so strained that the two men refused to meet without the presence of a tape-recorder. A positive influence on Russell was undoubtedly Ralph Schoenman, an American radical who later became Russell's secretary and who, because of his bluntness, succeeded in becoming the bête noir of large sections of the left.

Party. Gaitskell and Crosland saw the reasons for the defeat of the Labour Party as lying in its outmoded constitution. This still included the well-known Clause Four, which committed the Labour Party to full-scale public ownership. At the Labour Party conference at Blackpool in 1959, Hugh Gaitskell openly called for the elimination of the Clause from the party's constitution. The battle was not fought out in the open and Gaitskell capitulated at a closed meeting of the party's National Executive Committee (N.E.C.). Even the hardened right-wing trade unionists were not prepared to see Clause Four removed and their opposition was clearly decisive: in a sense the latter were merely trying to preserve the *tradition* of the party. Precisely because Clause Four meant nothing in practice there was opposition amongst the party faithful to attempts to get rid of it. If there had been a strong left force inside the party which showed signs of converting this traditional and sentimental Clause into a fighting reality, the fight would have been bitter and hard and Gaitskellism would have won the day. Precisely because Clause Four was merely a paper tiger it was decided to preserve it. The hard right of the Labour Party reflected the situation of capitalism in the 'fifties; the tail of the boom produced a change, and the complacent Gaitskell-Crosland thesis as contained in the party manifesto *Industry and Society* was abandoned and replaced by an anti-complacent document, *Signposts for the Sixties*. The latter admitted the failure of British capitalism and proposed methods of trying both to rationalize and humanize the system: the thesis was put forward that instead of nationalizing existing industries, the Labour Party would build up the public sector side by side with them. This sector would be 'science-based' and attuned to 'growth'. The first hints of Wilson's later rhetoric and the much-vaunted 'white heat of technology' were projected in *Signposts for the Sixties*.

The next annual conference of the Labour Party met at Scarborough in 1960. In previous years the pro-C.N.D. wing had been mustering an increasing number of votes and therefore the set piece of the conference was quite clearly the debate on defence. In 1958 Nye Bevan, the erstwhile leader of left social-democracy, had capitulated completely and had been instrumental in preventing the Labour Party Conference from taking a stand in favour of unilateral nuclear disarmament. Bevan had used his rhetorical gifts to argue that he did not want 'to appear naked at the Summit Conference'.[4] However, all Bevan's prestige could not prevent the movement from gaining strength. The failure of the 'Blue Streak' missile gave a certain impetus to the unilateralists as the Macmillan government had to admit that the country had been incapable of ensuring its own nuclear-missile armament and had to borrow its weapons of mass destruction from U.S. imperialism. The unilateralists inside the Labour Party received the support of several big unions, especially the T. and G.W.U., the A.E.U., and N.U.R. Even the N.U.M. hedged its bets. As a result unilateralism won the day. The Scarborough Conference rejected Gaitskell's compromises and voted for the C.N.D. proposals. What was the reaction of the Labour left to this? Did it see this verdict as a mandate which gave it the necessary go-ahead to take the fight to the Labour rank and file and destroy the right? The sad answer is no. The Labour left was

[4] Nye Bevan was without doubt the most talented of left social-democratic leaders in British history. See Michael Foot, *Aneurin Bevan* (Four Square, London, 1966), for an uncritical account. We are still waiting eagerly for volume 2, to see how Foot deals with the political about-turn effected by Bevan and his incorporation into the Labour establishment. In his early period Bevan personified the best qualities of social-democracy and in one sense was the Jaurès of the British proletariat. At the same time he was the faithful mirror of all the weaknesses and inadequacies of British 'socialism'. He had no doctrine. He was a pure empiricist, who was satisfied to solve problems only when confronted with them. He was not opposed to national defence under the capitalist regime; he did not want to break with the Atlantic Alliance, but only to obtain a greater independence within that alliance. He did not want to overthrow capitalism, but only to speed up the rhythm of social reforms. He obstinately refused to build a tendency in the Labour Party and as a result when he capitulated he did so alone. His death followed not much later and marked the beginning of the death of left social-democracy. Wilson was to drive the last knife into this decaying corpse not long after he assumed office.

more surprised than elated and even the surprise was tinged with a mixture of regret that they had been put on the spot and were expected to lead some sort of struggle. This the left had never any intention of doing, and if one recalls that most of the leaders of this victory later turned up in Harold Wilson's Labour government one has an insight into the minds of these people.

Gaitskell, Brown, Healey and Strachey were not beset with pangs of conscience at the decision of the Party Conference. From the conference hall itself, Gaitskell made this clear in his 'Fight, fight and fight again' speech. He needn't have bothered even that much because the fight was to be against men of straw who were as frightened as Gaitskell by their own victory. Some of them even applauded Gaitskell's speech and in the corridors whispers were heard that 'Hugh had been at his best'. The parliamentary majority was solidly behind the Gaitskellites and it went about its business as though the conference had not taken place.[5] The liberal press which had openly supported Gaitskell in his fight against unilateralism[6] now continued its campaign with greater vigour. *The Economist*, that well-known believer in democracy, proved that it meant by this democracy which suited the interests of its owners, as it advised Gaitskell to defend his minority position with 'the right mixture of butchery without spitefulness'. At Blackpool the following year, 1961, Gaitskell was successful in getting the decision reversed with the aid of a compromise motion, one of whose authors was Richard Crossman. Even the compromise, once its main purpose of defeating the unilateralists had been achieved, was quietly buried and forgotten.

[5] Thus we see that the Parliamentary Labour Party is virtually an independent force which disregards conference decisions at will, in opposition as well as in government.

[6] Thus the *Observer* published a full-page article by the reactionary John Strachey on the day of the Scarborough Conference arguing in favour of nuclear power and making constant use of the word 'surrender'. Similarly the *Guardian* virtually reprinted Gaitskell's speeches as its editorial comment. Both newspapers took an inordinate delight in attacking the Labour left.

The main lesson of this whole series of incidents is very clear: that paper victories such as the one in 1960 are totally meaningless unless they go hand in hand with a plan to mobilize the movement as a whole. Clearly the C.N.D., if it had had a politically conscious leadership, would have stormed the bastions of the Labour Party and used the 1960 decision either to break the right-wing leadership or to smash the Labour Party and lay the base for a new party. This it was totally incapable of doing. First because a large section of the leadership was dominated by the nauseating ideology of Labourism, and secondly because the rest of it was abstentionist (both its pacifist and semi-anarchist wings) and opposed to any action. There was a third trend which argued that linking C.N.D. to Labour would antagonize Tories and Liberals, some of whom supported the campaign. Thus the contradiction between the politics of the C.N.D. leadership and the revolutionary implications of the size and degree of commitment exhibited by the independent mass movement they had helped to build remained dominant.[7]

The failure to resolve this contradiction was a function of the weakness of the organizations to the left of the Labour Party and of the revolutionary movement in general. The Communist Party, not surprisingly, was nowhere to be seen at the start of C.N.D., and while it joined in later, and its militants supported the Scottish anti-Polaris demonstrations, it never attained any decisive independent influence on the politics of the campaign because when it was not actively engaged in aiding Soviet foreign policy, it was tail-ending the miserable lefts of the

[7] The failure of the C.N.D. leadership was a political one and it reflected the historical weakness of English liberalism which could never dominate British society. This liberalism has always dominated the diverse forces of the 'left' inside the Labour Party (represented today in a much weaker vein than ever before by Michael Foot, probably the last of the politicians in the radical tradition of liberal England), and the alliance between them and the C.N.D. liberals was a foregone conclusion. The interaction between the two liberalisms did not induce a cataclysmic change in Labourism; instead it provided material for the next Labour government.

Labour Party. The most significant of the non-Communist-Party-left groups at the period was the Socialist Labour League (S.L.L.), which had an important influence in the Labour Party Young Socialist organization. While it participated fully in the early years of the campaign, its sectarianism only succeeded in alienating it from the large numbers of youth active in the campaign. Instead of recognizing the potential of the campaign and utilizing it to combat the weaknesses by building a strong revolutionary-socialist wing inside it, the S.L.L. stood outside and made formally correct criticisms, while failing to gain any significant influence in this milieu. No other revolutionary tendency at that time existed which could play an influential role, and an important opportunity was lost of winning over hundreds of young people to revolutionary Marxist positions.

The left tendency which existed inside C.N.D. consisted of the group around the *New Left Review*.[8] The intellectual weaknesses and origins of this group are discussed elsewhere in this book.[9] What characterized it and determined its inability to act was its heterogeneity and its almost total distrust of organizations and also, unfortunately, *organizing*. The nearest it got to organization was the brief period in which the 'Left Clubs' flourished around the country. They were responsible for giving some C.N.D. supporters a confused theoretical grounding, and bringing half-baked socialist ideas to a large number of young activists. The notion was seriously entertained that these clubs constituted the embryo of a new socialist movement, but they disappeared without a trace in a couple of years. The weaknesses of the clubs reflected the weaknesses of the New Left: they were not founded on the basis of a political programme *of action* nor were they nationally co-ordinated. In each locality they reflected the specific preoccupations of the

[8] This was very different from the present editorial board of the *Review* and a very sharp distinction should be made. There are some similarities, but these are discussed in Chapter 7.

[9] See Chapter 7.

individuals who led them: more often than not they were pure and simple discussion clubs dominated by university-based intellectuals and engaged in social surveys rather than political action. Only very rarely were they capable of co-ordinating campaigns. Nevertheless, the New Left upsurge was an important component of the radicalization of youth in the late 'fifties and early 'sixties. It was, however, a victim of its own diversity and proved incapable of giving even an ideological lead to the movement.

The failure of virtually every section of the left and revolutionary left to meet the challenge of this first wave of youth radicalization gave the initiatives of the Committee of A Hundred a certain importance. The committee had been set up in 1960 as a protest against the C.N.D. leadership and out of frustration with the inability to make any impact on government policy. It was felt that one of the reasons for this was the conventional forms of protest to which the C.N.D. leadership had restricted itself. Bertrand Russell, who had up till then been the president of C.N.D., gave his blessing to the new actions which were proposed; namely to launch a campaign to carry out a series of mass sit-downs in central London as the beginning of a programme of mass non-violent civil disobedience whose open purpose would be to force the government to abandon Britain's nuclear weapons. Needless to say, the whole conception of the campaign was utopian. Not only was it not linked with an overall strategy relating nuclear weapons to the concrete issues of the class struggle, but even within its own encapsulated framework its terms of reference were at best limited. Added to this was the fact that, like C.N.D., its leadership was very diverse. Russell had recruited a whole number of literary, artistic and show-business personalities to add weight to the 'struggle'. Their drop-out rate was, however, quite phenomenal and the actual conduct of the campaign was left to a motley band of pacifists, social anarchists, a few C.P. members and other left organizations, notably the group around the paper Solidarity.

The sit-downs escalated rapidly in size during the summer of 1961, and following the Berlin Crisis of September 17th at least five thousand people squatted in Trafalgar Square after being prevented from marching to Downing Street. The police brutality at the conclusion of the demonstration provided many young militants with a salutary lesson in the realities of class power in Britain.

It began the process of breaking the widespread fetishism of non-violence which had fixated the entire movement in a Gandhian seance. The imprisonment of Russell and other members of the committee immediately prior to the demonstration merely increased the sense of impotence, as did the meting out of vicious eighteen-month sentences to six key leaders. September 1961 marked the turning-point of the Committee of A Hundred. Though there were some later exploits, in particular the exposure of the R.S.G. (secret nuclear war shelters reserved for the great and near-great), the methods of the committee proved as abortive as those of C.N.D. as far as producing short-term results were concerned, and within a short period the committee disintegrated into its constituent parts.

However, its importance cannot be measured by its eventual collapse. In contrast to the C.N.D. leadership, the committee promoted the idea of independent mass action without placing any reliance on the traditional political leaderships, and the attitude of the latter towards the sit-ins was marked by its hostility. Of course there was a negative side as well: the committee tended to throw out the baby with the bath water. It rightly rejected the left Labourites, but it also dismissed the Labour Party and, more important, the labour movement. As a result very few of its predominantly petty-bourgeois leadership were active in this milieu. Such attitudes were nourished by the writings of certain New Left academics like Wright Mills, who proclaimed the death of working-class activism and class solidarity. Thus the immense energy was never canalized in the direction of the labour movement and as a consequence proved to be a comparative waste. Instinctively hostile to the

bureaucratization of Labour politics and the conservatism of
the Labour bureaucracy, the average C.N.D. member and
Committee of A Hundred supporter recoiled from being tarred
with the Labour brush, thus leaving the field clear to the
opportunist lefts and the trade-union bureaucrats. The latter
revealed themselves in their true colours after the death of
Gaitskell. They immediately rallied round the opportunist
Wilson and brushed aside political differences in the interests of
'unity against the Tories'. They were aided in this by the decline
of the mass movement against the Bomb, which further paved
the way for their total betrayal and even relieved them of the
need to adopt a left posture. The election of Wilson as the leader
of the Labour Party was regarded by many C.N.D. leaders as a
victory for unilateralism (many C.N.D. members in the
Labour Party had actively canvassed for Wilson against the
nasty right-wing George Brown). Many genuine unilateralists
simply retreated from politics, either by an anarchist rejection
of politics of all sorts or by the futility of setting up independent
candidates. The latter were thus confined to playing the electoral game without the backing of a mass party. However, one
positive fact which emerged was that a significant number of
young people accepted the conclusion that the Bomb could
not be fought on its own and that it was not simply a cancerous
growth of an otherwise healthy organism, but part and parcel
of the capitalist system itself. Hence the need to fight capitalist
society as a whole was clearly posed.

The one movement of any significance which understood the
necessity for revolutionaries to develop a voice inside the
Labour movement was the Young Socialists. This consisted
largely of recruits won from C.N.D. and many of them were
new to socialist ideas. It was further hampered by the pre-
ponderance in its revolutionary wing of the politics of the
Socialist Labour League. The latter succeeded in winning over
a large chunk of the Y.S., and its youth paper, *Keep Left*, was
finally proscribed by the N.E.C. of the Labour Party. Here was
a golden opportunity for the S.L.L. to take its politics into the

heart of the Labour Party and wage a big struggle against the party bureaucracy. Instead it chose isolation and isolated its youth by developing an organization outside the Labour Party, accepted expulsions in many cases without protest and sometimes even invited them, and thus succeeded in demoralizing a large section of the Young Socialists who left the Labour Party and followed the S.L.L. into the political wilderness. Thus on two counts the S.L.L. leadership holds a certain responsibility for the dead end reached by the movement by 1963–4: first, for its inability to realize the revolutionary socialist conclusions inherent in the C.N.D. protests; and secondly, for its failure to utilize its control of the Y.S. to battle with the Labour leadership. Even though it would have lost this battle it could have succeeded in demoralizing many rank-and-file delegates to the annual conference and certainly some constituency parties.

The political situation was to remain somewhat bleak for the years which followed. Inside the Labour Party the siren voices of unity had their effect and political debate virtually ceased as the party prepared itself for the coming general election. The C.N.D. declined at a rapid pace and became part of the national scenery, like the changing of the guard. Its annual picnic continued, but politically undeveloped as it was, it fell apart at the seams at the signing of the Test Ban Treaty. All the 'angry young men' who had been associated with it, such as John Osborne and John Braine, gravitated towards conservatism. Peggy Duff, whose brilliant organizing skills had not gone unnoticed, was offered various jobs by the financial establishment (to her credit she turned them all down). The Committee of A Hundred had died and the Young Socialists were decimated and bewildered in the absence of any clear-cut socialist leadership. Most of the old *New Left Review* hands had departed to academic pastures and reformism, thus leaving the magazine in newer and bolder hands.

Yet despite all its failures and weaknesses this first wave of British youth radicalization had many positive results. It produced a mass movement which remained outside the influence

of social-democracy and Stalinism and as such was pointing the
road to the future, though very few could at that time see it.
It had involved thousands of young people in dynamic action
and had provided them through this action with an understanding of the dynamics of social change. It had produced a
whole conglomeration of new ideas, and while most of them
were petty-bourgeois they marked a break with Stalinism and
implicitly refused to equate the latter with Marxism or communism. Thus political debate itself became more open. While
many of the militants of this period were lost to politics, a small
proportion were to provide the backbone of a growing anti-
Stalinist revolutionary movement. This movement in its own
way, in a radically changed situation, was able to assimilate the
lessons of C.N.D., reject petty-bourgeois politics and pave the
way for a return to the ideas of Lenin and Trotsky and to
the principles of Bolshevism.

5 The Revolutionary Left in Britain

Politically you have always been right, and now more
right than ever. Some day the party will realize it ...
Don't lose your courage if someone leaves you now,
or if not as many come to you, and not as soon as we all
would like. You are right, but the guarantee of the
victory lies in nothing but the extreme unwillingness to
yield, the strictest straightforwardness, the rejection of
all compromises; in this very thing lay the secret of
Lenin's victories.

ADOLF JOFFÉ,
Letter to Trotsky before committing suicide, 1928

I

The growing crisis of British capitalism creates, of necessity, a
generalized feeling of unease and insecurity which permeates,
in varying degrees, all the different layers of the bourgeoisie.
Thus the latter's press gradually begins to drop its liberal pretence and actively begins to participate in a crude and blatant
campaign to deflect the intensity of the class struggle by creating
divisions inside the working-class movement. One of the
methods[1] which the unfree press uses is as old as the capitalist
system itself. This is the technique of the 'red scare', which in
its different forms has been utilized by every single capitalist
government in the world at some stage. The purpose is to
isolate the militants leading the struggle from the mass of the
workers, many of whom are very susceptible to bourgeois
propaganda. The British press has had a lot of training in this

[1] See 'The Postal Workers' Struggle', *The Red Mole*, vol. 2, no. 3, for a description
of the role of the mass media in the postal workers' strike.

field and therefore the revolutionary movement was not really surprised to read, in the first few months of 1971, several articles on the 'revolutionaries' in the *Daily Express, Daily Mirror, Daily Telegraph* and even *The Times*.[2] What was striking was not that all the articles were inaccurate and badly-researched, even from the point of view of the unfree press itself,[3] but that in one sense they all reflected the changing relationship of forces on the left in Britain. There were none of the usual sneers about 'fellow-travelling' Labour left-wing M.P.s, but more important was the fact that the British Communist Party was no longer regarded by the press as the 'enemy in our midst'. It was either totally ignored or referred to with respect as a 'healthy' contrast to the wildness of the extreme left.

The fact that the C.P. has been *politically* eclipsed by the groups on its far left does not mean that its influence or effect on the advanced workers has been replaced as well. Even today the C.P. has more industrial militants than the entire member-ship of all the extreme left groups put together. Most of these militants are excellent fighters and are getting increasingly depressed with the industrial policy of their party, which is usually confined to following the line laid down by the 'left' trade-union leaders such as Jack Jones and Hugh Scanlon. Thus the possibilities for winning over C.P. militants to revolu-tionary political positions are at the present time fairly high. What is decisive is that the revolutionary left groups are capable of demonstrating *in action* their superior politics to thousands of shop-steward militants, because it is only through action that it will be possible to make a qualitative leap and develop an implantation inside the vanguard layers of the workers' move-ment. This process could well pave the way for the construction in Britain of a revolutionary party, which is an essential for the

[2] *The Times*, as the most 'civilized' voice of the British ruling class, does not compare at all well with some of its counterparts abroad. The *New York Times* is a far superior paper in every way, and *Le Monde* towers above them all and demon-strates what a good bourgeois newspaper can be like!

[3] Thus the *Daily Express* conjured up images of large numbers of 'red moles burrowing away' in industry to wreck capitalism. Flattering but, alas, untrue.

successful conclusion of any meaningful struggle. The problem of the revolutionary left in Britain has been that it has never developed out of any native mass struggle but has grown as a reflection of international events (the Russian Revolution led to the C.P.) or international struggles (International Left Opposition led to British Trotskyism). On its own this would not be important, but the failure to develop any real mass base has accentuated this weakness and imparted a certain element of artificiality to the revolutionary movement which began to disappear only in between 1967 and 1969 with the new rise of the world revolution. But even today the Marxist left in Britain appears to many people, and even to its sympathizers, as a welter of competing factions, divided on minor and somewhat obscure doctrinal points and engaged in a continual battle against each other. It is therefore necessary to explain the origins of the various tendencies on the left, and the nature of the differences which divide them.[4] We will discuss in Chapter 8 the possibility of unity among the left-wing groups.

It is essential to emphasize that the differences which exist on the left are not, in most cases, insignificant or irrelevant. They may appear so to many who are not members of the groups and who can therefore afford to mock or dismiss their polemics. This reflects not only the general contempt for theory which exists in Britain, but also the refusal of many people to commit themselves seriously to the revolutionary movement. After all, the accusation of sectarianism is not new to the revolutionary movement: Lenin was assailed in the most vigorous terms for splitting the Russian social-democracy.[5] In reply he used to

[4] I do not even pretend to be 'objective': (1) Because I do not believe that there is any such thing as objectivity; it is largely a bourgeois mystification. And (2) because I belong to one of the groups in question and therefore will obviously support its political positions.

[5] One of the accusers was the young Trotsky, who could not really grasp the importance of Lenin's theory of the party and thus subjected the latter to an extremely vehement critique. This was not only Trotsky's personal tragedy, it also affected his standing in the Bolshevik party much later on. The important fact is that Trotsky learnt from his mistake. The inhabitants of the political marsh and their latter-day descendants never did.

tell a story of Tolstoy's, in which a man was observed from a distance making weird and apparently almost insane gestures. It was only when the observers drew closer that they discovered what the strange man was doing: he was busy sharpening a knife! Lenin compared the disputes on the revolutionary left to the sharpening of revolutionary knives — an essential exercise if revolutionary theory is to be translated successfully into practice.

It could be argued with a certain amount of justification that sections of the revolutionary left in Britain seem to be blunting knives rather than sharpening them, but that reflects the historical weakness of Marxism in Britain which is discussed in some detail in Chapter 7. It should also be remembered that the process of splits has historically led to a qualitatively improved organization; which means not that one fetishizes a split, but that in most cases the reasons behind it are political. For instance social-democracy separated itself from the liberal populist and anarchist components of the First International through the building of mass working-class organizations during the intense development of capitalist industry in Europe. The Communist (Third) International was created when the majority of the Second International had capitulated to imperialism at the start of the First World War. It was the degeneration of the Third International, after the death of Lenin and the victory of the Stalinist faction inside the Soviet Union, that led Trotsky to start preparations for the construction of a new International. It was the last process which fathered most of the revolutionary left in Britain.

II

The Fourth International was founded in 1938, half a decade after the rise to power of German Fascism had conclusively proved the historic bankruptcy of the Third International and its different sections in this crucial test case. Before that the Trotskyists had acted as part of the International left opposition,

8

which had considered itself as part of the Third International confronted with the task of changing the leadership of the latter, but three events had been decisive in the total break with the Third International: the rise of Fascism, the defeat of the proletariat in France and Spain in 1936–8 and the complete incompatibility of a revolutionary Marxist programme with that of the Stalinist leadership of the Third International. The cynical role of the Stalinists in Spain and Germany had left only one course open to Trotsky and the International left opposition, and that was the creation of a new International.

However, the very events we have enumerated also coloured the existence of the fledgling Fourth International. Everywhere reaction seemed to be on the ascendant. In the Soviet Union itself the Moscow Trials were at their height and the third big trial had resulted in the execution of Bukharin and eighteen of his comrades, all of them leaders of the Third International, all of them old Bolshevik comrades of the dead Lenin. Stalin was destroying all the possible alternatives to him so that the C.P.S.U. would not even have the opportunity to think of the possibility of replacing him. The Second World War seemed to be approaching, and Stalin was staking his existence on an alliance with the 'democracies'. Class-collaboration was therefore to replace the policy of labelling all opponents social-fascists. Thus the Fourth International, unlike its predecessors, was born out of the big defeats suffered by the European working-class movement. Nowhere was it a mass organization. Persecuted by G.P.U. and the S.S. alike, the movement lost many of its leaders: Leon Sedov (Trotsky's son) died in extremely mysterious circumstances near Paris; Rudolf Klement, the international secretary, was kidnapped by the G.P.U. and executed; in Germany and Greece the Trotskyists were in the concentration camps; in Spain they together with the P.O.U.M.ists were being liquidated by the G.P.U. and Franco; in Mexico the plans of the Stalinists with Lombardo Toledano at their head to assassinate Leon Trotsky were well in hand. It was in this atmosphere of repression and persecution that the

Fourth International was born on September 3rd, 1938. The founding conference lasted only a day; thirty delegates were present from the U.S.A., the U.S.S.R., Britain, Germany, France, Italy, Poland, Belgium, Holland and Greece, and several observers. The precarious security conditions prevented the attendance of many other delegates. The Polish delegates (influenced by Isaac Deutscher) were the only ones who were seriously opposed to the creation of the new International on the grounds that the new International was isolated from the masses as the latter had not yet become conscious of the betrayals of Stalinism. There was of course general agreement on the isolation from the masses, and it was accepted that this would continue for a whole period for historical reasons. However, the Fourth International would be built on the wave of the revolutionary upheavals which followed on the heels of the imperialist war. It is not necessary to discuss in detail the early history of the Fourth International;[6] suffice it to say that the heritage of Marxism and Leninism was in those dark days defended *only* by the handful of Fourth Internationalists who had survived both the Stalinist and the Fascist terror. The theoretical acquisitions of Bolshevism were defended, improved and preserved by the Fourth International and it is this thin and frayed red line which has provided thousands of revolutionary militants today with a link to their own history.

The splits in the Fourth International centred around the pre-Second-World-War and the post-war periods. While these are discussed in detail elsewhere[7] it is important to pause over them briefly in order to understand the present state of affairs. The first serious division occurred during Trotsky's lifetime inside the Socialist Workers Party of the United States, and concerned the class nature of the Soviet Union. The Fourth International had maintained, despite its split from the Third, that the Soviet Union was a workers' state, a deformed and

---

[6] Cf. early issues of *Fourth International*, and Pierre Frank, *History of the Fourth International* (Maspero, Paris, 1968).

[7] Leon Trotsky, *In Defence of Marxism* (Pathfinder, New York, 1970).

bureaucratically degenerated one, but a workers' state nevertheless. The gains of the October Revolution, namely the abolition of capitalism and its substitution by a planned economy, created a new set of property relations which have been preserved despite the expropriation of *political* power by the Stalinist bureaucracy. Therefore defence of the Soviet Union against imperialism was an important tenet of revolutionary Marxism. Despite all the twists of the Soviet bureaucracy, despite the liquidation of Trotskyists, including members of Trotsky's own family, and in spite of all Stalin's crimes, Trotsky did not allow himself to be tarred even slightly with the idealist brush. Some of his co-thinkers were not as well versed in the dialectic and they began to wilt at the growing excesses of Stalinism. The Stalin–Hitler pact and the moral outrage of the hypocritical 'liberal democracies' also affected some of the petty-bourgeois leaders of the Socialist Workers Party (S.W.P.). They gradually began to abandon the concept of defending the Soviet Union and formulated theories of a 'new class' which had suddenly developed in the U.S.S.R., which was as oppressive as that of the imperialists, and therefore there was no qualitative difference between the capitalist states and the 'state-capitalist' or 'bureaucratic collectivist' states. The latter covered Germany, Italy, Soviet Union and New Deal U.S.A.! Trotsky's last great theoretical fight was thus waged against James Burnham and Max Shachtman of the S.W.P., a fight in which he was supported by the majority of the S.W.P. led by the well-known working-class leader, James P. Cannon. (Burnham later reneged completely and went over to the extreme right wing and Shachtman simply deserted to the bourgeois camp and later justified American imperialism's war against revolutionary Cuba!) Shachtman's theories were to find some response in Europe at a later stage and Trotsky's polemic against him is therefore of lasting value. In an important article entitled 'From a Scratch to the Danger of Gangrene',[8] Trotsky defined the Marxist method:

[8] Ibid., p. 103.

In Marxist sociology the initial point of analysis is the *class* definition of a given phenomenon, e.g. state, party, philosophic trend, literary school, etc. In most cases, however, the mere class definition is inadequate, for a class consists of different strata, passes through different stages of development, comes under different conditions, is subjected to the influence of other classes. It becomes necessary to bring up these second and third rate factors in order to round out the analysis, and they are taken either partially or completely, depending upon the specific aim. But for a Marxist, analysis is impossible without a class characterization of the phenomena under consideration.

The skeletal and muscular systems do not exhaust the anatomy of an animal; nevertheless an anatomical treatise which attempted to 'abstract' itself from bones and muscles would dangle in midair. War is not an organ but a function of society, i.e., of its ruling class. It is impossible to define and study a function without understanding the organ, i.e., the state; it is impossible to gain scientific understanding of the organ without understanding the general structure of the organism, i.e., society. The bones and muscles of society consist of the productive forces and the class (property) relations. Shachtman holds it possible that a function, namely, war, can be studied 'concretely' independently of the organ to which it pertains, i.e., the state. Isn't this monstrous?

This fundamental error is supplemented by another equally glaring. After splitting function away from organ, Shachtman in studying the function itself, contrary to all his promises, proceeds not from the abstract to the concrete but on the contrary dissolves the concrete in the abstract. *Imperialist* war is one of the functions of finance-capital, i.e., the bourgeoisie at a certain stage of development resting upon capitalism of a specific structure, namely, monopoly capital ... But by extending the term *imperialist* war to cover the Soviet state too, Shachtman cuts the ground away from under his own feet. In order to reach even a superficial justification for applying one and the same designation to the expansion of finance capital and the expansion of the workers' state, Shachtman is compelled to detach himself from the social structure of both states altogether by proclaiming it to be—an abstraction. Thus playing hide and seek with Marxism, Shachtman labels the concrete as abstract and palms off the abstract as concrete!

The assassination of Leon Trotsky by a Stalinist agent and the beginning of the Second World War marked the end of the first phase of the Fourth International (F.I.). The war years saw attacks on the S.W.P. by the U.S. government and an increase in the general problems which confronted the sections in Europe. Normal communication between groups was virtually impossible, but the publication of F.I. journals was carried on clandestinely. In those parts of Europe occupied by the Nazis the militants of the F.I. participated actively in the workers' resistance, and some of the leaders of the French section were executed by Fascist firing-squads. At the same time propaganda was distributed amongst German workers and soldiers when the opportunity allowed.

The post-war years saw Europe ravaged by the imperialist war and a pre-revolutionary situation in France, Italy and Greece. Trotsky's prophecy of revolutionary upheavals had certainly come true, but he had underestimated the mystifying capacities of Stalinism as part of the whole mystification of the 'democratic anti-fascist struggle' which enabled the C.P.s to lead the resistance (i.e. the workers in arms) and so retain their dominance over the workers' movement. Thus in France and Italy the C.P.s turned their respective proletariats to the task of salvaging capitalism, handing in their weapons and preserving the status quo. Both C.P.s then joined the National Governments together with the bourgeoisie. In Greece, pressure from Stalin resulted in an abandonment of the armed struggle against British and American imperialism. Yet again the objective conditions had been ripe for a social revolution and the revolutionary forces had been too weak to take advantage. Also American capital was forced to revive European capitalism to confront the Soviet Union and the Eastern European states, most of which had been de-capitalized by the Soviet Army. Thus the strengthening of European capitalism and what appeared as the strengthening of Stalinism confounded two of the premises on which the Fourth International had been based. The opportunists immediately took this as the starting-point for a new revision of Marx and began once again to challenge the class nature of the Soviet Union and proclaim the stability of capitalist society. There followed various discussions on Stalinism and the class nature of the buffer states (Eastern Europe) which were finally sorted out during the early 'fifties. However, the defeat of the working class produced another period of cynicism which was sharpened by the fact that some of Trotsky's predictions had not been proved correct. The intensification of the Cold War produced further pressures and the F.I. projected a thesis that argued the possibility of a Third World War between the Soviet camp and imperialism and re-affirmed the need to defend the Soviet Union.

At the same time the F.I. put forward the concept of 'entrism', which implied that Trotskyists should enter the working-class parties (in certain cases this included the C.P.s) and by patient work develop a strong faction which would be able to dominate the leftward currents which were bound to develop in these parties and split the party, thus creating a new revolutionary party or at any rate a party which could be won over to revolutionary positions. Various interpretations of this as well as other theses led to a split in the F.I. in 1953, when the British and American Trotskyists withdrew and set up a rival organization, which had a small following in parts of Latin America and France.[9] In 1963 a Reunification Congress took

[9] 'A Recall to Order: An Open Letter from the International Secretariat of the Fourth International to the Members and Leadership of the Socialist Labour

place where a large majority of the groups met and agreed on a common programme and analysis. The exceptions were the Socialist Labour League of Britain and their followers in France. Since 1963 the F.I. has grown at a very rapid pace and has established sections in new parts of the world as well as increasing the size of the other sections. The French section, the Communist League, today plays an important part in French politics and dominates the revolutionary left. The S.W.P. in the United States, which is barred by reactionary legislation from affiliating to the F.I., and its youth organization, the Young Socialist Alliance, form the largest organization on the revolutionary left. In West Bengal in India the Fourth Internationalists are engaged in leading a peasant struggle against the forces of the Indian State. In Argentina the F.I. leads the People's Revolutionary Army. In Ceylon it dominates the largest trade union, and in other countries too it is making a growing impact.

III

The long period of political quiescence among the working class meant that there was no necessity to forge a unified strategy, and instead an atmosphere was created in which doctrinal disputes were the only relief from the mundane task of keeping small groups together, maintaining small newspapers and trying to influence a labour movement which was not merely reformist but anti-communist. It was in this atmosphere that post-war British Trotskyism developed.

Of all the tendencies on the left the S.L.L. is probably the best-known 'Trotskyist' tendency, if only because a large number of people have seen its paper, *Workers' Press*, being sold on the streets every day. Thus for many people interested in revolutionary ideas the S.L.L. *is* Trotskyism, and this leads

League' (*Fourth International* [Autumn 1959]) will give readers the flavour of the split and an idea of the issues involved. (Limited copies are available from Red Books, 182 Pentonville Road, London N1.)

them to regard Trotskyism with a certain degree of repugnance. This is doubly unfortunate because it obscures the political relevance of Trotskyism and also the positive aspects of the S.L.L. itself. The fact that many young people can be persuaded to devote a large portion of their time to selling newspapers and engaging in political propaganda is in itself not a bad thing. What is futile is that many of these young people have very little idea of what they are engaged in doing, very little time to be politically educated, and are dominated by an organizational apparatus which must make the C.P. look on with some envy and reminisce about the good old days of 'Third Period' Stalinism.

The S.L.L. stems from a group which was known as the Workers International League and was set up in the mid 'thirties. During the war it carried out the workers' struggles based on anti-capitalist demands and immediately after the war it joined with the larger Revolutionary Socialist League to form the Revolutionary Communist Party which was probably the most effective revolutionary organization of the left in Britain. The R.C.P. succeeded in penetrating some trade unions, but its internal life was marked by an intense factional struggle on the question of 'entering' the Labour Party.

The result of the 1945 general election had been to establish the Labour Party, with a sizeable left wing, as the undisputed political expression of the British working class. One tendency within the R.C.P. advocated 'entry' in order to penetrate the structures of the Labour movement and lay the base for the construction of a revolutionary party. The majority of the R.C.P. was opposed to 'entry', and a section led by Gerry Healy left the R.C.P. in 1947 and entered the Labour Party, calling itself 'The Group'. The R.C.P. leaders who were opposed to this waited in the wings, hoping for a quick split in the Labour Party which would lead to the creation of a centrist-left organization. This did not happen, and the R.C.P. declined in numbers and influence and gradually capitulated to reformism. In 1949 a truncated R.C.P. entered the Labour Party and a fusion took place, Healy's Group demanding and obtaining a majority on the executive bodies of the new group. Many of the old R.C.P. leaders grew more disillusioned and left revolutionary politics for good. At the same time the internal regime of the organization became more and more authoritarian.

The initial period of 'entry' was modestly successful and a number of militants were recruited from the Labour Party. In the entire history of the Trotskyist movement in Britain, this was the golden age of 'entrism'. The entry paper of the Trotskyists, *Socialist Outlook*, acquired a wide circulation, basing itself on an alliance between Healy and sections of the social-democratic left, particularly the Bevanites. A libel suit destroyed *Socialist Outlook*, but this was not a major setback. For a time the group oriented to *Tribune*, which was sold by all its members and was promoted as the 'paper of the left'. In fact some of the verbal concessions made to Bevanism went well beyond the limit and provide a somewhat amusing comparison with the present-day antics of the S.L.L.

The big break for Healy came not so much in the Labour Party as in the C.P. The combination of the Khrushchev revelations and Hungary created a twin crisis for many loyal C.P. members and there was a mass exodus from the party in Britain. While a majority bade farewell to left politics, a tiny portion moved leftwards and Healy made an intensive drive to win some of them to his organization. He succeeded, and through the doors opened by the C.P. militants the Healy group was soon to gain influence amongst a good number of industrial workers. This enabled the group to establish its industrial reputation through the Shell-Mex strike and in the role it played in the London bus strike. The entry of many C.P. militants and a few 'red' professors created an enormous pressure on Healy to withdraw from the Labour Party. Many ex-C.P. members did not understand the importance or the necessity of mole-like work in the latter and following a series of expulsions from the Labour Party by Transport House, Healy's group took a conscious decision to start the process of withdrawal. The Socialist Labour League, an open and public Trotskyist organization, was launched in 1959 without any discussion with the membership, an extraordinary fact when considering the total change of orientation. Obviously it was felt that any discussion might provide an unnecessary encumbrance. The reason advanced for leaving the Labour Party was that the Trotskyists were faced with a witch hunt of massive proportions and had no public means of answering back. The fact that only a small proportion of the founding members were not members of the Labour Party, and that the majority of members operated exclusively within the L.P. until 1964 tends to refute the idea that the repression was so fierce as to make the precipitate launching of the S.L.L. unavoidable.

Whatever the internal constitutional implications (and the membership did not protest too loudly), the S.L.L. was a partial success. Its paper, *The Newsletter*,[10] soon increased in size and the circulation leapt forward; its theoretical magazine, *Labour Review*, established itself with a reputation for fair polemic. Its tone was remarkably free from the hysteria which surrounds all the S.L.L. publications today. In those early days the principled flexibility of the S.L.L. in relation to British politics made many think that it was capable of changing the whole face of left politics in Britain. However, the R.C.P. had coloured the entire outlook of all the tendencies which emerged from it. At its height the R.C.P. had seen the Trotskyist movement as the only revolutionary tendency in the world since the degeneration of the Third International. This had led to the assumption that it was the *only* force capable of overthrowing capitalism anywhere in the world. This had certainly not been Trotsky's view, but it became a dogma for a tiny, isolated group of people,

---

[10] The founding editor of the paper was Peter Fryer, who was the correspondent of the *Daily Worker* in Hungary during the rising. His dispatches were not published, one of the factors which led to his resignation. Fryer edited the paper very ably, but, like many others, could not stomach the internal regime of the S.L.L., having left an odious one in the C.P., and resigned. While not active in politics, he still remains a socialist and has *not*, as some allege, 'sold out'.

who could not for a long time readjust to the death of a leader who had outshone them all. This led to certain difficulties which a more flexible and realistic outlook could have avoided. The overthrow of capitalism in Eastern Europe, the Yugoslav revolution, the Chinese Revolution, the struggle in Indo-China, thus created problems for sections of the Trotskyist movement. The events in China, in particular, were inexplicable to many militants and thus their understanding of the motive forces of the Third and successful Chinese Revolution was impaired. In some groups this attitude was encouraged and sustained not by critical examination of new developments, but by a glib dismissal of all other movements and tendencies. The majority of the Trotskyist movement was able to transcend this, but the children of the R.C.P. could not. This led to an extreme organizational sectarianism which marred the development of any meaningful Leninist practice. This flaw was most marked in the Healy tendency, though not confined to it, and despite its political flexibility the S.L.L. has been chiefly characterized and marked by it.

The first indication of the lack of internal democracy in the S.L.L. was the spate of expulsions and resignations in 1959–60. One after the other, the ablest leaders of the S.L.L. broke with Healy: Peter Fryer, Brian Behan, Constance Kirkby, Peter Cadogan, Chris Pallis and Bob Pennington, whose weight inside the organization had been immense. These breaks were accompanied by a great number of accusations, counter-accusations, reports in the bourgeois press, rumour-mongering, etc., but when the dust was beginning to settle one fact emerged clearly: Healy was left in undisputed leadership of the S.L.L. He consolidated his forces, ensured their personal loyalty and started taking advantage of the opportunities which were opening up within the Labour Party.

The break in the C.P. had sent many of its militants scurrying across to left social-democracy; coupled with C.N.D., this had strengthened the formation of a left in the Labour Party and, as we read in a previous chapter, resulted in the defeat of the leadership at Scarborough in October 1960. The failure of the left to organize its support and its refusal to fight had paved the way for a right-wing victory the following year.

This was the greatest opportunity the S.L.L. had faced and its decision to withdraw from the Labour Party on the eve of the unilateralist struggle obviously affected its credibility. Not that it could have crystallized a 'left current' and split the Labour Party, but at least it could have waged a battle and dented the party apparatus, apart from withdrawing with many more supporters. However, even from the outside it could have done more. The incapacity of the Tribunites to stand up to Gaitskell left the rank and file leaderless against the right wing. A revolutionary tendency, well organized and disciplined, could have taken the lead, built up a united front which transcended the limits of left social-democracy and embarked on a struggle against the Labour bureaucracy. There was, after all, still considerable support for unilateralism.[11] The S.L.L. was content with making simple propaganda. It could not differentiate between agitation and propaganda and this led them to a sectarianism which only repelled people who were sympathetic to socialist ideas. Thus while *The Newsletter* condemned the sell-out week after week the only alternative they could offer the mass of the Labour left was the Socialist Labour League. Political propaganda combined with organizational sectarianism made this upheaval within Labour's ranks the S.L.L.'s greatest lost opportunity. More important, it projected a certain picture of 'Trotskyism'—a mirror-image of Stalinism—which haunts us even today.

The S.L.L.'s characteristics were also transferred to a field where a new generation of revolutionaries were emerging; the Labour Party's new youth movement, the Young Socialists (Y.S.). This was initiated after the electoral defeat of 1959 for the purpose of infusing some fresh blood into the ageing veins of the Labour Party, but the blood transfusion was from

[11] The 1962 Aldermaston March was the biggest ever, with over 100,000 people participating.

the very start hampered by the fact that the Y.S. members were more sympathetic to the revolutionary left. Even *Tribune* was regarded with suspicion in the Y.S. The task confronting the S.L.L. was to win them over *politically* and turn the Y.S. into an effective socialist battering-ram within the Labour movement. This was not a utopian dream. Most Y.S. members were not only active in their local L.P.s, but a good many were also trade unionists. A decisive factor in the initial success of the Y.S. had been the 1960 engineering apprentices' strike. This spontaneous action, which had started in Clydeside and spread to the rest of Britain, although at first dominated by the Y.C.L. won over a considerable number of young militants to the Y.S. because of the very effective solidarity action which the Y.S. mounted and in which the S.L.L. played a key role.

But the S.L.L. fumbled this opportunity. It tried to win the leadership of the Y.S. through a series of hysterical campaigns against the L.P. bureaucracy, which culminated in an attempt to 'rush the platform' at the first Y.S. National Conference in the Beaver Hall in London at Easter 1961. This tended to isolate the S.L.L. from the main core of the young people who had come into the Y.S. who, while revolutionary in sentiment, were still confused as regards the Labour Party which they regarded as 'their' party, and the hysteria of the S.L.L. was not a sufficient substitute for political education. A meaningful campaign for democracy in the Labour Party and for the removal of all bans and proscriptions would have educated many Y.S. members by taking them through a positive experience, but this was not done and instead the Transport House bureaucracy succeeded in isolating the S.L.L. by getting two successive conferences to pass resolutions against the S.L.L. paper *Keep Left*.

However, the fact that the S.L.L. was well-organized gave it an immense advantage and by a radical change in its attitude to building Y.S. branches it gained a numerical majority inside the organization. As the Y.S. had a certain effect on the development of the S.L.L. it is worth discussing this question in some detail. The concept that the Labour Party had of the Y.S. was of a group of middle-class (ideologically if not socially) youth, organizing dances and socials and occasionally gathering round the feet of some Labour Councillor or M.P. to hear the good news pertaining to the future social-democratic utopia. Needless to say, not many young socialists shared this absurd vision and there was constant friction over the question of whether branches should be based on a social or political basis. The S.L.L. was, to its credit, firmly opposed to the concept of dance-hall recruitment, but an accident occurred which was to have profound effects on the S.L.L. In Wigan, of all places, a Y.S. branch under S.L.L. control organized a regular dance and enrolled *all* those who attended as members of the Labour Party. This enabled the Y.S. branch to make the local Labour Party financially dependent on it and this feeling of power resulted in a complete turnabout of policy in the S.L.L. It proclaimed the need for the Y.S. to turn to 'working-class' youth, by which it meant an attempt to win non-political youth to the Y.S. through social activity. It was this turn that enabled the S.L.L. to fight its way through its initial setbacks to win a majority in the Y.S. In almost all areas the S.L.L. members in the Y.S. began to centre their political work around regular social activity. Gradually a pattern developed: the S.L.L. would organize a dance or record hop, it would leaflet the local youth employment office and would try and get the young people attracted to the dance to join the Y.S. In most cases this was superficially successful and they could build branches of between thirty and forty young workers. However, the turnover rate was extremely high, and the branch would usually be reduced to the initial S.L.L. members in a few months, if not weeks. Despite this, the very fact that they were able to mobilize such numbers, albeit for short periods, gave them an advantage over other sections of the left in the Y.S., who restricted their influence to those whom they could convince politically. This combined with three other factors to gain the S.L.L. a majority within the Y.S. First was the organizational superiority of the S.L.L. compared to the other tendencies, plus the fact that the S.L.L. was seen to be engaged in activity while the others were largely confined to propaganda. The second factor was that the factional atmosphere and the rigid sectarianism of the S.L.L. resulted in large numbers of youth simply withdrawing from both the Y.S. and politics.

Also the way in which the majority had been gained had been totally unrelated to any struggle within the Labour Party and by 1964 most of the Y.S. branches were operating independently and had no connections with their local Labour Parties. Since the Y.S. had not been used to fight against the Labour bureaucracy there was no sympathy for it within the broader labour movement or from the Labour Party rank and file. Having decided that there was nothing more for them to do inside the Labour Party, the S.L.L. decided to leave and accordingly the Y.S. split, two-thirds leaving with the S.L.L. and immediately launching their own youth movement in Morecambe (February 1965). This was also called the Y.S., and despite the semi-religious fervour with which recruitment plans were drawn up it declined rapidly. The reason was simple: the method of recruitment (socials, picnics, etc.) combined with the organizational sectarianism was sufficient to kill the organization as a stable political youth movement. The turnover was very rapid and virtually the entire leadership at the time of the break with the Labour Party left the organization, politically disillusioned and broken by their experience. This reduced the leadership to a group of colourless, unimaginative, uninspiring but staunch Healyites! Since that time Healy, like the Bourbon monarchs, has learnt nothing and forgotten nothing. The outward show of large conferences and demonstrations at the end of which the Leader, appears and greets the assembled masses, has not been able to conceal the high turnover.[12]

---

[12] It is in that light that the achievement of a daily newspaper must be regarded. The efficacy of the S.L.L.'s intensive campaigning methods cannot be denied. When they fix on an objective, it is usually gained. However, the achievement of a

Today the S.L.L. continues on the same road. Confusing the development of their organization with the building of real support within the workers' movement for revolutionary politics, continuing to recruit non-political youth on a non-political basis to sell newspapers, the S.L.L. today stands out as the best and classic example of a sect as defined by Marx: 'You yourself have experienced in your own person the opposition between the movement of a sect and the movement of a class. The sect sees the justification for its existence and its "point of honour" — not in what it has in *common* with the class movement but in the *particular shibboleth* which distinguishes it from it.'[13]

While the rhetoric of the S.L.L. and its formal programme proclaim its adherence to Trotskyism, its methods and practice are much closer to Stalinism. Its methods of dealing with political opponents, of slandering other tendencies on the revolutionary left, have nothing in common with the Fourth

---

daily newspaper is not in itself a major breakthrough in political influence. For an organization the size of the S.L.L. it means that their members spend a great deal of time as newspaper-sellers. Also, the violent and ultimatistic language of the paper with regard to all other left tendencies makes it impossible for the rank and file of the labour movement to take it seriously. Many of them do not understand the need to have serialized articles in never-ending parts denouncing people of whom they have never heard, e.g. Michel Pablo. Besides these attacks on other tendencies, the S.L.L. often prints interviews with right-wing trade-union leaders; its questions are critical, but at least these men are allowed to reply — a privilege not accorded the left. A daily paper with the correct method and politics would have had no real difficulty in completely eclipsing the *Morning Star* in working-class circles. Instead militant workers are presented with a self-parody.

It is not essential to discuss in detail here the amazingly sectarian position which the S.L.L. has on the colonial revolution. Thus it regards the Cuban regime as qualitatively no different from that of Batista's, and refuses to engage in consistent united actions in defence of the Vietnamese Revolution. If Fourth International militants are involved with struggles in the Third World, they are denounced as agents provocateurs. This is how the S.L.L. and its degenerated *Workers' Press* performs its internationalist duty. Everything is seen from the interests of the Clapham High Street leadership (or should we say 'caste').

[13] Marx to Schweitzer, October 13th, 1868, *Selected Correspondence of Marx and Engels* (International Publishers, New York, 1964).

9

International or its programme. Totally incapable of developing theory, the S.L.L. tends to make a fetish of existing texts and use them in a completely mechanistic fashion. It treats the writings of Trotsky in much the same way as the Stalinists treat the writings of Lenin. Its political attitudes lead it to strange analyses of the world revolution, which are developed not so much on the basis of fact, but in order to prove that the S.L.L. has been correct all along. The tragedy is that the S.L.L. contains many honest, sincere revolutionaries who actually believe the myths propagated by their leadership only to be totally demoralized later when they discover that they have been duped. The number of cadres who have left revolutionary politics because of their experiences with the S.L.L. must be fairly high. An offshoot of this is that the S.L.L. is scared of united-front activity with other revolutionary tendencies lest its members are forced to enter into a real political discussion and become disillusioned even sooner than they would other- wise be. For this reason, organizational exclusiveness is a cornerstone of S.L.L. practice, and the concepts of 'party loyalty' and 'party pride' are forced down the throats of its members. Its very lack of political confidence in its own ideas and its failure to educate its members politically causes the demonology and the paranoia. Hence also the tarred image in Britain of 'Trotskyism', which does not appear in practice, particularly to many dissident members of the C.P., to be much different from the C.P. in the hard-line days when no differ- ences were permitted. Can this jerry-built 'Trotskyism' survive for long? The answer depends on the ability of the revolu- tionary left to grow and the development of the mass movement in an anti-capitalist direction. For the masses are themselves the best antidote to sects and sectarianism.[14]

[14] For further reading on the antics of the S.L.L. and how they have used the technique of slander, see Ernest Germain, *Marxism vs. Ultraleftism* (Fourth Inter- national, London, 1967), and Tony Whelan, *The Credibility Gap: The Politics of the S.L.L.* (I.M.G., London, 1970). Both are available in limited editions from Red Books, 182 Pentonville Road, London N1.

IV

Lenin's most important contribution to revolutionary ideology was his constant stress on the nature of our epoch. He and Trotsky characterized it as the epoch of decaying capitalism, as the age of permanent revolution. Lenin firmly believed that the processes of revolutionary upheaval would multiply and spell the death sentence of capitalist society. In brief, as Lukács expressed it very succinctly, for Lenin the main characteristic of our epoch was the 'actuality of the revolution', the belief that not only were revolutions on the agenda, but that the task of revolutionaries was to prepare for them.[15] And if we look back we see that despite the many defeats that have taken place since the victory of the Russian Revolution, just over sixty years ago (not a long time in a historical sense), there have also been victories, and today a large part of the world's population is not dependent on the vagaries of the capitalist world market.

As we saw earlier, Trotsky overestimated the ability of revolutionary Marxism to replace the traditional Stalinist parties following the Second World War and this created dissension in the Fourth International. As in the 1930s there had emerged an idealist current in the S.W.P. in the States, now similar currents developed in Western Europe inside the F.I. In the period 1947–9, Tony Cliff developed some of Shachtman's themes and removed their most obvious absurdities. He propounded a similar theory which maintained that the Soviet Union was no longer a 'degenerated or deformed workers' state', but a class society where a new form of capitalism prevailed — 'state-capitalism'. There was nothing new or original about this theory, and not much attention was paid to it as the R.C.P., the British section of the F.I., was busy with its fight over the Labour Party orientation. It is possible that if the regime inside the R.C.P. had been democratic and allowed a free interplay of discussion, Cliff would not have

[15] Cf. Chapter 8.

emerged from his obscurity and would probably even have altered his views, but the authoritarianism of our old friend Healy only added spice to Cliff's view that to continue designating the Soviet Union, China, etc., as workers' states meant ending up as semi-Stalinists: as we have stressed, the organizational methods of the R.C.P. left a lot to be desired. The Cliff Group crystallized during the outbreak of the Korean War. As it did not regard North Korea as a workers' state it was only logical that Cliff refused to defend it against imperialism. Since Soviet 'imperialism' had mysteriously come into existence the war was quite clearly an inter-imperialist conflict and therefore 'revolutionists' could not support either side. The Korean War took place at the height of the Cold War period in Europe and the pressures on the revolutionary movement were very great. Cliff and his group capitulated to these pressures and abandoned a revolutionary Marxist position. At the same time they rejected the Leninist theory of imperialism and the concept of the Leninist Party. Though they have never stated so clearly, the logic of these positions was to challenge the nature of the epoch and certainly some of their practical conclusions did indicate that they recognized this. Because if Russia is state-capitalist, China, Cuba, Korea and Vietnam are 'petty-bourgeois' states, and poor old Lenin and Trotsky were completely wrong in their characterization of this epoch as one of proletarian revolutions. Then we are entering a new phase of capitalism and a new epoch—the epoch of the petty-bourgeoisie! Because if the latter is capable of making bourgeois-democratic or rather bourgeois-nondemocratic revolutions, then the theory of permanent revolution is simply hogwash and the Russian Revolution was a noble adventure carried out before its time and doomed to failure. In this case the only perspective is that of patient propaganda work for reforms within the working-class movement.

In the early years many members of Cliff's group, which later called itself *International Socialism* (I.S.), were virtually indistinguishable from left social-democrats, in the best sense of the word. Their refusal to distinguish between Soviet society, despite its flaws, and capitalist society made it difficult to distinguish some of them from the cold warriors whose entire energy was spent on producing books attacking the Soviet Union and China. The I.S. was at its weakest point between 1957 and 1959, when the limited success of the S.L.L. confined the latter to ephemeral and propagandistic political interventions. The sectarianism of Healy allowed I.S. to develop and gain strength.

The shift in the world situation and the new rise of the world revolutionary movement, symbolized by the staggering heroism of the Vietnamese N.L.F., created a new atmosphere amongst the youth which was far removed from the ideologies of the Cold War. Accordingly the positions of the I.S. began to shift as well and in 1967 it came out in support of the N.L.F.[16] How the N.L.F. or the North Vietnamese regime differed from North Korea has not so far been explained in detail. One can only conclude that either the I.S. were wrong in 1950 or they were unprincipled and opportunist in 1967. Because of the extreme heterogeneity of the organization both variations would apply to different members and tendencies inside I.S. However, the refusal of I.S. as an organization to take solidarity action with the Indo-Chinese revolution seriously after there was a general downswing on activity in this field, does testify to the opportunism of the majority of its leadership.

The May 1968 explosion in France also seemed to change their attitude to the concept of the Leninist Party. In the first edition of Cliff's book on Rosa Luxemburg, the chapter dealing with the question of revolutionary organization concluded: 'For Marxists in advanced industrial countries, Lenin's original

[16] Cliff has always been more 'flexible' than his American co-thinkers, who embraced monopoly capitalism/imperialism as being more progressive than Stalinism and thus advocated a 'state department socialism'. It was only in the last months of 1969 that the heirs of this tendency were able openly to support the N.L.F. *against* U.S. imperialism. However, even the I.S. did *not* prevent one of its leading theoreticians from working in collaboration with a Ford Foundation project in Pakistan, and thus providing Stalinists in that country with a ready-made excuse for denouncing 'Trotskyists' as 'imperialist agents'.

position can much less serve as a guide than Rosa Luxemburg's, notwithstanding her overstatements on the question of spontaneity.' This passage was completely deleted and a new one inserted after May 1968: 'However, whatever the historical circumstances moulding Rosa's thoughts regarding organization, these thoughts showed a great weakness in the German revolution of 1918–19.' The first position saw I.S. arguing that politics would emerge spontaneously from the shop stewards' movement. This was brought out by the Cliff/Barker pamphlet on Incomes Policy and declared that the 'nexus of reformism' had shifted to the shop floor and that a political movement would emerge from there. Hence it followed that the main task confronting socialists was to keep lonely vigils outside the factories with a few leaflets and patiently wait for this new movement to emerge. The second position saw a superficial change with a declaration that I.S. was to be a 'democratic centralist' organization, but this was interpreted as simply reorganizing the internal system of the group. There was a total inability to understand that democratic centralism was a *political* concept requiring a high level of political understanding. This inability was demonstrated when, frightened by the favourable response of a small section of dockers to Enoch Powell, the I.S. announced the danger of fascism and issued a four-point unity proposal to the left. These points were so liberal that they could be accepted by left M.P.s, for example Stan Newens.[17] Also they led to a large increase of I.S. members who did not have a clue as to what the basic theoretical positions of the organization were; this would not have mattered if I.S. had a well-organized system of internal education, but far from this they announced that theory was not important. In fact Cliff, in a frenzy to gain new members, went as far as saying that the theory of 'state-capitalism' had been formulated at the height of Stalinism to prevent a capitulation to the same, but that this problem no longer existed! After the membership had

[17] I.S. Executive Committee minutes, discussion of the situation in Harlow New Town before the general election in 1970.

risen a year or so later this old problem became dominant again.[18] The growth of I.S. (it is probably the largest of the left groupings today) also reflected a further deterioration of political standards. Thus the I.S. refrained from demanding the withdrawal of British troops from Northern Ireland for a considerable length of time. Their position on the fight against the Tory government and their total abandonment of any systematic work in the universities[19] lead to an organization which is thoroughly centrist in character.[20] Thus *Socialist*

[18] Thus at the debate between the I.S. and the F.I. in London in late 1970, Tony Cliff acquitted himself in the best tradition of the sectarian R.C.P. and even the S.L.L. Apart from hysterical ranting accusations that the F.I. had capitulated to Stalinism and that *The Red Mole* did not 'smell of the factory', his speech was not designed to promote left unity. Fortunately, many I.S. branches wrote to the I.S. centre to express their concern, and *Socialist Worker* did not even feel it necessary to report the debate which was attended by one thousand militants. For a good critique of recent I.S. positions, see Brian Grogan, 'New Developments (?) in State Capitalism', *International* (London), vol. 1 no. 6.

[19] Cf. the excellent editorial entitled 'Student Power' in *International Socialism*, no. 33 (Summer 1968[!]), to see how far the I.S. has moved since those days. To those I.S. members who claim that students as a group are 'petty-bourgeois' we would quote a section of the editorial: 'The students retain roots in the mass of the population, so that they are essentially ambivalent in class terms, pulled in both directions simultaneously at a time in their lives when they have not established what they believe.' And if there was still doubt, the editorial ended: 'On the other hand, committed revolutionaries who treat the student revolt as an idle game misunderstand the potentialities for change and the role of students as one of the most sensitive indices of social disorder. We need a new movement on the left, and in present conditions, students must play a vital role in it.' And today any serious effort to organize in the universities is immediately labelled by the I.S. as 'abandoning the working class'.

[20] There is a scientific meaning of the term 'centrism' and it should not be taken to mean 'in the centre'. Basically centrists are those who constantly vacillate between revolutionary and reformist positions on various political issues of the day and are guided by the political pressure of the milieu they are working in. This pressure could lead in either direction. Thus Trotsky in his classic text on Germany, 'What Next?' in *Germany 1931–1932* (New Park Publications, London, 1970), p. 146, defined the term thus: 'While Centrism *in general* fulfils ordinarily the function of serving as a left cover for reformism, the question of to which of the basic camps, reformist or Marxist, *a given* Centrism may belong, cannot be solved once for all with a ready-made formula. Here, more than anywhere else, it is necessary to analyse each time the concrete content of the process and the inner tendencies of its development.'

Worker, the I.S. weekly paper, published an article which proposed a right-wing policy, supporting the return of a Labour government and calling on the trade unions to support the same on the basis of the following demands:

1. Unqualified repeal of the Industrial Relations Bill and all anti-union laws.
2. No incomes policy under capitalism.
3. Restoration of all welfare cuts. No welfare charges.
4. Work or full pay at trade union rates for the unemployed.
5. Re-nationalization without compensation of all sectors of nationalized industry returned to private hands.[21]

This amazing list of demands which poses as a 'minimum' programme is to the right of even the C.P.(!) and could be supported by 'left' M.P.s and 'left' trade-union bureaucrats without too much trouble. Thus does I.S. abandon completely the tenets of the Transitional Programme and prepare to build a centrist party. The only likely result is demoralization of its cadres at the first signs of fluctuation in the class struggle. This, coupled with an increasing adaptation to left social-democracy, will mark the decline of I.S. as an organization containing many dedicated revolutionaries.[22]

V

The refusal of Healy and his group to enter the re-unified Fourth International in 1963 and the disinterest of I.S. in an organization which was 'capitulating' to Stalinism, meant that for a long period there was no British section of the Fourth

[21] Cf. *Socialist Worker*, March 20th, 1971.

[22] For detailed discussion of the economic perspectives and the policies of I.S., see Ernest Mandel, *The Inconsistencies of State-Capitalism* (I.M.G., London, 1969), and by the same author, 'The Mystifications of State-Capitalism', *International*, vol. 1, no. 2 (September 1970). Also John Walters, 'The Theory of State Capitalism; The Clock Without a Spring', *Marxist Studies*, vol. 2, no. 1 (winter 1969–70).

International. The crisis of Stalinism also produced many militants who left the C.P. but refused to work within any of the other organizations for the reasons detailed above. Thus the roots of the International Marxist Group (I.M.G.), the British section of the F.I., are not tangled with those of the R.C.P. A group of militants who left the C.P. in 1956 in Nottingham formed the basis of what is the I.M.G. today. After a few futile attempts at working in a common organization with a small grouping known as the Revolutionary Socialist League (R.S.L.), the pre-I.M.G. militants started the production of a cylostyled weekly bulletin known as *The Week*. As they were engaged in doing 'entry' work inside the Labour Party, this journal gathered as its sponsors a mixed bag of centrists, left social-democrats and Bertrand Russell (!), in addition to certain Marxists. The I.M.G. was formally constituted in 1965; its early life was dominated by the Labour Party and its strategy premised on the emergence of a left current inside the Labour Party which would raise the banners of revolt against the Wilson clique. This never took place despite the vicious and reactionary policies of the Wilson administration. Thus the policy of 'waiting for lefty' had to be adjusted.[23] The left of the Labour Party destroyed itself and the changing world situation saw the growth of a new radicalized milieu. Thus while the I.M.G. played a decisive role in setting up the V.S.C. it was still committed to entrism on paper. This reflected a certain weakness theoretically as (of course it is easy to say this with

[23] It is only too easy for 'ultra-lefts' like myself to mock at the period of 'entrism'. Apart from anything else it reveals a certain political backwardness common among those militants who have never given serious thought to the building of a revolutionary party. However, 'entrism', unless carried out very clearly, also leads to the danger of adaptation. Thus while the bulk of the I.M.G. made the revolutionary choice when faced with extra-parliamentary action, one of its leaders preferred to continue the 'entrist' mentality and the evolution of the Institute of Workers Control is a sad testimony of how this process works. I still believe that a 'waiting for lefty-type entrism' was a bit utopian and that a well-planned entry purely for the purpose of raiding members would have proved much more worthwhile. This could also have been coupled with short-term battles against the Labour Party bureaucracy.

hindsight) a decisive and sharp turn away from social-democracy and the establishment of an embryonic youth organization
could have altered the balance of forces very radically on the
revolutionary left. The I.M.G., together with every other
revolutionary tendency, underestimated the breadth of the
radicalized youth milieu and its capacity for responding in a
revolutionary manner to the Vietnamese struggle. Once V.S.C.
had got off the ground the I.M.G. cadres devoted themselves
to the task of building it with a single-minded devotion, and
while the decision to put the needs of the Vietnamese Revolution above the interests of I.M.G. was thoroughly commendable,
the organization suffered and in fact it was I.S. which filled the
gap and recruited most of its members.[24] In fact I.M.G. overestimated the capacity of militants to recognize its 'superior
political programme' without any real ideological effort by the
I.M.G. itself which is so essential for creating a socialist and
totalizing consciousness.[25] For this it was vital for I.M.G. to
pose as a clear pole of attraction with a distinct ideology and
programme *apart* from, but at the same time in addition to its
excellent work in the V.S.C.

A similar error was made in the building of the workers'
control movement. It was I.M.G. which took the initiative in
launching a movement for workers' control, but at that time it
was engaged in 'entry' work in the Labour Party and this led
to an absurd fetishization of the question of security in relation
to the Transport House bureaucracy. A section of the I.M.G.
leadership were even opposed to recruiting militants to the
organization except in the most stringent circumstances. (This
turned out to be a trifle ironical as the most security-conscious

[24] This was both ironic and tragic. Ironic because of I.S.'s extremely Eurocentric
positions on the social revolution in semi-colonial countries, and tragic because
once it had gained members I.S. withdrew totally from V.S.C. and constantly
groaned about the futility of 'solidarity demonstrations'. Thus when imperialism
escalated the war it was difficult to mobilize large numbers of people.

[25] Even in the Labour Party a similar mistake had been made. *The Week* comrades had expected a spontaneous generation of socialist consciousness which
would automatically move towards them because of their superior programme.

I.M.G. leader, Ken Coates, was expelled from the Labour Party, while the most 'open' members were not discovered!) This over-caution led to a situation where virtually no attempt was made to draw the worker militants involved in the workers' control movement into the I.M.G. This was doubly tragic as it was the I.M.G. which organized the early conferences of the workers' control movement and serviced its needs. The leading comrade involved in this work broke with the organization when it insisted on criticizing Jack Jones of the T. and G.W.U. for betraying the dockers' strike in October 1967. Unfortunately he had found alternative means for servicing the movement and the I.M.G. was virtually excluded. The Institute for Workers' Control, helped by the Bertrand Russell Peace Foundation, established for itself a place on the political stage, but its politics moved further and further to the right. Thus when *The Times*, in its fatuous series of articles 'The Revolutionaries', implied that the Institute was inspired by Marxist ideas, one of the leading lights of the Institute hurriedly wrote a letter of protest to *The Times*:

> The statement that the Institute is 'attempting to translate Marxist aspiration into fact' is misleading. The truth is that the majority of our members and councillors are *not* Marxists at all; they find their commitment to workers' control coming from a variety of Humanist and Socialist traditions. Aspirations towards industrial democracy are by no means the exclusive prerogative of Marxism.[26]

Even if the I.M.G. had recruited a *handful* of worker militants in those early days it would have secured for itself a base from which limited actions could have been mounted, particularly in this period of heightened class activity when the weakness of the entire revolutionary left is so painfully visible.

[26] The letter, signed by a Ken Fleet, was dated March 4th and published a couple of days later. So keen to clear up the confusion was Mr Fleet that he could not wait for the conclusion of the postal workers' strike. Also worth study is the Ken Coates/*Red Mole* polemic in early 1971.

However, one can say that the lessons have been learnt and that I.M.G. has established itself as an organization of the revolutionary left; it has participated in the creation of a youth organization, the Spartacus League, and it has acquired a distinctive press. The latter is extremely important, as the period in which revolutionary left groups do not have any real implantation inside the working-class movement makes it all the more necessary that their propaganda is not merely agitational, but, like all good agitation, is also educative. For a certain period the I.M.G. had only a duplicated weekly paper, then it developed a printed montly, *International*, whose existence was a bit schizophrenic as its real role was never understood. At the same time *The Black Dwarf* emerged; its politics were similar to those of the I.M.G., and its editorial board was fully committed to V.S.C., so that many I.M.G. militants were prepared to sell the paper and use it as a means of organizing. This created problems, particularly as the downswing of the V.S.C. and the student movement meant that the newspaper had lost its mobile base and its milieu. Some of us on the editorial board therefore argued that the paper should develop a political programme and issue a call for the setting up of a revolutionary youth organization. This was regarded with utter horror and when it became clear that united work was impossible, rather than have a protracted struggle with nasty backbiting and rumour-mongering we decided to leave *The Black Dwarf* and organize a new paper.[27] This was done and *The Red Mole* came

[27] Various papers were circulated inside the *Dwarf* editorial board, where there were three tendencies: I.M.G., a wing of N.L.R. and non-affiliated militants who were paranoid about organizations and thus tended to oppose I.M.G. on principle. One of them, the poet Adrian Mitchell, actually resigned from the editorial board in protest against the I.M.G. presence and wrote a sweet non-sectarian little poem in *Peace News* (January 16th, 1970): 'If your comrade has less guts than you, call him a reformist. If he has more guts, call him an adventurist. Right, now that you've graduated and I've resigned, with some bitterness, from the *Black Dwarf*, I'd like you to join the chorus of The Red Rag. Altogether now:

> *I'm an entrist, centrist, Pabloite workerist —*
> *Sweet Fourth International and never been kissed.*
> *I've got a mass red base, that's why I'd rather sit on the floor.*

into existence with the avowed purpose of helping in the creation of a revolutionary youth organization; and if a balance
sheet were drawn, we could say that we have had a modest
success. More important, *The Red Mole*, while clearly the paper
of the Fourth International in Britain, has broken with the
image so often associated with newspapers of the revolutionary
left: either a mindless sectarianism or a drab, paternalistic
economism or even the feeling that a revolutionary newspaper
has to be dull in order to appeal to workers and 'serious
socialists'. *The Red Mole* has established itself as an all-embracing
revolutionary newspaper: its political coverage of all struggles,
its interest in youth culture, its interviews with shop-floor
militants and its insistence on providing regular articles on the
history of the labour movement and on Marxist theory has
won for it a readership that extends far beyond the actual
strength of both the I.M.G. and the Spartacus League. Red
Circles organized to discuss all aspects of revolutionary politics
are springing up everywhere and are attracting young workers
and other layers not involved in the educational system.
Whether or not the I.M.G. will be able to establish its authority
over the revolutionary left in Britain depends on the capacity

---

If you want to be a Vanguard, better join Securicor.
My daddy was opportunistic.
My mama was mystified.
I want to be a movement
But there's no-one on my side . . .
NO REVOLUTION WITHOUT COMPASSION
NO REVOLUTION WITHOUT COMPASSION.'
The I.M.G. argued that the *Dwarf* itself would cease to exist unless its base was
organized and in a prophetic few paragraphs we outlined the process of the
Dwarf's demise: ' ... The *Dwarf* could attempt to carve some other role out for
itself, but if this were in the direction of loose, perspectiveless politics, meandering
from one issue to another and one group to another without much forethought, the
paper would soon disappear. And its disappearance would then be well-merited
for it would have failed to be a Marxist paper, to look creatively at its environment,
to see what are the possibilities and the opportunities for changing the situation ... '
Soon after the split our non-sectarian friend, Adrian Mitchell, re-joined the board.
A few months later the paper had ceased to exist.

and capability of its militants to intervene in the different sectors of struggle and project a programme which will draw to it the politically advanced worker militants.

VI

It would be wrong to maintain that the Trotskyist movement in all its variations exists on its own on the revolutionary left in Britain. There are other tendencies, but none of them have been able to make any serious impact on revolutionary politics to date. The most important of these are the two Maoist organizations, the Communist Party of Britain (Marxist-Leninist) and the Communist Federation. The former is composed of dissidents from the C.P. who moved away during the Sino-Soviet split and is led by Reg Birch, the militant trade-union leader of the A.U.E.W. Despite the fact that Birch has been recognized as the 'official' group by Peking, his influence is restricted largely to a few pockets of industry and is largely industrial. Because of their refusal to break with Stalinism the political impact of both groups has been minimal. The Federation also contains a fair proportion of industrial militants, but is in certain ways more political. Neither of the groups grew out of a solidarity with the Chinese Revolution and the colonial revolution in general, nor are they the result of the global impact of the Chinese Revolution. They tend to be rather dependent on Peking for their political line and therefore any reconciliation between the Chinese and Soviet bureaucracies will leave their friends in Britain stranded in mid-air.[28] Also the Cultural Revolution did not have the same impact in Britain as it did in Western Europe and so we have fortunately been spared, at least till now, the development of an anti-Stalinist, but ultra-left Mao-spontaneist current which would

[28] We should by no means discard the possibility of a Sino-Soviet rapprochement after Mao's death as the interests of both the bureaucracies could easily begin to coincide. Of course, the recent sharp right turn by the Chinese state and party will also have its effects.

correspond to the Weathermen in the United States or La Gauche Prolétarienne in France. There do exist, however, small groups (literally consisting of less than ten members) who call themselves Maoist, but hate each other more than anyone else. In 1969 an unofficial survey unearthed twenty-eight such groups, but their membership seems to have declined since then. Another interesting sidelight is that Britain is probably unique in possessing a small group which denounces Mao, attacks the Soviet Union, and is inspired by Liu Shao-chi, the main victim of the Cultural Revolution. Any serious discussion of this group would require a knowledge of matters not related to politics and therefore it is best to leave it at that.

The anarchist movement continues to produce its paper, *Freedom*, but is itself not very strong and has declined considerably since the days of the Committee of A Hundred and C.N.D., when it was the scourge of Canon Collins and his associates. There has, however, been a proliferation of 'libertarian socialist' groups, particularly in certain universities, who are opposed to the very idea of organization and violently opposed to Leninist–Trotskyist currents. While many of them withdraw from politics on leaving universities, there is a fairly solid base around the journal *Solidarity*, whose main inspiration is an ex-S.L.L. member, Chris Pallis. Without doubt the formative influence as far as he is concerned has been the S.L.L. and its brand of 'Trotskyism'. Despite differences which one has with *Solidarity*, there is absolutely no doubt that it has produced extremely useful information from time to time. Even when one disagrees with it, one is forced to take its articles seriously, but *Solidarity* does its best work by producing excellent little pamphlets analysing particular strikes, which can be and *are* used by many shop stewards. However, its belief in a spontaneously generated political consciousness, and hence no real need for any organization, could demoralize its own militants in the not-too-distant future, as could its analysis of the colonial revolution.

VII

The whole question of how to build a revolutionary party in neo-capitalist societies is therefore posed. From our point of view we discuss the whole question of the party in Chapter 8, but it is important to discuss the attitude to the Labour Party which still obsesses the entire left. There has been no real discussion of the Labour Party except in the period immediately preceding the 1970 general election when there was an exchange in *The Red Mole* between Robin Blackburn and Pat Jordan (National Secretary of the I.M.G.). The main disagreement was as to whether the Labour Party could be considered a *totally* bourgeois party or not.[29] As far as tactics in the General Election were concerned, once again I.M.G. differentiated itself from the other tendencies by concentrating on revolutionary propaganda, rather than canvassing for the return of a Labour government. We discussed the C.P. attitude in Chapter 2, but even some 'Trotskyist' organizations fall into confusion and serve up re-hashed formulas which only reveal their own static concepts. Thus the S.L.L. raises the hoary slogan of 'Labour to power with a Socialist programme'. Apart from the fact that the most militant workers have, for the time being at any rate, no illusions regarding the Labour Party and its parliamentary leadership in so far that they have been through an experience, that of a Labour government from 1964–70, and they have learnt from this experience, the slogan raises other questions. Who, for instance, is going to ensure that the Labour Party has a socialist programme? The entire Labour Party, at the time of writing, is characterized by a complete decline in its internal life. More than 25 per cent of the constituency parties could not be bothered to send delegates to the Labour Party Annual Conference in 1970; Barbara Castle, the union basher, once again headed the poll for the election of members of constituency parties to the National

<hr>

[29] Cf. *The Red Mole*, vol. 1, nos 3, 4 and 5.

Executive Committee. Hardly a reflection of the struggles taking place in British society! There is *no* force today *inside* the Labour Party which could fight for a socialist programme. And that brings us to the second weakness of this grotesque slogan. It suggests that revolutionary socialists can actually gain control of the Labour Party. This is a totally revisionist concept which today borders on absurdity.[30] The Labour Party is totally bureaucratized and the *only* orientation which revolutionaries can have to it is to devise a strategy of destroying it, which means in effect breaking its links with the trade-union movement. The five-point charter of the I.S. is worse than the slogan we have just discussed in that it *creates* the worst illusions inside the working-class movement and encourages rightward moves by shop-floor militants.

Both these approaches lead to one logical conclusion: the need for 'revolutionaries' to enter the Labour Party in order to *change* it—or in other words the 'peaceful road to a Socialist Labour ... Party'. However, none of the organizations or even individuals who raise this slogan accept that logic because of the practical consequences involved. It would involve their becoming political necrophiliacs. That is the only description for those who want to 'enter' a corpse. Of course, it cannot be ruled out that out that the Labour Party will be revived by a mass influx of workers at the constituency level, but this is rather unlikely at present.

This incorrect perspective flows largely from an essentially propagandist approach to politics. It equates disillusionment with social-democracy as a development of political militancy, whereas it could lead also to political demoralization. It is essential for political militancy that the vanguard layers of the working class see in *practice* and in *action* that there exists an alternative way of carrying on the struggle. Revolutionaries, although they are few number, must at all times attempt to

---

[30] Trotsky certainly speculated about this possibility in the early 'thirties, but he was wrong. We are not cultists in any way and have to accept the fact that most revolutionary leaders have, despite their genius, made certain mistakes.

lead and analyse concrete struggles. The days when revolutionaries could conceive of their main task as 'defending' the programme are over. But to lead struggles it is essential constantly to develop theory. Any belief that at some point in the past the ideal programme was drawn up must be rejected.[31]

But what does 'lead' mean? Some 'Trotskyists' use the word and others interpret it simply as an administrative concept. That is certainly how Stalinists view it even today. Nothing could be further from Lenin's definition of democratic centralism, which was anything but administrative. The role of revolutionaries is to advance perspectives that will be seen to lead to a solution of the problems which confront the masses. That is why the I.M.G.'s perspectives are politically more advanced on the question of the Labour Party and governmental slogans, namely the call for 'a workers' government based on democratic control of the trade unions'. This lays down an orientation of activity and leads to policies which will help break the mass of the organized working class from the Labour Party by recognizing that the differentiation inside the Labour Party will arise between the constituency parties and the trade unions and not inside the former alone. That is why it does not lead to the bizarre conclusion that we should be inside the Labour Party today. Also it does not project the I.M.G. as an alternative to the Labour Party, a pit into which both the S.L.L. and I.S. tend to fall. A serious period of crisis could well lead to the formation of a National Government and in this eventuality all the anti-Labour Party propaganda which is being conducted *now* would only aid in detaching the trade unions from the Labour Party and the creation of a new party, not revolutionary, but in which revolutionaries will be able to

---

[31] The founding document of the Fourth International, The Transitional Programme, contained a 100 per cent correct evaluation of the situation as it existed then, and above all used a correct method to reach that evaluation. The method is more important than some of the demands, which have today been overtaken by history. Trotsky himself viewed the programme in this light, as his discussions on its nature with several S.W.P. comrades revealed.

operate with ease. The present period therefore means working outside the Labour Party and this demands greater resources than are at the disposal of the revolutionary movement today. We will discuss later how these resources can be increased.

6   The New Youth Radicalization

> We need young forces. I am for shooting on the spot
> anyone who presumes to say that there are no people
> to be had. The people in Russia are legion; all we have
> to do is to recruit people, young people, more widely
> and boldly, more boldly and widely, and again more
> widely and again more boldly, *without fearing them* ...
> The youth — the students, and still more so the young
> workers — will decide the issue of the whole struggle.
>
> LENIN,
> *Letter to Bogdanov and Gusev, February 11th, 1905*

I

The Labour Party achieved its narrow victory in 1964 partly
because there had been a shift to the left among a substantial
layer of young people: the only political means by which this
could be expressed at that time was through the Labour Party.
Although the support the latter received was often fairly critical,
nevertheless it cannot be denied that it still successfully mystified
most newly-radicalized people. As we saw in Chapter 4, this
radicalization had earlier expressed itself through C.N.D. and
the Committee of A Hundred, but the political bankruptcy of
both these organizations drove people to a left-reformist outlook; they had not been educated at all regarding the real
nature of the Labour Party as a party within the framework of
capitalism and obeying the dictates of that system. A Labour
victory was seen as a big step forward not because it would
help to remove the many illusions which existed regarding
social-democracy, but as an end in itself — people could be

convinced about the wickedness of nuclear weaponry and the few unconvincable evil men of the Labour right could be isolated. This was the barren message which left social-democracy broadcast to British youth.

The problem which faced the new Labour government and its parliamentary coffin-bearers was that it was entering not only a different period from the point of view of British capitalism, but also a fundamentally changed political period on a global scale. The previous generation had lived through some extremely disheartening and demoralizing experiences. They had witnessed the degeneration of the Russian Revolution and the triumph of Stalinism. They had seen the resulting betrayals in Spain, witnessed the victory of Fascism first in Italy and then in Germany. The prospects for world revolution seemed to be gloomy and this undoubtedly affected the view of large numbers of people throughout Europe. An outlook emerged which mixed cynicism with an extreme pessimism and saw no way out of the existing crisis. True, the aftermath of the Second World War had seen important new changes and up-surges: socialist revolution in China, and victories in Yugo-slavia, North Vietnam and North Korea. But the British working class was not really stirred by these victories and not only the workers' movement but even the left failed to under-stand the real significance of the social upheaval in China. A major change in the political situation in Western Europe would have been needed to affect radically the consciousness of a sizeable mass in Britain. In the absence of this, chauvinism and a narrow outlook governed the British Labour movement: thus there was no protest when British troops marched into Saigon, butchered many Vietnamese militants and paved the way for the return of French imperialism.[1] Nor was there any real action when the Labour government of 1945 supervised the butchery of the Malayan communists and British troops

[1] G. Rosie, *The British in Vietnam* (Panther, London, 1970). The author gives an extremely interesting account of the policies of the first Labour government (remember — the good one!) in relation to Vietnam.

posed for souvenir photographs with a few chopped-off communist heads lying at their feet.[2] By 1964, fortunately for us,
the situation had altered and a new generation which had not
lived through a period of defeat had matured and was accordingly much more open to political ideas. Even if the Labour
left had been able to play a mystifying role the response would
have been extremely critical as the large numbers of young
people who actively campaigned for a Labour victory were a
highly volatile mass who desired real changes which pointed
towards a solution of some of the problems and threats which
capitalism had spawned.[3]

But the Labour left had mystified itself so thoroughly that it
was not really capable of mystifying anyone else. As we mentioned briefly earlier, the Labour left had put all its heart into
the fight to get Wilson elected as the leader of the Labour
Party. Having succeeded in this purpose they actually believed
that this was a victory for left social-democracy and at last
they would have a government which they could identify with
fully. There was not going to be the vacillating Attlee or the
reactionary Bevin or the 'traitor' MacDonald. Gaitskell was
dead and Wilson was king. The votes of the left had been
decisive in putting him on the throne and the left naively
believed that he would behave differently from other Prime
Ministers.[4] This belief was not only manifested in Michael

[2] These photographs were published in the *Daily Worker*, but because this paper
had lied so often in the past and because the Stalinists were not averse to faking
photographs when it suited their purpose (cf. the famous photographs of Lenin
from which Trotsky has been removed!), the bourgeoisie spread rumours that it
was all 'communist propaganda'.

[3] Although many of these people did not consciously realize it at the time, the
whole logic of this position led to a break with the capitalist system because this
was the only way in which these problems could be solved. Hence a break with
capitalist politics and capitalist parties was essential.

[4] Wilson, of course, encouraged this belief and his pre-1964 election rhetoric
was full of choice phrases. Thus at a meeting in Birmingham he pledged: 'We
want to give our people a new Britain and we are going to bring home to the
people the excitement there will be in building it ... We want the youth of Britain
to storm the new frontiers of knowledge, to bring back to Britain that surging
adventurous self-confidence and sturdy self-respect which 1964 can mean. A chance

Foot's pictorial and adulatory biography of the Leader, but in the role played by left-wing M.P.s in trying to damp down opposition to the Wilson regime outside Parliament. Many student militants will remember the left stalwarts touring the universities, speaking to Labour Clubs and Socialist Societies and reassuring them that all was well. The main excuse of the Labour left was that Wilson had a small majority of three and this is what was preventing the Labour government from dynamically moving forward to newer pastures. In fact the left signed its own death warrant, because it was precisely with a small Labour majority that the left group of twenty-five M.P.s could have played a decisive role in Parliament. They could have prepared a modest list of demands concerning the economy, Vietnam, Rhodesia and Immigration and they could have warned that unless these were implemented they would have no hesitation about bringing the Labour government down. Instead of doing this the Labour left became apologists for the Wilson regime and explained that it was the majority of three which was preventing Wilson from adopting socialist policies and that once Labour had a larger majority all would be well. Thus left social-democracy, whose main leaders anyhow had been integrated by being included in the Wilson government, killed itself.

When Labour returned with a majority of ninety-seven after the 1966 election the state of British capitalism demanded further attacks on the living conditions of the working class. This meant more reactionary policies, and though *Tribune* proclaimed boldly that: 'AT LAST SOCIALISM IS ON THE AGENDA', what the electorate actually got was a dose of good old-fashioned capitalist medicine. The Labour left found that even if it had wanted to protest, the large majority meant that it would be meaningless and indeed the Labour leadership

---

for change! A chance to sweep away the grouse-moor conception of Tory leadership and refit Britain with a new image, a new confidence.' Though these hollow remarks would today draw only ironical laughs and heckling, in those days they were taken more seriously and greeted with rapturous applause.

allowed the 'left' to protest now and again to keep up the morale of the party. This virtual collapse of left social-democracy paved the way for the development of an extra-parliamentary opposition and the revolutionary left in general. The man largely responsible for destroying left social-democracy as a serious current in the politics of the labour movement was undoubtedly Harold Wilson, and the revolutionary movement owes him a certain debt in this regard.

The policies of the Labour government on the war in Vietnam, on the trade unions and immigration at home, undoubtedly provided the platform from which revolutionists could mount a critique of the entire capitalist system as such and thus radicalize an increasing number of young people. It is therefore essential to discuss these three components separately and in detail before describing the evolution of the milieu on which they had the greatest effect: the student movement.

1. *The Vietnam War and its international consequences*

To understand and appreciate why the Vietnamese Revolution has had such an enormous impact in shaping the consciousness of the newly radicalized layers, one must go back in history a little and examine the Cold War period and the general atmosphere it engendered. During the late 'forties, the 'fifties and the early 'sixties, revolutionary consciousness was at a very low ebb. The struggle was seen by both sides as a choice between bourgeois democracy and Stalinism, and neither of these apparent options was very appealing to large masses of people. The working class in particular was not attracted to the model of the Soviet Union, and the bourgeoisie played on this feeling to engender a vicious anti-communism which not only affected the workers' movement but toppled many left-wing intellectuals as well. The Cold War thus consolidated the ideology of capitalism and temporarily stabilized the system.

The war in Vietnam pierced the myths of the Cold War with the shaft of the National Liberation Front. From the very beginning of American involvement the situation excited the sympathy of young people: a colonial people in arms on the one side and the armies of the most 'advanced' industrialized nation in the world on the other presented a clear choice. However, this in itself would not have been sufficient. What was absolutely decisive was that the Vietnamese, far from losing the war and accepting imperialist rule in South-East Asia, showed that they were capable of taking the offensive, and their immense reserves were brought into play during the Tet offensive. The fact that the N.L.F. could inflict defeats on the American Army aroused the enthusiasm and admiration of youth throughout the world. In that sense the Vietnamese Revolution also broke through the mystifying effects of Stalinism and provided a new and attractive pole of attraction on a global scale. They themselves were fully aware of this fact. When I was in Hanoi in January 1967, the North Vietnamese leader Pham van Dong said quite unequivocally: 'Tell the comrades in Western Europe that the Vietnamese people are fighting for them as well. Tell them that internationalism is in our blood ... ' In an article commemorating the October Revolution of 1917, Le Duan, the Secretary of the Vietnamese Workers Party, wrote: 'The Vietnamese Revolution is part of the world revolution and its success cannot be dissociated from that of the world revolution.' Thus the struggle in Vietnam emphasized and furthered an internationalization of anti-imperialist consciousness which had already begun to take shape with the victory of the Cuban revolution.

It was on this of all issues that the Labour administration first displayed its totally reactionary nature. Without equivocation the government of Harold Wilson gave open support to American imperialism in Vietnam, and Wilson advised demonstrators to go and demonstrate outside the Chinese Embassy! Michael Stewart, the Labour Foreign Secretary, won for himself the permanent admiration of the entire Tory Party in the way he handled some mealy-mouthed liberal protests from his own backbenchers and in fact was the most sickening apologist for American actions in Vietnam. The Labour 'lefts' urged both sides to come to the conference table, asked Wilson to act as 'honest broker', pressed for intervention from U Thant or a 'third force' — in short, worked to encourage everything but the real task : to support an oppressed people in its struggle against the mightiest imperialist nation in the world. In this the Communist Party initially tail-ended the fake-lefts; in one of the earliest Vietnam demonstrations, in 1965, some of us who had come with banners demanding 'Victory to the N.L.F.' were told by C.P. stewards that these banners would not be allowed, and when we persisted the police were called to ask us to leave. But here the C.P. completely miscalculated. It thought, like the reformists, that simple and straightforward reformist slogans would rally the largest number of people. They completely misjudged the depth of feeling on this question.

It was in this atmosphere that the Vietnam Solidarity Campaign was founded, largely on the initiative of the Bertrand Russell Peace Foundation and the International Marxist Group (the British section of the Fourth International). The latter was acting on the call of the Fourth International to all its sections and supporters to make solidarity with the Vietnamese Revolution a political priority and to mobilize support for its success. Despite its limited resources at that stage the Fourth International felt that in the face of the total incapacity of the Stalinist parties in Western Europe to wage a consistent campaign, this task fell on its shoulders and that therefore it should do all in its power to make this a key task. The success of the Vietnam Solidarity Campaign astounded even its most ardent supporters. Though the Campaign had been founded in 1966 it had concentrated first on propaganda and had been involved with the work of the International War Crimes Tribunal which had been set up by Bertrand Russell. The Tribunal denounced the systematic genocide which was being conducted against the Vietnamese people long before the massacres of My Lai were brought to the attention of the general public. The

Tribunal played a crucial role in focusing attention on the struggle in Vietnam and had an important effect in many parts of Western Europe, particularly Scandinavia. Both Harold Wilson and de Gaulle had refused permission for the Tribunal to meet either in London or in Paris and the British press accordingly virtually boycotted its proceedings.[5] At any rate an important start had been made.

From its very inception the Vietnam Solidarity Campaign (V.S.C.) had stressed its complete break with the politics of the reformist organizations. It had declared itself completely in solidarity with the N.L.F. and the struggle to *defeat* American imperialism in Asia. It was these politics which made V.S.C. attractive to thousands of young people and it was the continuation of these politics on to the streets and its style of demonstrations which won it the active support of the revolutionaries. Many intellectuals and old workers who had grown disgusted with reformism and Stalinism and had slunk into an isolated existence dominated by both despair and cynicism were suddenly rejuvenated by the new rise of revolutionary consciousness. Thus V.S.C. was startled when its first well-publicized demonstration appeal brought ten thousand militants to Trafalgar Square in October 1967. The ensuing march to Grosvenor Square resulted in the first violent demonstration for decades. The demonstrators found that the American Embassy was protected by policemen and they took both themselves and the police by surprise by charging the police lines and actually reaching the steps of the imperialist fortress in Grosvenor Square. A battle took place and finally the demonstrators were driven back, but the feeling was one of total euphoria and elation. The fact that the *Guardian* referred to us as 'thugs' only generalized a feeling of happiness. What was important about this demonstration was not so much the confrontation with the fuzz, but the fact that a large number of militants had got

[5] With the partial exception of *The Times*, whose correspondent Malcolm Southan sent in some balanced reports till *The Times* decided to stop publicizing the Tribunal's activities.

together and identified themselves with the struggle of the
N.L.F. Despite its growth, the V.S.C. lost an important ally.
Because Ralph Schoenman was not allowed back into the
country, the Bertrand Russell Peace Foundation fell into
the hands of people who did not attach much importance to the
task of mobilizing militants and thus severed their connection
with the V.S.C. by asking the latter to move out of the premises
of the Foundation within a specified period of time. While this
affected the orgnizational efficiency of V.S.C. it did not prevent
the latter from attracting increasing numbers of supporters.
A demonstration was called by V.S.C. for March 17th, 1968, in
response to an appeal by the Vietnamese for increased activity
in the imperialist countries. Those who had been alarmed by
the success of the 1967 action now trained their guns at V.S.C.
and its leaders. A very strange alliance developed between
Peace News, the Communist Party and the Socialist Labour
League. All these organizations shared a common hostility to
the V.S.C. for one basic reason: they were frightened by
spontaneity, and contemptuous of any real mass action outside
their control. The most detailed and sustained criticism of
V.S.C. came from *Comment*, a C.P. publication meant for its
active members. Exactly a month before the March demonstration the paper carried an article by our old friend Mrs
Betty Reid entitled 'Diversions in the Fight for Peace', which
contained attacks on the Fourth International and the Chinese
Communist Party. What struck one about this article was its
intellectual dishonesty. In an article dealing with Vietnam,
Mrs Reid did not mention once the semi-pacifist front organizations through which the C.P. directed its own Vietnam activity.[6]
The Vietnamese had publicly criticized the chairman of one
of these front organizations, Lord Fenner Brockway, in very
strong terms for suggesting that U Thant had a role to play.[7]

[6] The British Council for Peace in Vietnam (B.C.P.V.) and the British Peace
Committee were the two dynamic organizations through which the C.P. participated. The average age of their members must have been between 40 and 50.

[7] Cf. *Vietnam Courier*, Hanoi, July 24th, 1967.

Mrs Reid argued that the solidarity position (i.e. demanding victory to the N.L.F.) 'narrows down the movement for Vietnam'. This was written when V.S.C. was beginning to draw more support than the C.P. had ever done on the question of defending the colonial revolution. Thus the C.P. opposed the demonstration of March 17th and actively canvassed support for one a week later which had been called by the Youth C.N.D. In the event history made its own judgment: the V.S.C. demonstration attracted 25,000 people, all chanting the slogan which upset Betty Reid so much: 'Victory to the N.L.F.!' and packing Oxford Street with red flags and the N.L.F. banners. At Grosvenor Square the police very clearly provoked a confrontation and got one in which they did not fare so well and finally had to summon mounted police to clear the Square. A Granada TV film made by World in Action showed some interesting examples of police brutality against the demonstrators. This violence established very clearly the identity of interests between American imperialism (represented by its Embassy) and the British state (represented by its repressive apparatus charging at demonstrators on horseback and truncheoning them). More important, the strength of feelings and solidarity on the demonstration reached the entire world. In the United States the liberal Senator McCarthy assailed Lyndon Johnson for creating a situation where the U.S. Embassy in the capital of 'our closest ally in Europe' was 'besieged by thousands of demonstrators'. In South Vietnam, the puppet Foreign Minister called a special press conference to denounce V.S.C. as being part of a communist conspiracy. This was true, but, as we saw, not part of the tactics or strategy of official 'communism'. The *Morning Star* reported the demonstration without mentioning the V.S.C., a feat which was much envied by the capitalist press. The bourgeois press, as expected, went berserk. The fact that a large contingent from the German S.D.S. had participated and the fact that I was a Pakistani and on the national committee of V.S.C. was used to stir up all the latent prejudice which British imperialism

injected into the minds of its populace.[8] In comparison with the
V.S.C. demonstration, the one supported by the C.P. and the
'left' Establishment only a week later turned out to be a
miserable flop. Only three thousand demonstrators attended
and they were led by the banners of the London C.P. They
marched in good step and were saluted by the bourgeois press
for their good humour compared to the thugs of the previous
week.[9]

V.S.C. continued to escalate the protests and the October
1968 demonstration mobilized 100,000 militants in solidarity
with the Vietnamese struggle, the largest demonstration with
revolutionary implications in post-war Britain. The hysteria
of the bourgeois press, which was reflected in front-page
articles in *The Times* predicting the violent capture of key
installations in London, created a situation to which the
demonstrators were forced to respond. After long discussions
inside the V.S.C. leadership a compromise was agreed upon:
the demonstration would not go to Grosvenor Square but to
Hyde Park.[10] If the police interfered with the demonstration at
all we would fight back, otherwise discipline would be maintained, as indeed it was. Because of the rapid decline of V.S.C.

[8] For instance Callaghan and Bob Mellish exchanged public letters about the
legal problems which lay in the way of getting me deported. Callaghan also, for
some curious reason, referred to me as a 'rich playboy', a comment which was
used a lot in those heady days by the Young Communist League (Y.C.L.) leaders
and the S.L.L.

[9] Some Y.C.L. branches had started defying the C.P. and marching with V.S.C.
and under its slogans. This began to become rather widespread and finally forced
the C.P. to change its policy and participate on the October 27th demo as a small
minority!

[10] There were three points of view: I.M.G. was in favour of Grosvenor Square;
I.S. wanted to go to the Bank of England; a third group wanted the South
Vietnamese Embassy! Hyde Park was therefore agreed on as a shabby compromise.
On reflection I think we were wrong in accepting the compromise and that
Grosvenor Square should have remained the main target. The overwhelming
weight of the bourgeois state and its use of the press to engender hysteria un-
doubtedly affected many people, myself included. (This is intended as a self-
criticism.) For an analysis of the way in which the mass media handled the demonstration, see J. D. Halloran, P. Elliot, G. Murdoch, *Demonstrations and Mass
Communication* (Penguin, Harmondsworth, 1970).

as a mobilizing force there were countless post mortems and inquests. Most of them centred round the fact that it was the lack of violence on October 27th which caused the decline; others argued that V.S.C. should have declared itself into a multi-issue organization whereas some pointed the way to community work. All these reasons were far from the real reasons for the decline which lay in the inability of the revolutionary student movement to organize itself and the weakness of the only organization which had a global view of politics and which would appeal to the mass of militants. Within its limited framework V.S.C. was a tremendous success. It fulfilled the role it had set out to play. Its sudden collapse had its roots in the politics of the revolutionary left as a whole. It should be pointed out that while V.S.C. faded from the headlines and did not organize any mass demonstrations it has remained the *only* organization which has maintained a regular journal and has carried out small propagandistic actions in solidarity with the Vietnamese, or rather the Indo–Chinese, Revolution.

2. *The black citizens of Britain and how Labour and Tory alike have treated them.*

We do not intend to deal here with a history of immigration into Britain. That has been done effectively elsewhere.[11] After the Tory government restricted immigration in 1962 many black people came to regard the Labour Party as a party which would defend them against racism. Indeed, Gaitskell had encouraged this belief with his moral outrage at the racist Immigration Act of 1962 and his pledge that Labour, when elected, would repeal it completely and without equivocation. Even in those days, however, many Labour M.P.s talked in terms of 'constructive alternatives' and were not too happy with the enthusiasm of their leader in defending the blacks. Fortunately for them Gaitskell died and was replaced by Harold Wilson, who had no similar moral hang-ups and who

[11] P. Foot, *Immigration and Race in British Politics* (Penguin, Harmondsworth, 1965).

was interested above all in maintaining power. If this meant that the Labour government should inject a further dose of racism into British politics, then racism it would be. The Smethwick election in 1964, which was fought on an anti-immigrant ticket by the Tory candidate and resulted in the defeat of the Labour reactionary Patrick Gordon Walker, obviously stunned the Labour Party. Wilson's first reaction in Parliament was to denounce the victorious Tory as a parliamentary 'leper' who would spend his time in isolation. But soon the leprosy spread very rapidly and infected a large chunk of the parliamentary Labour Party. The illusions of the black people were severely dented when in 1965, a year after they had been in office, the new Labour government introduced laws making it much more difficult for black people to come to Britain. This they referred to as 'tightening the loopholes' which the Tories had left open in the 1962 Act![12] Labour policy continued on these lines and culminated with the Labour government and its Home Secretary, Callaghan, writing racism officially into the statute books by barring Kenyan Asians with British passports from entering Britain! The wheel had turned full circle. In addition, the Labour government further capitulated to racism in Southern Rhodesia when they failed to take any effective action to deal with Ian Smith's attempts to South Africanize Rhodesia. Wilson's readiness to compromise with the White racist regime contrasted only too clearly with his patronizing and paternalistic attitude to the Black African leaders when they reprimanded him in no uncertain terms for his dealings with the Smith clique.

All these events had their effect on the black population, and

[12] This was a far cry from Harold Wilson's statement, printed in *Hansard*, November 27th, 1963: 'The committee will recall that, when the Commonwealth Immigrants Bill was introduced, we on this side strongly opposed its particular terms for three main reasons. We opposed it first, because it was, in fact, based on race and colour discrimination, however much attempts were made to suggest otherwise. Second it discriminated against the Commonwealth ... Our third reason for opposing the Bill was that it was not based on consultation, still less on agreement with Commonwealth countries ... '

slowly but surely the leadership of the black community began to slip away from the 'Uncle Tom' figures, the advocates of working within the system, and began to pass to the more militant elements. The latter are making even more headway now with the Tory government's new Immigration Act[13] which distinguishes between patrials and non-patrials (i.e. blacks and whites!). The development of black organizations, the increasing harassment and brutalization of black people and black militants by the police are factors which are going to play an important role in the development of the revolutionary movement in Britain. As the capitalist class utilizes the fragmented consciousness of workers and plays on racism to divide the workers' movement the need for an articulated and aggressive response will become even more necessary.

3. The trade unions and the Labour Party

It is not necessary to discuss the relationship between the two in any detail as we have indicated, particularly in the first two chapters, how their strained relations reflected the situation of British capitalism. The important factor is that the Wilson attack on the trade-union movement, and particularly the shop stewards, brought home to many revolutionaries, who had developed largely outside the traditional labour movement, the important understanding that the working class was the only agency for social change in late-capitalist societies. While this is obvious to most socialists today as the class struggle intensifies, it was certainly not clear to many revolutionary students in the heady days of 1967–8. The bombshell which hit Gaullist France in the form of the social explosion of May–June 1968, and revealed the capacity of the working-class movement to the entire world, had an important effect in combating some

---

[13] No other governments have passed so many Immigration Acts as have the Labour and Tory governments from 1962–71. Tory and Labour politicians shouldn't be too complacent about this. The chickens will soon start coming home to roost!

Marcusianisms which totally rejected the working-class movement and claimed that it had been integrated into the structures of the bourgeois state. The May revolt shattered the
complacency of even the British ruling class and brought home
to hundreds of thousands of people the actuality of the revolution
in capitalist society. This realization, which dawned late on
some militants, caused many to yearn for contacts with workers;
we shall discuss in the last chapter the danger of making these
contacts without a clear-cut understanding of the uneven
development of consciousness; mistakes can be made which
lead to serious demoralization.

In addition, the general growth of education, the immense
power and wide availability of the mass media, particularly
television, and the rise of working-class pop groups brought
about the narrowing of cultural differences between young
workers and large sections of students. Many of these young
workers were more attracted to certain styles of student activity,
both cultural and political, than to the heavily bureaucratized
trade-union structures with which they could not identify.
While this revealed a certain backwardness, and meant that
many of them equated the trade-union bureaucracies with the
trade union itself and so refused to take part in trade-union
activities, at the same time it promised a healthy future, and the
militancy displayed by many young workers in the class
struggles which dominate British politics today is a sign that
the balance is being restored.

These three factors have dominated the politics of the
revolutionary students in the universities, and to understand
why the students have reacted to these issues as a mass and
have solidarized with them, we must understand the changing
nature of the bourgeois university and the role which a large
majority of students will be expected to play after they have
left universities and polytechnics. It is important to analyse
these developments in some detail as most of the existing revolutionary groupings are still composed predominantly of students.

Unfortunately most of them, instead of trying to understand why this has happened, are busy trying to forget this fact as fast as possible and are engaged in breeding a strange and bizarre masochism inside their own students. While this is understandable, it nevertheless distorts existing realities and creates a demoralization inside the student movement itself.

II

The political situation has changed to the advantage of the revolutionary movement as a whole. The problem is whether the existing revolutionary groups will be able to seize the time, whether they will be able to grasp the opportunities in the present period and develop from organizations which simply carry out propaganda activity into organizations which can begin to make limited but influential interventions in the working-class movement.

One of the reasons that the universities and, particularly in Britain thanks to the binary system, other institutions of further education have very rapidly become open to the spread of revolutionary ideas is because they themselves have been in a state of transition over the last two decades. The role of the university has traditionally been to provide for the general diffusion of bourgeois culture, thus training the future ruling class of capitalist society. This situation has changed fundamentally because of the increasingly complex nature of neo-capitalism, which needs technically specialized labour to cope with the new technological processes which are reshaping the industrial development of the entire capitalist world. The universities are trying to adapt to these changes and their failure to do so efficiently or rapidly provides one of the causes for the student revolt. At the same time the adaptations profoundly change the nature of the university. We see the rapid multiplication of new sociology, economics, statistics departments and special courses in industrial relations whose aim is to provide the cadre for *helping* to manage industry and the growing apparatus of the state itself. Thus in many universities we see the development of a 'labour market' for university graduates. Firms send in their 'talent scouts' to pick graduates once a year and the law of supply and demand is beginning to determine the wages of intellectual workers as it has done those of manual workers for the last two hundred years. The university is thus no longer a training ground for the ruling elite (a few particular universities are sufficient for that particular task), but increasingly a mass university. Intellectual labour is thus becoming proletarianized, but,

> Proletarianisation does not mean primarily (or in some circumstances at all) limited consumption or a low standard of living, but increasing alienation, increasing subordination of labor to demands that no longer have any correspondence to the special talents or fulfilment of the inner needs of men. If the university is to fulfill the function of training the specialists wanted by the big corporations, higher education must be reformed in a functional direction. Specialists on economic growth have 'discovered' that one of the reasons for the slow growth of the gross national product in Great Britain has been the overstressing of theoretical science in the universities at the expense of applied science ... [14]

Many of the entrants to the universities do not come from the ruling class. Although they still desire privileges, they do not necessarily expect to occupy ruling positions. These changes were heralded by the red-brick universities, but are now taking place on a vastly increased scale. The problem for the bourgeoisie is that while these changes are important to it, it is incapable of financing the change on an adequate scale, and sometimes unwilling to do so. Hence ambitious projects for the rapid creation of new universities are slowed down because too little money for adequate buildings is given to the universities

[14] Ernest Mandel, *The Changing Face of the Bourgeois University* (Spartacus League pamphlet, 1971), Red Books, 182 Pentonville Road, London N1.

by the University Grants Committee (U.G.C.). Pressure on accommodation, catering facilities and libraries has brought home to many students that their position is becoming steadily less favoured. This contradiction has been seen with more explosive force in the rest of Western Europe. In Britain itself, tight control of admission to university has both relieved the pressure to some extent and helped preserve illusions among those who 'made it'. Also the relationship of the student to the institution of the university is mediated in Britain by the tutorial system. As we mentioned earlier, British universities are a relatively privileged section of higher education; it is in the other section of the binary system that the poverty of facilities really revealed itself, with some sharpness, and the 'seventies will see an escalation of struggles in this sphere as the objective conditions exist for a big upheaval.

The changing character of the university has also affected the credibility of bourgeois ideology. Today the values, objectives and history of the bourgeoisie inspire only disgust and horror, where once they inspired enthusiasm. Large numbers of students do not need to be told of the vast gap which exists between the promises and hopes of the bourgeoisie and its performance. The crimes being committed daily in Asia, Africa and Latin America have become too glaringly obvious to be ignored: hence the massive response of students to the struggle in Vietnam. In addition, the increasingly functionalized nature of university courses results in a growing sense of alienation. Both what he studies and the grading process seem more and more irrelevant to today's student. The ideological atrocities which the bourgeoisie carries out in the universities are beginning to be challenged more often. The revolt against bourgeois ideology (seen more clearly in Germany and the U.S. than in Britain) expresses itself in the mushrooming of free universities, critical universities, and so on, at a time of sharp conflict within the university itself. This opposition becomes increasingly part of the accelerating discontent of the professional layers of society (teachers, television journalists, etc.) who begin to question the overall social significance of their daily activity (cf. the media workers in France in May 1968).

Students find themselves in the midst of a contradiction which they try to surmount in various ways, but which they can never resolve as it involves the fundamental contradiction encompassing capitalist societies: that between the development of productive forces and at the same time the preservation of the existing relations of production. In brief, the socialization of production contrasts sharply with the ownership of the productive forces, which affects the universities by compelling them to develop the productive forces while at the same time retaining existing productive relationships through the fragmentation and compartmentalization of knowledge, by discriminatory recruitment and a respect for the private profits of capitalists as individuals.[15]

But it is important to understand that the student population lacks both social and political homogeneity, and is not the natural ally of the workers. The school-leaving age has been extended; the university population is larger than ever before; and through the diversification of university recruitment and professional careers, university students have strengthened their ties with the rest of their generation in the polytechnics, colleges of further education and the factories. But there is still no objective basis for bringing the students as a social layer over to the side of the industrial proletariat. There are no homogeneous student interests to defend as such. On the other hand, neither can the students be characterized as petty-bourgeois, a common mistake of philistines and vulgar 'Marxists'. The student milieu has created political currents whose poles lie outside the university, in the class struggle between the bourgeois state and the proletariat. A section of

[15] The only meaningful analysis of the evolution of the student movement and the effects on it of neo-capitalism has come from the Fourth International. See in particular the special *Cahiers Rouge* (Maspero, Paris, 1969), on the student movement, and also an article by Bensaid and Scalabrino in *The Black Dwarf*, vol. 14, no. 29 (February 20th, 1970), and Ernest Mandel, 'The New Vanguard', in *New Revolutionaries*, Tariq Ali, ed. (Peter Owen, London, 1969).

students align themselves with the ruling class whose benefits they are designed to share; another section have gone over to the proletariat because they realize that the student movement by itself is incapable of solving the contradictions of the university, which is dependent on the very foundations of capitalism. Thus despite the fact that the uneven development of political consciousness can sometimes put the students in a vanguard role of articulating the demands of the working class as a whole, this role can at best be temporary and of an exemplary character.

The student movement is incapable of political and programmatic independence from the working class, though this does *not* mean that they are not capable of attacking the reformist and fumbling leadership of the working-class movement which exists at the present moment virtually throughout Western Europe. As a result of this the student movement is torn between its revolutionary desires and its objective limits, between its mass potential and its role as a substitute political vanguard, particularly at a time when it finds itself thrown into struggles.[16] Hence the importance of transcending studentism and linking up with the embryonic vanguard organizations of the revolutionary left which exist outside the universities and are slowly being implanted in the working-class movement. In addition the vanguard groups have a certain historical past, whereas the student movement as such has neither memory nor history and is usually absorbed in temporary actions or in short-lived but spectacular demonstrations. The revolutionary group, by intervening in the universities, can organize and train militants and thus start the process of weaving the fabric of political memory of the student movement itself. The task

[16] Students in colonial and semi-colonial countries play a somewhat different role as a temporary vanguard because of the immaturity of the proletariat. This is nothing new: Engels, Trotsky and Mao Tse-tung hailed the leading role played by students in Austria in 1850 and China in 1919. Today, the vanguard role of the student movement in certain capitalist countries is not a sign of the insufficient maturity of the proletariat, but of the total bankruptcy of its social-democratic or Stalinist leaderships.

which confronts revolutionary Marxists is to win over not simply individual student militants but masses of students to their organizational and political ideas; then the propaganda they have been carrying out inside the workers' movement can begin to be transformed into action, and the workers can feel that if they reject social-democracy or Stalinism they still have a strong organizational alternative which is capable of intervening on the national political stage. Linking with a revolutionary organization thus offers the only way for revolutionary students if they are to transcend the limits of their objective situation.

The other strategies offered to the student movement have shown their weaknesses on an international scale and have ended in failure. The 'theoreticians' of the Free University reduced the student struggle to simply an ideological struggle against the bourgeois university and did not permit it to develop any further. The criticism of the university is meaningless however if not related to the criticism of society, and once students move to a criticism of society as a whole then the question of revolutionary strategy and tactics is posed, a question which can only be solved within a revolutionary organization. Similarly the propagators of 'revolutionary trade unionism' in the student milieu, however well-intentioned they may be, lead the students towards reformism. The application of an all-embracing design for society as a whole which students in fact can put into practice only in universities and there, too, only temporarily, reveals the limitations of the movement. Even the most extreme-sounding slogans, like student control, student self-management, student power, thus turn out to be, if isolated from the overall situation of the class struggle, thoroughly reformist. The Red University is not so much a slogan as a theme of struggle which has to be filled in with concrete slogans in concrete situations. The Red University is therefore not an institution that one counterposes to the bourgeois university; it is a movement of struggle by which revolutionists attempt to direct the student movement as a permanent striking force against the system.

It is not a strategy for the university, but a tactic used by revolutionary militants in the universities which remains a subordinate part of its overall strategy.

There has been an increase in graduate unemployment throughout the advanced capitalist world, including Britain.[17] This means either that many students after they leave university remain unemployed, and thus if they have been won over to revolutionary politics can be prevailed upon to work as full-time revolutionaries, or that they are forced into jobs as manual workers, where they can play a useful role as red moles. Graduate unemployment is going to increase; it can be curtailed only by a vicious educational policy which will determine the number of students engaged in any particular subject. This policy is inevitable in neo-capitalist societies and will further accelerate the contradictory processes in institutions of higher education and thus increase the objective causes for the student revolt. Whether this revolt can be channelled into a revolutionary opposition against the bourgeoisie depends on the strength — both ideological and political — of the revolutionary vanguard organizations. Thus the struggle is a test of the vanguard's capacity to lead the mass of students away from reformism and Stalinism and engage in a continual polemic against the basically liberal, but spontaneously generated ideologies.

III

The level of student organization in Britain has been fairly low compared with other countries — there is the S.D.S. in the United States and West Germany, for example, the Zengakuren in Japan and the March 22nd Movement in France. In Britain the early student radicalization was dominated by Vietnam and the V.S.C., and it was not till June 1968 that an attempt was

[17] 'Ten per cent of the graduates who left university last summer have still not got a proper full time job. Five years ago it was 5 per cent. Next year the figure could double again ... ', *The Economist* (March 6th, 1971).

made to set up a Revolutionary Socialist Students Federation (R.S.S.F.). Unlike some of its counterparts on the Continent, R.S.S.F. did not develop from the youth organization of a social-democratic party. It was a direct attempt to start from scratch by sections of the left. The first conference of R.S.S.F. attracted 650 militants from almost every university and college in the country which had a Socialist Society. This was a response to May 1968 in France and the tremendous upsurge of the student movement in Western Europe, symbolically illustrated by the convergence of revolutionary militants in London for a BBC TV jamboree on the eve of the conference. The major participants in the founding of R.S.S.F. were the Maoists, I.S. and some independent militants from the *New Left Review*. The main decision the conference took with unanimity was to work for the October 27th Vietnam demonstration. This commitment to an anti-imperialist demonstration allowed for a clear united front in which all political tendencies could participate and thus give R.S.S.F. a tremendous opportunity to win thousands of new people to its politics.

This opportunity was missed because of the uncertainties that afflicted the I.S. group. Although it was the leading force in R.S.S.F., it could not make up its mind on three crucial questions. Firstly, on the role of the student movement in the overall revolutionary strategy (this reflected the absence of any clear programme for the group). Secondly, on whether the student movement could maintain and develop its own revolutionary leadership, or, on the other hand, needed a strong Marxist leadership. Thirdly, on whether I.S. should devote its entire organization to build and service R.S.S.F., and if so whether it should aim to transform R.S.S.F. into an I.S. youth organization or continue with the policy of a broad united front with other political groups that had attended the founding conference. We do not know if these questions were ever formally asked and answered, but I.S. answered in practice by not participating seriously in the leadership of R.S.S.F. and by refraining from giving the organization political perspectives. In

London, the Maoists were allowed to take over the field and the local R.S.S.F. organization. The result was that on the V.S.C. demonstration there was no effective intervention by R.S.S.F. and a big opportunity was thereby lost. Also preparations for the next conference were abysmal. It met in an atmosphere of demoralization, thanks to the record of the co-ordinating committee, and the discussion which followed was unprepared and chaotic. Nevertheless, the conference managed to take a few decisions: it approved a manifesto and a constitution, and established a new leadership which provided an infrastructure for the organization in the form of a national office, a news-sheet, membership requirements and a regular meeting of the co-ordinating committee. These changes corresponded to the leadership of R.S.S.F. being taken over by the *New Left Review* militants with at least the tacit agreement of I.S. After Conference No. 2 the organization was set in the mould in which it was to continue until its final disintegration. The questions were resolved in one particular direction, namely the model of the German S.D.S.

Three key factors brought about the downfall of R.S.S.F.: characterized by ideological and strategic evasion. Firstly R.S.S.F. did not take a well-defined position on the key issues of the world workers' movement: it had an inadequate understanding of the role of American imperialism, and made no clear analysis of the degeneration of the Russian Revolution and its side-effects. Secondly, the domination by I.S. provided a slight contradiction as the latter attached little importance to the struggle for social revolution in the semi-colonial world and dismissed the Chinese, Vietnamese and Cuban Revolutions, whereas a large mass of students had been radicalized on precisely these issues! Thirdly, R.S.S.F. did not succeed in laying down clearly its strategic perspectives, and as a result it was not able to act in a unified manner or as a unified organization; this almost settled its downfall. (A comparison with the S.D.S. in Germany and the U.S.A. would be in order here: both organizations, despite their federalism and heterogeneity, never had any doubts at all as to the central strategy, namely the defence of the oppressed people in their struggle against U.S. imperialism. However much the R.S.S.F. might state its solidarity, the dominance of the I.S. group acted as an impediment and instead of hammering out the politics of the matter, the *New Left Review* militants tended to obscure these questions in the interests of 'non-sectarianism'.) [18]

The third and final conference was held when R.S.S.F. was in its last throes, and thus the serious attempt which took place to try and orientate the organization towards Ireland failed completely. [19] By this time the failure of the organization to deliver the goods in terms of providing ideological and political perspectives had caused many student militants to look in other directions.

After the lengthy struggle at the London School of Economics in early 1969 had ended with the defeat of the student strike and the ultimately successful victimization of two L.S.E. lecturers, Robin Blackburn and Nick Bateson, the student movement went into a decline, only occasionally punctuated by upsurges such as the files issue at Warwick University, the 1970 occupation at the North-Western Polytechnic and the sit-in at Southampton University. (The last two were related to the appointment of men who were regarded as politically suspect.) Indeed, it is difficult at the time of writing to speak in terms of a 'student movement' in Britain. The short-lived R.S.S.F. experience demonstrated, as did the experience of the international student movement, the difficulty of building an organization based solely on university students, for reasons which we explained in the previous section of this chapter. Although British universities have a higher percentage of

[18] The I.M.G. was unfortunately not strong enough to play a leading role in R.S.S.F. as well as V.S.C. to which it was heavily committed. Also there were very few students in the organization at that stage, particularly in London.

[19] The only useful things which emerged from this orientation were a well produced R.S.S.F. broadsheet on Ireland and an interesting interview with some Irish militants in the *New Left Review*, no. 55 (May–June 1969), back copies of which can be obtained from 7 Carlisle Street, London W1.

working-class students than do universities in the rest of Western Europe, the division in higher education has managed to prevent the flooding of the universities,[20] and thus made the task of university mobilization more difficult. The potential, however, is there, as the large mobilizations during the Spring-bok tour at the end of 1969 vividly demonstrated. However, this campaign was led by liberals and thus the political education of militants was nowhere near as effective as that achieved by V.S.C.

The way out of this impasse was clearly the formation of a youth organization of sufficient organizational and political maturity to learn the lessons of R.S.S.F.'s collapse and transcend the limitations of the student movement in general. Some I.M.G. militants created the Spartacus League in July 1970. Although at its founding conference the backbone of the organization consisted of students, it was formed specifically as a revolutionary youth organization rather than a student organization—to work among school students and young workers as well. Its aims were to provide a milieu in which student revolutionaries could easily continue in revolutionary politics *after* they had left their university or college, and to break down the barriers between student revolutionaries work-ing in the deliberately isolated atmosphere of the universities and youth in general. The League was formed on the political basis of solidarity with the programme of the Fourth Inter-national and its British section, the I.M.G. It trebled in size between its first conference and the second, which was held seven months later in February 1971. By this time it had become an effective national organization. Its demonstrations in soli-darity with black people in the face of repression, its initiative in setting up the Black Defence Committee, its activities during the Dock Strike of 1970 and its solidarity demonstrations with

[20] Cf. Ralph Miliband, *The State in Capitalist Society* (Weidenfeld and Nicolson, London, 1969), p. 43. Miliband cites *The Times*'s report which stated that 'over a quarter of the British university population are the sons and daughters of manual workers. This compares with 14 per cent in Sweden, 8·3 per cent in France and 5·3 per cent in West Germany.'

the Indo-Chinese revolution have shown its growing maturity: in particular its understanding that the lack of internationalism for which the British left is noted has to be combated vigorously and permanently.[21]

The present phase of the class struggle in Britain, despite the reformist trade-union bureaucrats, only emphasizes the necessity for students to intervene as an organized group rather than as individuals. This is not to say that they must abandon their working-class orientation, or stop attempting to detach by propaganda some of the militant rank-and-file leaders; merely that a 'serve-the-workers' type of populism is not as effective as organizing in one's own milieu and giving a practical demonstration of solidarity. Of course, this requires the political education of the student population in the nature of capitalism and the basis of the attack on the working class, an uphill task requiring patience and persistence, but nevertheless essential. The basic contradiction of the movement is in a way accentuated: the uneven development of consciousness has often meant the existence of a youth vanguard with incipient socialist, even revolutionary, consciousness, but no autonomous weight inside the working class; on the other hand there is the tremendous potential power of the working class, but only a reformist consciousness. There is no easy solution to this problem. The creation and development of revolutionary nuclei is a step in the right direction, but from there to the development of a revolutionary party firmly rooted in the working class is a long journey along a path which is full of pitfalls, both of an opportunist and an ultra-left nature. The task is to continue the journey and avoid the pitfalls.

[21] This should not imply that the League is not active in the student movement. Indeed, its activities have often aroused the wrath of the police and the Special Branch. The *Guardian* reported on January 29th, 1971, how Chris Pailthorpe, a Spartacus League militant at Hatfield Polytechnic, was harassed by the police who visited the polytechnic and demanded to see the secret file relating to him. The President of the Students' Union told the *Guardian* that when protests were made about the incident a senior police officer told him, 'There is a very thin line between political and criminal activity.' At the time of writing, the league was considering a fusion with the I.M.G.

7 Marxism and the British Intelligentsia

We have said that *there could not have been* social-democratic consciousness among the workers. It would have to be brought to them from without. The history of all countries shows that the working class, exclusively by its own effort, is able to develop only trade-union consciousness ...

> V. I. LENIN, *What is to be Done?* (1902)

Without a sense of theory among the [German] workers, this scientific socialism would never have entered their flesh and blood as much as is the case. What an immeasurable advantage this is may be seen, on the one hand, from the indifference towards all theory, which is one of the main reasons why the English working-class movement crawls along so slowly in spite of the splendid organization of the individual unions ...

> F. ENGELS, *The Peasant War in Germany* (1850)

I

The lack of a Marxist culture and tradition in Britain has always bedevilled the revolutionary movement. It is responsible for the contempt in which theory is held by certain sections of the British left today, and it reflects the British bourgeoisie's worship of practicality and 'common sense'. In a negative sense, the weakness of Marxism in Britain also explains a certain ingrained anti-intellectualism on the part of the British left: unable to develop its own theoreticians who could contest bourgeois ideas and publicly challenge bourgeois ideologists, the left often retreated into an extremely backward defensive posture and implied that 'too much theory never did anyone any good'. This amounted, in fact, to a rejection of all theory. The rejuvenation of the revolutionary movement, and the current interest in revolutionary history and ideas, makes it essential to combat vigorously the anti-theoretical prejudices which still exist.

Today it is almost a truism to say that there can be no revolutionary practice without revolutionary theory. The success of the Bolshevik Party in 1917 vindicated Leninism, but in practice many people demonstrated their inability to assimilate this basic tenet of Leninism. A key to the understanding of the relative weakness of Marxism in Britain, therefore, is the extreme theoretical weakness of British Marxism. This failure cannot be explained in terms of the personal psychology of H. M. Hyndman or any of the other leaders of the early S.D.F. One of the reasons for the S.D.F.'s weakness was the peculiar course of bourgeois development in Britain. It has deep social and historical roots. Perry Anderson has argued that Britain's failure to produce a native Marxism resulted in its failure to produce a vigorous sociology which could attempt to tackle Marxism:

The peculiar destiny of the nineteenth century industrial bourgeoisie in Britain is the secret of this twin default. The class which accomplished the titanic technological explosion of the Industrial Revolution never achieved a political or social revolution in England. It was checked by a prior capitalist class, the agrarian aristocracy which had matured in the eighteenth century, and controlled a State formed in its image. There was no insuperable contradiction between the modes of production of the two classes. The industrial bourgeoisie, traumatised by the French Revolution and fearful of the nascent working class movement, never took the risk of a confrontation with the dominant aristocracy. It never evicted the latter from its hegemonic control of the political order, and eventually fused with it in a new, composite ruling bloc in mid-century. It thus remained socially and politically hetero-nomous, even in the years of its economic apotheosis. The result was that it never generated a revolutionary ideology, like that of the Enlightenment. Its thinkers were confined by the cramped horizons of their class ... they failed to create any general theory of society ... [1]

The only ideologies the British bourgeoisie could evolve were empiricism and utilitarianism, and Trotsky, always an ex-tremely perceptive observer of the British political scene, wrote:

... historical dialectic played an evil game with Britain, transforming the advantages of her earlier development into the causes of her backwardness. We see this in the realm of industry, in science, in the state structure, and in political ideology. She was not able to search for and find in one of the leading countries an indication of her own future. She moved forward gropingly, empirically, drawing generaliza-tions from her road and looking ahead only insofar as it was unavoidable. The traditional way of thought of the British, that is first of all the British bourgeoisie, is impressed with the stamp of empiricism, and that mental tradition has passed on to the upper circles of the working class. [2]

Scientific socialist theory is not plucked from the air. Rather it is formed by constant struggle against the ideology and practice of the bourgeoisie and as such it exists as a dialectical antithesis to that bourgeois ideology. Empiricism which per-meated British bourgeois thought also affected the radical movement. In the early nineteenth century there were im-portant British radical theorists. Hodgkin had evolved a proto-socialist theory of value by the 1820s, but this coexisted in his

[1] Perry Anderson, 'Components of the National Culture', *New Left Review*, no. 50 (July–August 1968).
[2] L. Trotsky, *Where is Britain Going?* (New Park Publications, London, 1970).

system with an extreme laissez-faire liberal view of the state. The upsurge of Chartism produced Ernest Jones and George Julian Harney, the latter re-interpreting the Jacobin tradition in terms of the struggle of the working class. There were sharp insights, but no system of thought developed which could encompass an overall critique of capitalist society.

One of the minor, but contributory, factors to the weakness of British Marxism was conjunctural. Marx's ideas were about to reach a British audience[3] when Chartism was rolled back and the working-class movement retreated from the political stage. Comparative class peace existed in Britain from 1850 until the early 1880s, and this time was used effectively by the ruling class: leading manufacturers fostered and moulded the political aspirations of the emerging labour aristocracy. Successive governments, their complacency shattered by the revolutionary potential of Chartism, carried out reforms and achieved a flexibility unknown to the bourgeoisie of the Continent. It was the development of this strategy which gave birth to an undeveloped and sickly ideology—Labourism. It has proved to be the most superficial and shallow, but at the same time the most tenacious of working-class ideologies; it has not changed much since its inception and still haunts the working-class movement of Britain. Although the British working class created its own party two decades after the working class on the Continent, it did not learn from the Continent's experiences. Marxism did not touch it, and when the fledgling Communist Party sought affiliation (under advice from Lenin) it was firmly refused admittance.[4]

The workers' militancy in the last two decades of the

---

[3] The publication of 'The Communist Manifesto' in Harney's *Red Republican*.

[4] It is sadly typical that when Hyndman published *England For All*, the first essay in British Marxist theory, it largely consisted of a paraphrase of *Capital*, but more characteristic was that Marx's name was studiously avoided. The reason given was that 'The English don't like to be taught by foreigners'. The early British Marxists were brave, tenacious and dedicated, but they possessed little theory and produced virtually none. Engels accused the S.D.F. of reducing Marxism to 'a rigid orthodoxy' which was considered 'a credo and not a guide to action'.

nineteenth century destroyed the class peace, but British capitalism—its monopoly weakened—immediately set about attempting to re-establish social stability on new foundations. The epoch of imperialism opened up new possibilities, and the division of Africa and the discovery of gold in the Transvaal created conditions which made it possible to buy off the top crust of the working class yet again. The new discoveries produced two new ideologies, imperialism and Fabianism; however, the prophets of imperialism were not ideologues, but politicians or adventurers (Joseph Chamberlain and Cecil Rhodes). The imperialist poet, Rudyard Kipling, much taught and appreciated in British and colonial schools, was the least intellectual of the new wave of British writers. With the establishment in 1880 of the London School of Economics, the reconstruction of British capitalism in the late 'eighties, and the establishment during the same period of the red-brick universities, the basis was laid for the existence of 'Fabian Socialism', or rather for the development of an upper petty-bourgeois layer of the intelligentsia which would help preserve the profit mechanisms of the ruling class in the name of humanitarian principles. Since it was not directly engaged in the processes of capitalism (i.e. it was tied up as teachers, local government officials, factory inspectors, etc.) it projected the belief that it was 'above' classes and defended the interests of 'society as a whole'. As such this new intelligentsia was not attracted to socialist ideology,

... but its appearance was nevertheless a symptom of the same crisis, of which the chief symptom was the new wave of acute struggles of the proletariat—the 1886 demonstrations of the unemployed and the strike of 1889—and which was the beginning of a turnover on the part of the working class from traditional liberalism to an independent class policy. The spectre of social revolution which had not visited Great Britain since the days of Chartism once again showed in its ominous form, and it was inevitable that some more intelligent members of the new intelligentsia should understand that it was up to them to make up to the new revolutionary movement, in order to master it and deflect it into some harmless channel.[5]

This was the job which the Fabians allocated to themselves and they were, unfortunately, quite successful in completing it. The grip of reformist ideology ensured that even the limited Marxism which developed in Britain was subject to extremes of insular opportunism and a protective and introverted dogmatism and sectarianism. What dominated and obsessed the Fabian mind was the prospect of a bloody revolution. In a letter to Sorge, Engels expressed this accurately and referred to the Fabians as 'an ambitious group here in London who have understanding enough to realize the inevitability of social revolution, but who could not possibly entrust this gigantic task to the rough proletariat alone and are therefore kind enough to set themselves at its head. Fear of the revolution is their fundamental principle.'[6] The Fabians understood that the social peace which British imperialism had tentatively succeeded in establishing could not last for very long. They therefore turned themselves to the task of searching for new formulas and methods which could ensure periods of class stability. They were forced to make some sharp critiques of British capitalism in the era of trade monopoly 'and its oligarchic

[5] Dmitri Mirsky, *The Intelligentsia of Great Britain* (Gollancz, London, 1935). Mirsky was a Bolshevik stationed in Britain during the Third Period who wrote this extremely perceptive and vigorous critique of British society. Despite the fact that he uses the Third Period jargon (i.e. Laski and Cole are constantly referred to as 'social-fascists'!) the book remains valuable. On his return to Moscow, Mirsky 'disappeared' and was shot like numerous others, which is why the British C.P. never really used the book. The style of the book is reminiscent of Trotsky's *Where is Britain Going?*, op. cit., and it is interesting that there is no mention of Trotksy; Mirsky carefully refrains from slandering him or attacking him. Could it be that this is what made him suspect on his return? We'll only find out the truth when the K.G.B. archives are thrown open after the successful political revolution!

[6] Cf. Letter of January 18th, 1893, *Correspondence of Marx and Engels* (Moscow, 1956).

debris taken over from the century-old partnership between the British bourgeoisie and the dividend-drawing aristocracy'.[7] Thus Britain produced an intelligentsia which was extremely conformist and geared to the preservation of the existing social structure. In the early years of the twentieth century this intelligentsia could not be separated from the bourgeoisie of which it was part, and in whose disciplines it educated itself and later educated others.

The leading lights of the British intelligentsia had all reached their formative years in the period preceding the First World War. The Fabians, symbolized by the triumvirate of the Webbs and Bernard Shaw, had already demonstrated their aloofness from such nasty things as wars. Thus during the Boer War the Fabian Executive Committee had declared that the war was an issue 'which Socialism cannot solve and does not touch'. However, as the war continued and chauvinism increased in Britain, the Fabians were forced to abandon their aloofness. Accordingly, Bernard Shaw wrote an appalling pamphlet, *Fabianism and the Empire*, in which after his customary veil of mystificatory prose had been torn down he came down solidly on the side of the Empire and defended its right to 'civilize' those areas of the world which were 'backward'. It was not therefore surprising that the First World War found the Fabians solidly behind the bourgeoisie. Their historian, Pease, actually boasted that Fabianism had been responsible for weaning Bernstein away from Marxism and thus creating a schism in German social-democracy!

The reason for the Fabians' support of the war was simple: they never understood the nature of capitalism or the real significance of the birth of imperialism. It would be wrong, therefore, to characterize their support of the war as a betrayal. There was nothing for them to betray and they acted as good Fabians were expected to act. The Webbs and Shaw were the three blind mice of British capitalism. They could not see what was before their very eyes. A liberal writer, J. A. Hobson, had, in

[7] Mirsky, op. cit.

contrast, written a fairly extensive text, *Imperialism*, in 1902 establishing the economic causes of imperialism and explaining the roots of the inter-imperialist war. This liberal writer showed more perceptiveness and a greater understanding of some of the dynamics of capitalism than all the Fabian 'theoreticians' put together.[8] The latter were more interested in the question of municipal reform, and devoted their time to analysing the problems which confronted parish councils as the capitalist world was moving inexorably towards conflict. Few members of the intelligentsia provided a socialist critique of the war. Those that did not surrender to the prevailing militarism retreated to a noble pacifism, like Bertrand Russell, and were universally vilified. The war struck the social-democratic parties in Western Europe severely and, with few and honourable exceptions, even those parties trained in Marxism put themselves at the service of their respective bourgeoisies. It is hardly surprising, then, that in England no Marxist voice was heard; but shrill English chauvinism did not prevent the emergence of opposition elsewhere. Two brave voices spoke up and denounced the war vigorously: one was in Scotland and the other in Ireland.

John Maclean and James Connolly stand out as two outstanding working-class leaders who always put the interests of the proletariat above everything else and who saw the war for what it really was, as Lenin saw it, and Karl Liebknecht, Rosa Luxemburg and Trotsky. The Irish left had suffered a setback as a large section of the working class had deserted internationalism and rallied to the bourgeoisie, but the leaders of Irish labour met the challenge which the war posed, denounced it as an imperialist war and challenged the recruitment policies. Its main leader, James Connolly, understood as Lenin did the need for striking against imperialism while the time was ripe. He immediately set about the task of training the Irish Citizens'

---

[8] In his celebrated text on imperialism, Lenin admitted his debt to Hobson and later wrote that his text was better than the writings of both Hilferding and Kautsky on the same subject.

Army. Liberty Hall, the headquarters of the Irish Transport and General Workers' Union, openly flaunted the slogan 'We serve neither King nor Kaiser', and became the focus of resistance to British imperialism. Connolly founded a new paper, *The Workers Republic*, which constantly reminded the workers of the need to emancipate themselves. Every industrial dispute was used to strengthen the Citizens' Army and propagandize against imperialism. Thus while British imperialism was involved in a war across the channel, the Citizens' Army challenged the might of British imperialism on the barricades in Dublin on April 24th, 1916. They were let down by the failure of the radical middle-class Irish Volunteers to rally to their help as they had promised: only one thousand men came to aid Connolly and Pearse. The fighting continued for five days, but the British succeeded in crushing the revolt and its leaders were captured and executed. Connolly, too badly wounded to stand up, was shot strapped to a chair.[9] In this one murderous blow British imperialism silenced the voice of the Irish Revolution which had dared question the motives behind the imperialist war and explain them to the Irish working masses. More important, they executed the leadership of the Irish Revolution and the absence of a strong leadership partly accounts for the abortion which took place in the 'twenties when Ireland was divided. The middle-class were able to withstand the tremors

[9] Connolly's capture and execution is similar to that of another great revolutionary, Che Guevara. Both Connolly and Che were accused of putschism, militarism, etc. Lenin defended Connolly against this charge in terms which apply to Che as well (in particular against his Stalinist detractors). Lenin wrote: 'The term "putsch", in its scientific sense, may be employed only when the attempt at insurrection has revealed nothing but a circle of conspirators or stupid maniacs, and has aroused no sympathy among the masses. The centuries-old Irish national movement having passed through various stages and combinations of class interest ... manifested itself in street fighting conducted by a section of the urban petty-bourgeoisie and a section of the workers, after a long period of mass agitation, demonstrations, etc. Whoever calls *such* a rebellion a "putsch" is either a hardened reactionary or a doctrinaire hopelessly incapable of envisaging a social revolution as a living phenomenon ... ' (*Collected Works*, 45 vols. [Progress Publishers, Moscow, 1964], vol. 22, p. 355, from an article entitled, 'The Discussion on Self-Determination Summed Up').

of the national struggle, become its leaders and behead the Irish Revolution. Connolly's contribution to the Irish struggle was not only in the field of struggle. He helped to develop socialist thought in Ireland, and though a controversy rages on the interpretation of some of his theoretical texts, this in a sense is itself an eloquent testimony of both their relevance today and their general validity.[10]

John Maclean was a Scottish teacher, who studied socialism, understood its importance and became an energetic Marxist. He was an expert popularizer of Marxist ideas, a brilliant mass agitator who was known by the Scottish working class as a tireless fighter against capitalism. Always conscious of the importance of theory, he set about establishing the Scottish Labour College which was attended by crowds of young Scottish workers. Many of the shop stewards who led industrial battles in the next few years had graduated from the Maclean University. He was undoubtedly one of the most important British Marxists and the fact that very little is known of him in England testifies to the intellectual chauvinism of sections of the English left. It was as a Marxist that Maclean took the lead in opposing the war, in opposing conscription and in actively encouraging the continuation of the class struggle. As his presence posed a threat to the interests of British capital, he was arrested during the war, but he converted his trial into a platform for revolutionary propaganda and began his brilliant speech from the dock by declaring: 'I stand here not as the accused, but as the accuser, the accuser of capitalism dripping with blood from head to foot ... '[11] After the Russian Revolution

---

[10] Cf. D. R. O'Connor Lysaght, 'The Unorthodoxy of James Connolly', *International*, vol. 1, no. 3 (January–February 1971). In his assessment of Connolly, Lysaght defends him against both the Green Tories in Dublin who claim his heritage and the Stalinists who distort his message.

[11] John Maclean's speech has been reproduced as a pamphlet by the I.M.G., with an Introduction by Bob Purdie. That Connolly and Maclean, the only two great creative Marxists these islands have produced over the last century, came from the same background—the early Scottish Marxist movement—was no accident. In contrast to the prevailing philistinism of English culture, Scotland

the Bolsheviks paid tribute to Maclean by appointing him the first Soviet Consul in Scotland.

When the Bolsheviks seized state power in Petrograd and declared the existence of the infant Soviet Republic, the effect on the intelligentsia throughout the world was electric — with the exception of Britain. Connolly was, alas, no longer alive. Maclean understood the impact of the revolution and what it meant for the old order all over the world. The effect on British workers was so tremendous that the Labour Party felt obliged to organize several meetings in defence of the Russian Revolution. It was this mood among the British proletariat, symbolized by the *Jolly George* strike,[12] that seriously hampered the ability of Winston Churchill and other reactionary leaders to aid the counter-revolution in Russia. But while the British

---

provided an intellectual environment which encouraged the development of theory. This stemmed from two main sources:

(1) *The French Enlightenment.* Because of Scotland's historical ties with France, the French Revolution had a tremendous impact on every level of society, and evoked a number of diverse responses, including the Radical Rising of 1820 (see some of Burns's more radical poems — 'The tree o' liberty', 'For a' that and a' that', and 'Scots wha hae', for example), and, most important, the 'Edinburgh Enlightenment'. Maclean's Marxist economics can be traced to the influence of Glasgow University, where the tradition of Adam Smith was still very much alive. Now, however, Glasgow is politically one of the more reactionary universities, as I can testify from personal experience.

(2) *The Church.* The Church of Scotland differs from the Church of England not just in being Presbyterian, but also in representing a much higher level of the struggle of the bourgeoisie on an ideological plane. The 'Great Disruption', or the split between the liberal and reactionary elements in the Church, although fought out in theological terms, created an atmosphere in which discussion of, and respect for, ideas was much more advanced, and penetrated more deeply into the population, than in England (e.g. Burns, a small farmer, was much involved in the debates).

In addition to these two sources, Edinburgh University, at the beginning of the century, contained a small number of European émigré Marxists, who were instrumental in forming the early Marxist movement in Scotland.

[12] Dockers had refused to load munitions destined for the Whites in Russia on to the *Jolly George*, and had withdrawn their labour. One of their leaders was a man named Ernest Bevin, who was later to become the most vilely anti-communist of Labour Foreign Secretaries — more vile than Michael Stewart, in so far as he was more effective and powerful.

workers demonstrated their solidarity with the Russian Revolution, what a gulf there was between them and the intelligentsia.
The latter was initially surprised and then disturbed, particularly as the post-war period led to severe class struggles, and in
certain parts of Scotland the possibility of dual power was
constantly posed. The tide of working-class struggles was in a
process of ebb well before the 1926 General Strike. The T.U.C.
had chosen the wrong moment for the strike and this, coupled
with the reformism of the 'left' leaders, condemned the strike
to failure before it began. The small but well-placed Communist Party was unable to play any meaningful role because of
the cover which the Soviet leadership provided the T.U.C. 'left'
leaders, such as Purcell, through the existence of the Anglo-
Soviet Committee.[13] The intelligentsia, needless to say, regarded
strikes of this sort as 'distasteful' and with certain exceptions
they backed the authority of the bourgeois state and constantly
strove to reinforce it.

II

It was not until the 'thirties that Marxism showed any real
signs of advancing in Britain and the main reason for this was
the economic crisis in 1931 which struck at the roots of the
capitalist world. Despite the bureaucratization of the Soviet
Union and the triumph of Stalinism, the strength of its social
base, which had existed since October 1917, prevented the
crisis from affecting the Soviet economy in any meaningful way.
This fact became obvious to a large section of thinking people

[13] The Anglo-Soviet Committee had been set up by Stalin to improve the state
interests of Soviet foreign policy. It consisted of the then equivalents of Daly,
Scanlon and Jones, and the young C.P. was asked to subordinate its activities and
support the committee. Needless to say, in the face of the General Strike the
committee was disbanded because the 'left' trade-union leaders withdrew to sell
out the strike. Thus the opportunism of the Stalin leadership played a significant
part in paralysing the development of the British C.P. If the latter had played an
independent role and fought for revolutionary positions, it might have seriously
dented the trade-union armoury of social democracy.

throughout the world. It was the intellectuals on the left of the Labour Party who first started re-thinking some of their earlier positions. This included men like Cole and Laski, who had claimed some kinship with Marxism but none with Leninism, and a wider grouping which included Tawney, Cripps and Trevelyan, and who based their critique of the crude utilitarianism of the Fabians on the radical liberal tradition of Victorian England.

The 'shock' of the 1931 debacle forced Laski to question whether 'evolutionary socialism deceived itself in believing that it can establish itself by peaceful means within the ambit of the capitalist system'. This was the burning question that other Labour left intellectuals struggled to answer. The struggle did not last very long. All the problems were to be resolved by a retreat to liberalism. Laski was to develop his writings on the British Constitution and argue in favour of a pacific syndicalism: having discovered the power of the British trade-union movement Laski maintained that provided the movement became more politically astute, it could actually force the capitalist class to bow gracefully off the stage of world history. Thus were the consciences of the Labour left salvaged, and they could sigh with relief at the realization that they did not have to become revolutionaries. Some of them understood the importance of Marx in the sense that in a period of economic crisis many young people would be attracted to Marxism. They therefore sought to explain Marx and this task was taken up by Cole and Lindsay at Oxford. Mirsky commented aptly that 'G. D. H. Cole, a veteran in this culinary art, has from his academic eminence in Oxford been busy preparing many young people in the art of pot-roasting Marx (or cooking Marx in his own steam in order to de-Marx him) ... '[14]

But the 'thirties did radicalize many young intellectuals. The 1931 crisis, the Civil War in Spain and the threat of fascism were the chief recruiting agents of Marxism. The Soviet Union, interestingly enough, became popular in intellectual circles

[14] Mirsky, op. cit.

only after the Stalinist Thermidor, and a monstrous regiment of fellow-travellers was raised to defend this edifice. Even Beatrice Webb declared that she approved of the 'spiritual' tone of Stalin's Russia. It was during this period that the C.P. began to attract its intellectuals.[15] But many of these intellectuals were not won to Marxism; rather they were won over to a formula which offered easy answers and easy solutions to the existing crisis. They were attracted by the liberal popular frontism spiced with a dash of Marxist rhetoric. What became important to them was not the methodology of dialectical materialism, but its result, namely a system of criteria which attracted them as they discarded their empiricism. However, the mere fact that they turned towards what they considered Communism was a sign of the times. One of the most brilliant of bourgeois minds, a product of pre-war liberalism, J. M. Keynes, understood these intellectuals perfectly. In a revealing letter to Kingsley Martin he wrote:[16]

> There is no one in politics today worth sixpence outside the ranks of the Liberals except the postwar generation of intellectual Communists under thirty-five. Perhaps in their feelings and instincts they are the nearest thing we have to the typical nervous, non-conformist English gentlemen who went to the Crusades, made the Reformation, fought the Great Rebellion, won us our civil and religious liberties and humanised the working classes during the last century.

Keynes was, unfortunately, correct. British Marxists were confronted with the task of moving beyond the radical tradition

[15] Harry Wicks, one of the first British C.P. members to break with Stalinism, told an educational school on the History of the Fourth International, organized by the Spartacus League in February 1971, that very few liberal intellectuals were prepared to sign an appeal demanding an inquiry to challenge the Moscow Trials. Bernard Shaw wrote in reply to a request to sign the appeal: 'Trotsky is the prince of pamphleteers. He does not need my help to defend himself ... '

[16] Cf. Neal Wood, *Communism and the British Intellectuals* (Gollancz, London, 1959).

of liberal England and developing a totalizing Marxism. What happened was that their 'Marxism' was, in fact, a radical liberalism which was moulded by the tactical demands of the Soviet bureaucracy. When Stephen Spender wrote *Forward from Liberalism*,[17] he expressed a desire that was never translated into reality. And later, when he had left the embrace of the C.P., he admitted:

> When I considered the existing injustices and the future destruction which were involved in the system in which I lived, I longed to be on the side of the accusers, the setters-up of world socialism. But at this stage, having shifted the centre of struggle within myself from the bourgeois camp to the communist one, I failed to find myself convinced by Communism. Even when I had accepted in my own mind the possibility of having to sacrifice everything I gained by living in a bourgeois society, I still could not abandon my liberal concepts of freedom and truth.

Never able to understand Marxism, many of these intellectuals equated it with the Stalinist distortion in the Soviet Union. This meant that they were unable to withstand shocks, and the first test which was required of them proved to be too much for their frail little intellects: the approach of the Second World War and the Ribbentrop-Molotov Pact was the end of the road for them. Of course, there were honourable exceptions who have to this day preserved their beliefs, but the experience with Stalinism was responsible for inoculating British culture against the Marxist disease and it was only in the late 'sixties and the early 'seventies that this vaccine seemed to be losing its original powers. Very few intellectuals had even read Trotsky or his searing critique of Stalinism, and his impassioned defence of revolutionary Marxism and of Leninism. For them Stalinism was Marxism and that was the end of the story. This myth which has been implanted so firmly in British society, and is one of the central myths of bourgeois ideology, was also, but

[17] Victor Gollancz, 1937.

for completely different reasons, nurtured by the British C.P. British Stalinism was not really interested in the development of theory and did not look kindly on intellectuals who seemed to look beyond the narrow horizons of Stalinist orthodoxy. And therefore very little theoretical advance was registered during the 'thirties by the Marxists of the C.P. One gauge of this is the list of sterile books produced by the Left Book Club at that time. Very few have stood the test of time. Strachey has shrunk in estimation and it is difficult, now, to regard his books as other than mediocre popular introductions to Marxism of a rigidly economic determinist type. Only in the works of Christopher Caudwell does Marxism begin to take on some meaning. Caudwell was killed fighting in Spain and the controversy which developed in the C.P. journal in the late 'forties and early 'fifties regarding his *Studies in a Dying Culture*[18] and other works was one indication of how he would have been treated if he had survived Spain. Also the end of the 'thirties did bear fruit in the sense that it produced serious Marxist historians of the calibre of Christopher Hill and, somewhat later, Eric Hobsbawm, both of whom challenged the historicism of bourgeois historians.

But the failure of the C.P. intellectuals cannot simply be explained away by the extreme weakness of the British Marxist tradition. The C.P. only wanted hack writers to 'explain' the 'successes' of Stalinism. Thus men like D. N. Pritt, who could use their talents to justify the purges of the 'thirties in Moscow and the liquidation of virtually all of Lenin's old comrades, were much in demand, as were abject apologists like Klugmann, who at that time was not engaged in a respectable dialogue with Christianity, but was writing books like *From Trotsky to Tito*,[19] in order to endear himself to his Stalinist masters. Thus the C.P. had nothing to gain in trying to break many of its pet

18 John Lane, 1938.

19 Lawrence and Wishart, London, 1951. Maybe Klugmann missed his real vocation. He might have been more suited to writing scripts for Hammer Films, or at any rate the titles.

intellectuals from the grip of liberalism. In fact this liberalism came in handy during the war, when the task of a communist was supposedly that of preaching an end to class warfare, and after the war, when it was to call not for an election, but for a continued National Government, and to adopt various other charming Stalinist postures as we indicated in Chapter 3. The effect of Stalinism on the radicalized intelligentsia should by no means be underestimated.[20] It set back the development of a real revolutionary movement by at least two decades. And twenty years is a very long time in revolutionary history.

III

By the time the war ended the processes which had been moulding the new intelligentsia were almost complete. The liberals who had joined the C.P. had recoiled in horror at the perfidy of the Stalin-Hitler pact and rejected the defence of the Soviet Union; later they had been forced by the Stalin-Churchill alliance to mute their anti-Soviet hysteria, and were now back in form as anti-Communist ideologists. They were the men who had been almost waiting for the Cold War to begin, and once it did they became the intellectual warriors of American imperialism; in many cases they were directly on the payroll of the Central Intelligence Agency. But even the most brilliant of them could not compare with the old giants such as Keynes, Russell, Huxley and Lawrence. In fact the intellectual life of the bourgeoisie was pulled out of the doldrums by the White émigrés from Continental Europe. The dominance of these extremely reactionary individuals over the academic life of capitalist Britain was a well-established fact. It was Perry Anderson who drew attention to the fact that it was not a simple coincidence that Britain had attracted the most reactionary émigrés. He argued, correctly, that the comparative stability of British society and its isolation from the upheavals in Europe

---

[20] Cf. Neal Wood, op. cit.

(the Russian Revolution, the collapse of the Habsburgs, the destruction of capitalism in Eastern Europe, etc.) made it a paradise for people who were frightened by violent change and permanent instability:

> The intellectuals who settled in Britain were thus not a chance agglomeration. They were essentially a 'White', counter-revolutionary emigration ... England was not an accidental landing-stage on which these intellectuals unwittingly found themselves stranded. It was often a conscious choice — an ideal antipode of everything that they rejected ... Established English culture naturally welcomed these unexpected allies. Every insular reflex and prejudice was powerfully flattered and enlarged in the convex mirror they presented to it ... [21]

What appealed to them most was the empirical tradition of the British intelligentsia, so conveniently free from the constant urge to find out why events were what they were and to try and root out their causes. The very fact that the émigrés came from Europe meant that they were able to dominate the cultural scene in Britain without much difficulty. They were seized on and lionized by the British bourgeoisie. Honours were bestowed on them and their leading representatives were knighted: Sir Lewis Namier, Sir Karl Popper, Sir Isaiah Berlin ... [22] And, as Anderson bitingly expressed it: 'This was not just a passive acknowledgement of merit. It was an active social pact.' The one émigré who did not belong to this tradition, and who was in one sense its antithesis, Isaac Deutscher, was ignored by the academic establishment. His crime was that he was a Marxist and this made it impossible for him to obtain a post in any British university. A Marxist, and an anti-Stalinist Marxist at that, could not be allowed to teach history. Some of the counter-revolutionary émigrés who dominated academic life in

[21] Perry Anderson, op. cit.
[22] The other luminaries of bourgeois thought: Wittgenstein, Malinowski, Gombrich, Eysenck and Klein.

some instances played an extremely vicious and underhand role in sabotaging a post he had been offered at Sussex University, a few years before his tragic and premature death in 1967. What annoyed our ideologues of bourgeois democracy more than anything else was the undoubted fact that Deutscher was by far the most brilliant historian resident in Britain.[23] He was a much more impressive figure than Namier, Popper and Berlin put together. His writings will survive the test of history and will be cited in years to come as an exception to the banal offerings of his contemporaries which characterized the 'fifties and 'sixties and are even now beginning to be forgotten. The chronic instability which confronts British capitalism also affects the credibility of its apologists.

In the face of this counter-revolutionary onslaught, Stalinism could not provide an answer. The *Daily Worker* had after all described the dropping of the atom bomb on Hiroshima and

[23] Deutscher was working on a biography of Lenin and desperately needed a university post so that he could work in peace, free from the tedious necessity of earning a living at the same time by writing for the bourgeois press. He completed only one chapter, which has recently been published and which gives us an indication of what we have lost. Deutscher stopped work on the book to serve on the International War Crimes Tribunal set up by Bertrand Russell. This was the latter's last act of revolt against the bourgeois Establishment and Deutscher could not turn down an appeal which involved Vietnam, a war which had excited his passions and compelled him to action.

While Deutscher is famous as Trotsky's biographer, and indirectly responsible for winning over many people to Trotskyism (myself included), it is ironic that in fact he disagreed with Trotsky on the setting up of the Fourth International and on the question of political revolution in the Soviet Union. Deutscher thought that the bureaucracy would reform itself and the 1957 promises by Gomulka must have reinforced this view, but already there were indications in *The Unfinished Revolution* (Oxford University Press, 1970) that he was veering towards the position that struggle would be necessary which would involve the might of the Russian working class. If he had lived, two events would undoubtedly have modified both his differences with Trotsky: May 1968 in France might have persuaded him that the Fourth International was a necessity, and August 1968 in Prague would almost certainly have convinced him that a violent overthrow of the bureaucracy in the U.S.S.R. was the only way out of the Stalinist impasse in Eastern Europe. One writes this because one knows that Deutscher's Marxism was anything but static. His brilliance as a historian lay precisely in his ability not only to understand events, but to forecast them.

13

Nagasaki as an event that 'will enormously increase the strength of the three great powers in relation to all other countries'. Refusing to understand the dynamics of the world capitalist system, the Stalinists judged American imperialist plans and intentions in terms of individuals. Roosevelt was good and if only he had lived, etc., etc., whereas Truman was bad and responsible for all the evils of the world. This process of continuous prostitution in the interests of the Soviet bureaucracy did not increase the credibility of C.P. intellectuals. Even their supposed anti-imperialism was turned into a chauvinist anti-Yank crescendo.[24]

Zhdanov and other cultural policemen of the Soviet party line made it easier for the intellectual not to pose critical questions, but to play safely in non-contentious areas with the old formulae. To read *Modern Quarterly* of the 'forties and 'fifties is to abandon reality and enter a world of sterile scholasticism interpolated by frenetic spasms of pseudo-controversy over non-issues, and even this was punctuated by nervous glances over the shoulder at Uncle Joe. Since the Soviet bureaucracy could neither afford a living Marxist theory nor to ditch Marxism entirely, it successfully perverted the mainstream of Marxism into an ideology, a form of false consciousness. For decades Marxism was forced to suffer this distortion. Later, after Stalin had died and the Twentieth Party Congress had become an old affair, the French ex-Stalinist Garaudy[25] could write of Stalin's dialectical method:

The entire system was synthesized in 20 dazzling pages which were held to contain the whole of political wisdom. After 'Latin without tears' we had 'instant Greek'; we had

[24] That is one characteristic the C.P. has adhered to in Britain up to this very day. Thus one often gets the impression that the problems of British capitalism might be eased if the dreaded 'Yanks' and their capital were thrown out of Britain. This education is carried out particularly when there are strikes in factories owned by U.S. capital.

[25] Garaudy was for a time the leading intellectual of the French C.P. Czechoslovakia convinced him that he had been wrong all his political life and he rebelled against the French C.P., thus creating a minor sensation not only in France but

philosophy brought within every man's reach in three easy lessons. Ontology: the three principles of materialism. Logic: the four laws of dialectics. Philosophy of history: the five stages of the class war. Far from being a guide to research, this concept of dialectics and philosophy in general acted as a brake upon it.

Thus dialectics was turned into a three-card trick and Marxism into a religion. In Britain the Stalinist 'night of theory' was darker than elsewhere because of the weakness of theory in general. While clearly the C.P. intellectuals were in a state of decline after the Second World War, they could always point to those who were even worse than them: the Labour left. The responsibilities of office had sobered the demagogy of the left-wingers of the 'thirties (in much the same way as it did when Wilson came to power and brought Castle (anti-apartheid) and Greenwood (C.N.D.) into the government). Stafford Cripps became the promulgator of the wage-freeze, 'Red' Ellen Wilkinson became Minister of Education and in the front line of defence of the grammar school. The total failure and death of the Labour left in 1964–70 can be historically traced to its failure to understand the nature fo capitalism in 1945. Also the virus of the Cold War bit deep and hard. Thus Michael Foot could write at the time of the Korean War: 'American soldiers are fighting in Korea ... to uphold the principles of collective defence against wanton aggression.' Such an attitude could only facilitate a resurgence of right-wing ideology.

The default of the left, the Cold War and the capitalist boom provided a big boost to the right. The major 'intellectual' journal of the 'fifties was the C.I.A.-financed *Encounter*, which

---

also in Moscow where he was on first-name terms with leading members of the Politbureau! He denounced both the French C.P. and the Soviet Union and was consequently expelled from the party. His book *The Turning-Point of Socialism* (Fontana, London, 1970) is a right-wing text which reveals all the confusions of an ex-Stalinist and in fact marks a turning-point for Roger Garaudy more than anything else. Where and in which quarter his evolution will end cannot be predicted with certainty at the time of writing.

gathered together both remorseful ex-C.P. members like Spender and a new generation of American and British hacks. Maudlin essays by ex-Stalinists[26] were churned out as examples of theoretical brilliance, along with complacent little exercises in myopic pragmatism.[27] The vacuum was filled by the right-wing ideologues of the Labour Party, Crosland and Strachey. Crosland equated Marxism with Stalinism. The latter was said to be the inevitable result of a revolution. The second premise was that the economic boom was now a permanent feature of capitalism and hence the only sensible policy was a little piece-meal social engineering on the home front and an alliance with democratic America against totalitarianism in foreign affairs. The class struggle was, according to Mr Crosland, now obsolete since capitalism in Britain had been reformed out of all recognition and we were living in a 'post-capitalist' society. Permanent full employment, Mr Crosland told us, was now on the agenda and therefore the period which lay ahead would be one of abundance for all.

The response of the left to this onslaught was pathetic. Within the Labour Party itself the 'left' demanded a return to 'socialist principles', but their moralizing went unnoticed, particularly after they revealed that even when they won the Party conference to unilateralism, they were totally incapable of following this up with a sustained campaign. The majority of Marxists consigned themselves to the task of monotonously worded dark warnings of the imminent slump and the wrath to come, while the C.P. and its fellow-travellers juggled with figures for future five-year plans and informed the workers via their press of the role which grass-roots democracy played in the Soviet Union.

The year 1956 marked a turning-point in left politics. Two major crises had occurred and had forced a new assessment of both Britain and the world by large numbers of people. The Suez disaster revealed the impotence of British imperialism as

[26] E.g. R. Crossman, ed., *The God that Failed* (Bantam, New York, 1964).
[27] E.g. Daniel Bell, *The End of Ideology* (Collier–Macmillan, 1965).

an independent force, and U.S. policy brought home to many the reality of inter-imperialist contradictions. At the same time a similar crisis shook the Stalinist world: not long after the liberalization which followed Khrushchev's speech to the Twentieth Party Congress, Soviet armour had entered Hungary to crush the workers' uprising in Budapest. The political effect of these two crises was explosive. Suez had succeeded in dissolving the apathy of the young and radicalizing a sector of students. The party faithful could not stomach the invasion of Hungary so soon after discovering the crimes — or some of them — of Stalin, and one-third of the members of the British Communist Party left.

The fusion of these two experiences produced what has been known as the New Left: its birth then was conjunctural as its death was to be in a few years' time. The intellectuals who formed the core of the New Left were grouped around two magazines: *The New Reasoner* and the *Universities and Left Review*. The aim of the New Left was to bring together ex-Stalinists (before they became too bitter and disillusioned), left social-democrats and radicalized students under a new banner which would have written on it in big letters: SOCIALIST HUMANISM. It would attack Stalinism, but at the same time keep its supporters away from Stalinism's 'stunted opposite, dogmatic Trotskyism ... '[28] The 'humanism' of the New Left was, in fact, a pre-socialist populism. Instead of coming to grips with the realities of class society, and understanding that the fundamental contradiction between Labour and capital remained, despite all the taunts of social-democracy, the New Left tried to talk in terms of 'the interests of ordinary human beings', 'people before profits' and other nice phrases which on their own simply reflected a moral feeling. In one sense we can even say that some of the New Left's leading ideologues became the stunted, empirical opposites of the right in the Labour Party: Stuart Hall and E. P. Thompson were the New

[28] E. P. Thompson and John Saville, *The New Reasoner*, vol. 1, no. 1 (Summer 1957), p. 2.

Left's answer to Crosland and Strachey. Thus in their intellectual manifesto, E. P. Thompson could write that pragmatism

> has served the British people a great deal better than most Marxists have been prepared to admit. Pragmatism combined with parochialism have served it least well in international affairs; and far more often than not they have served the colonial peoples very badly indeed. And yet even in international questions, Marxists tend to overstate the case; we should not forget that the British people played their part—with high and conscious morale—in turning the tide of fascism in Europe.[29]

Harold Wilson could have said exactly the same at that period! Also there was a tendency to refurbish the move away from revolutionary Marxism by emphasizing the young Marx and creating a dichotomy between his early work and his later writings. In doing this the New Left were implying that the Stalinist distortions followed from Marx's later works and therefore the latter should be discarded. This atrocity could be perpetrated because Marx's *Grundrisse* had not seen the light of day.[30] But even in their assessments of the young Marx, the New Left could not produce any material which could compare to the work which was being done in Continental Europe. Thus E. P. Thompson could write: 'I believe that George Lichtheim's "Marxism" and Wright Mills' forthcoming study of "The Marxists" provide the basis for a complete revaluation of the Marxist tradition.' It would be easy to be patronizing about this statement, but it does adequately pinpoint the theoretical level of the British Left: its most important theoretician could seriously argue that Lichtheim and C. Wright Mills were the Way and the Truth.

Another current attempted to reassemble from the indigenous radical tradition a theoretical heritage which could become the

[29] Ibid.
[30] Cf. Martin Nicolaus, 'The Unknown Marx', *New Left Review*, no. 48 (March–April 1968).

basis of the new socialism. In this sphere some extremely useful work was done and a lot of material unearthed which is indispensable to any student of labour history. John Saville, E. P. Thompson and Raymond Williams made the most serious attempt to build on the old foundations. Williams argued that there was a literary tradition from Blake through Carlyle, Mill, Arnold and right up to D. H. Lawrence that criticized the inhuman priorities of capitalism: 'The moral critique of industrial capitalism, which has mainly informed the British working-class movement, has been paralleled throughout by a literary tradition of comparable importance ... What is asserted in this tradition is the claim to life, against the distortion of humanity by the priorities and disciplines of industrial capitalism.'[31] The importance of this work was that it criticized Crosland and other defenders of the 'affluent society' by reference to the quality of life and culture. Raymond Williams was the most important influence on the New Left, but he cast a shadow that covered far wider areas. Richard Crossman lavished extravagant praise on *The Long Revolution*[32] and wrote that it was 'The book I have been waiting for since 1945 ... '

While this book and its predecessor *Culture and Society*[33] were important, they were grossly overestimated. The whole tone of Williams laid itself open to extreme variations in interpretation. What exactly was the revolution he was talking about? Whom or what was it directed against? The revolution was to overthrow 'non-democratic patterns of decision', 'older human systems' or a 'familiar inertia of old social forms'. Is it therefore all that much of a surprise that Crossman claimed this as his tradition? Some of the New Left were themselves forced to make a critique of Williams, notably E. P. Thompson, but the vast majority chose to bask in the reflected glory of their hero, too enraptured to do more than stud their articles with extensive quotations from Williams who was vested with an aura of

[31] Raymond Williams, *The Long Revolution* (Chatto and Windus, London, 1961).
[32] Penguin, Harmondsworth, 1965.
[33] London, 1958.

supreme authority and even finality. In the main, the partisans of Raymond Williams and the rigorous denouncers of the 'superstructure/base dichotomy' ended up as rather flabby liberals reduced to writing essays with inspiring titles such as *Forward From Marxism*. What had been meant to lead to an enrichment of radical theory ended up as reformism. It became an exercise in submitting reports to the Pilkington Committee and finally reflowered, briefly, in Mr Wilson's 1964 election rhetoric against the 'candy-floss society'.

Because of its own theoretical weakness and ambiguity the New Left could not provide an ideological leadership to C.N.D. At times it attempted to provide a strategy and analysis for the movement, and sometimes it even succeeded in moderating the old-fashioned liberalism of some sectors of the C.N.D. hierarchy; at other times it crumpled and retreated to moralism. Its failure to evolve a theory of the Cold War led it to further retreats and Stuart Hall and friends were left to propose 'responsible' pressure-group tactics and write *Steps to Peace*, a policy document that watered down the unilateralist case even further and was praised by the *Observer* as being little more than a repetition of the 'official policy of the United States government as explained by Walter Lippmann'. Also the New Left, from a position of total hostility to the very idea of revolutionary organizations or their necessity, turned to substitute themselves for the non-existing organization. Many of them saw the flowering of New Left Clubs all over the country as the dawn of a new phase in British political life, but the clubs failed to develop in any meaningful sense and thus the collapse of the New Left signalled the end of the clubs as well. Finally the death of unilateralism also became the death agony of its ideologues, and it was this that marked the downturn and rapid disintegration of the New Left even as an amorphous mass.

Where did the errors of the New Left come from? Firstly from their inability to understand the real nature of the society in which they were situated. Even today, when the objective conditions have eroded the props which ensured the hegemony of reformist ideology, it would be premature in the extreme to claim that a total analysis of neo-capitalism was in existence. However, the New Left's weakness lay also in their naive and semi-chauvinistic belief that an imaginative re-establishment of a purely British radical tradition would provide the necessary answers. They completely failed to grasp that a real synthesis could only develop in a dialogue with the world revolutionary movement and through conscious internationalism. The New Left was prevented from taking this proposition seriously, partly because of the insularity of the British left-wing tradition, and partly because of some left-overs from Stalinism. In fact the New Left stressed the opposite on certain occasions. Raymond Williams wrote that the 'campaign to "modernise" Britain, and to make it less "insular", is, in its most common forms, a campaign especially directed against the particular strengths of the British working class'. Now in a certain sense there is an element of truth in this, but it is a somewhat peculiar formulation for a socialist to use and, as the C.P. has discovered, some very funny allies can be accrued on this basis. E. P. Thompson showed himself susceptible to similar visions, of a character which seems nowadays to be unbelievably insular. Could he have been really serious in writing: 'Perhaps the key to change has been tossed into British hands and the world waits impatiently upon us to turn the lock.' And is still waiting, Comrade Thompson! The patriotic fervour of these and similar phrases completely blinded Thompson to a rational analysis of the dialectics of world revolution.

One of the greatest weaknesses of the New Left was its lack of understanding of Stalinism. A large majority never succeeded in disentangling Marxism or Leninism from Stalinism, and as a logical consequence ended up as liberal radicals or populists. Most of them behaved in an extremely sectarian way to the 'sectarian' Trotskyists. Now it is true that the Trotskyist movement in Britain had never been known for the intellectual brilliance of its cadres; it is also true that the Socialist Labour

League's methodology was a bit rigid and mechanistic,[34] but this was no reason for refusing to engage in a political dialogue with them or for refusing to accept articles for publication in the *New Reasoner*, whose pages were open to everyone else. Also none of the ex-C.P. intellectuals could claim clean hands as far as the witch-hunting and harassment of the Trotskyist movement in Britain was concerned. It was this that had given the Trotskyists of that time ('thirties, 'forties and early 'fifties) some rather negative and esoteric characteristics. However, despite the weaknesses it was clear that the Trotskyist analysis, however imperfectly interpreted, was the key to an understanding of Stalinism and Hungary and through this to regaining contact with the suppressed traditions of revolutionary Marxism. The failure of the New Left to relate in any way to these developments marked the end of its decline. Thus when Vietnam and the heroic struggle of its people traumatized the entire world, the old New Lefties were nowhere to be seen. They played *no* role in the V.S.C. and were to be seen now and again on C.N.D.

---

[34] Despite this rigidity, the S.L.L. at that stage was a different kettle of fish than it is today. Then it did not denounce political opponents on the left as 'traitors', 'revisionists', etc., but tried to argue politically. Thus in the S.L.L. journal, *Labour Review*, of March–April 1958, a reference to the differences was couched in ultra-reasonable terms: ' ... there has never been the slightest desire to widen the gap between these two trends; on the contrary we have desired, and still do desire, the utmost co-operation on matters of common concern ... ' and again none other than Cliff Slaughter wrote in the *Labour Review* of July–August 1959 the following amazing words: 'Many others in Britain today besides contributors to *Labour Review* are consciously trying to make a Marxist theoretical contribution to the socialist movement. Those connected with the *New Reasoner* and *Universities and Left Review* number avowed Marxists in their ranks and some of their work is of great value.'

Any other revolutionary tendency which used language like that today would be impaled in the columns of the S.L.L. press. One can almost imagine an article beginning with the magic sentence: 'It is no accident that *Labour Review* enters into a dialogue with semi-Stalinist middle-class intellectuals. It merely proves as we have said all along that *Labour Review* has been created to liquidate the S.L.L. into the C.P. middleclass and unstable elements such as Thompson, Saville and Company are the middlemen of this process, etc., etc., etc. ... ' For its own reasons the S.L.L. in those days did not behave in this fashion and there was no excuse for the New Left's contemptuous refusal to enter into a dialogue.

picnics complete with carrier bags bearing the slogan: IN ANY
WAR IT IS THE PEOPLE WHO SUFFER, or words to that effect.
Thus they proudly announced their total degeneration.[35]

IV

The New Left died with C.N.D., but the magazine which had
been born out of the marriage between *Universities and Left
Review* and the *New Reasoner*, namely the *New Left Review*, continued to exist. In 1962 it was taken over by a new team which
has provided a continuing change from its old traditions.
Despite the fact that in its early post-1962 issues, the *New Left
Review* (*N.L.R.*) still had some illusions regarding social-
democracy and Stalinism,[36] there was one distinguishing factor:

[35] A look at the back copies of the *New Reasoner* provides an interesting insight
into the workings of the *New Left* mind. In particular, readers are recommended
to read (for pure amusement) in *New Reasoner*, no. 7 (Winter 1958–9) and no. 8
(Spring 1959), an article by Alasdair MacIntyre entitled, 'Notes from the Moral
Wilderness'.

[36] A *New Left Review* editorial (*N.L.R.*, no. 28, November–December 1964),
published just after the Labour victory in 1964, could proclaim without embarrass-
ment: 'For a party with a small parliamentary and popular majority, the temptation is always the same: to do nothing, avoid controversy and provocation, wander
along in a 'centre-left' mediocrity and confusion of purpose. If the Labour Party
succumbs to this temptation, even minimally, it will lose everything. Its only hope
is to magnify the impetus which has carried it into power—by seeking controversy,
by creating genuine conflict in 'public opinion', and by thus mobilising the whole
of the working class out of its apathy at the next election. The Labour Party is
condemned to act radically or perish.

'Fortunately, it appears that Wilson understands this. Where Gaitskell would
have sought "moderation" at all costs, and wilfully sacrificed the class-character
of the Labour Party for the sake of the mythically conceived "middle-class" vote,
Wilson will be more ready to follow the logic of the situation.'

In addition, *N.L.R.* went through phases of popularizing certain C.P.s (in
particular the Italian C.P.) and fostering illusions regarding them. They were
also infected by some of Deutscher's misconceived theses regarding the 'regen-
erating' power of the Soviet bureaucracy. The latter assumption led to the
conclusion that inter-bureaucratic struggles could sort out matters in the bureaucratized workers states. However, despite a certain uncritical appreciation of the
Chinese 'Cultural Revolution', they have clearly broken with that past, as a
cursory glance at certain more recent issues of the *Review* would indicate.

while the old New Left had been rapidly extending the distance between themselves and Marxism, the *N.L.R.* was moving towards Marxism and revolutionary positions on a world scale. As the *Review* is still in a process of evolution, it is too early to comment with any finality on its role in the revolutionary movement of Britain. However, certain things can be and need to be said, particularly as the revolutionary left has often been dismissive, or pandered quite shamelessly to the anti-intellectual prejudices rampant on the British left. Sometimes it has combined both attitudes to project a mindless philistinism. We can say quite definitively that the *N.L.R.* has naturalized Marxism and has laid the foundations for the development of a viable Marxist tradition. They have done this both by publishing in English a whole variety of Marxist approaches that are evolving throughout the world, and also by attempting a Marxist analysis of Britain. In that sense the revolutionary left in Britain owes a major debt to the *N.L.R.*[37]

There are, however, aspects of their work that must be examined critically but fraternally. There has been a tendency amidst the *N.L.R.* which has ascribed the death of the New Left to the fact that it was side-tracked into activism at the expense of theoretical work during the C.N.D. upsurge. Now while it is true that the New Left did not develop theoretically, the reason for this cannot be ascribed to their activism; this creates the impression that it was simply a question of time, and that the shortage or even the waste of it led to disaster. The basic reason for the defeat of the old New Left was rooted in both its origins and the objective conditions in which it was placed. It proved theoretically incapable of transcending these two factors

---

[37] The popularization of European Marxism in Britain is largely the work of *N.L.R.*, and they have published articles by Sartre, Debray, Marcuse, Mandel, Gorz, Althusser, Colletti, Lukács, Dello Volpe, Magri, Adorno, Bettelheim. The recent formation of New Left Books (N.L.B.) is obviously going to help the process by ensuring the constant appearance of new Marxist books from the rest of Europe, something which has been badly needed in Britain for a long time. It should be added, however, that many militants feel a paperback publishing house would have been more accessible as far as the left was concerned.

because to have done so would have meant partially isolating itself from the main currents and swimming against the stream. The logic of this would have been to force some kind of organizational choice on to the New Left and that they were not prepared for and, in fact, were a bit paranoid on the question of organization in general. Thus the whole question of how Marxist theory is evolved is being posed.

The essence of dialectics is the interrelation between existing reality and consciousness. Thus merely to engage in a form of Marxist scholasticism and divide theory from practice was criticized most severely by Lenin in his polemical *Materialism and Empirio-Criticism* :[38]

> The standpoint of life, of practice, should be first and fundamental in the theory of knowledge. And it inevitably leads to materialism, sweeping aside the endless fabrications of professorial scholasticism. Of course, we must not forget that the criterion of practice can never, in the nature of things, either confirm or refute any human idea *completely*. This criterion too is sufficiently 'indefinite' not to allow human knowledge to become 'absolute', but at the same time it is sufficiently definite to wage a ruthless fight on all varieties of idealism and agnostocism.

The problem is not one of activism versus theory, but of how a group of people, with no generally shared system of theoretical concepts or political priorities, can act together to fight capitalism 'scientificially', to synthesize their shared findings in a disciplined way and finally, after the most democratic internal interplay of ideas, to validate its theory in action. The New Left could not do this in the past. Can the *N.L.R.* do it today? At times when the revolutionary movement is weak it is essential for intellectual groups to meet for the purpose of discussion and publication. Today the situation is slightly different. While the revolutionary movement is still weak, the possibility of

[38] *Collected Works*, 45 vols. (Progress Publishers, Moscow, 1964), vol. 14, p. 142.

making a breakthrough is much greater. The decline of social-democracy, the end of reformism and the dramatic disintegration of Stalinism provide opportunities which have never existed in Europe since the degeneration of the Russian Revolution. There are today politically defined areas where revolutionary Marxists can, in fact, intervene as revolutionaries. For us the era of commentary politics is over and that of intervention, albeit limited action, has begun. This fact decisively alters the relationships between even the most talented intellectuals and the revolutionary groups. In order to become effective, the latter will, in the next period, be forced to carry the major theoretical burden, and to the extent that they become effective their theoretical understanding will increase. The choice which is going to be posed more and more plainly is between helping to build a revolutionary organization or joining the marsh. In the marsh, priorities and ideas are not determined by the struggle, but by changing trends, for in the realm of 'pure' theory most ideas are attractive and the most attractive one predominates for the next period. There is considerable evidence that some members of the *N.L.R.* collective are only too aware of the need for revolutionary organization as well as the need for action,[39] but how far this awareness will transform itself remains an imponderable.

This choice is not a new one. Historically it has confronted both revolutionary intellectuals and revolutionary politicians who refused to take sides till the revolutionary movement was united, and thus failed to understand that the different groups were divided on important issues. Thus, for a certain period a whole group of revolutionaries vacillated on this question just before the Russian Revolution, the best known being Trotsky. Even though after he had joined the Bolsheviks he became, in Lenin's words, the best one, the very fact that he had not been

[39] Thus Robin Blackburn played an exemplary and heroic role during the L.S.E. struggle in 1969, despite the fact that he was a lecturer, and was dismissed from his teaching post. There are instances of lecturers, members of certain revolutionary groups, who far from acting in solidarity with the student struggles have supported disciplinary action!

with the party in the days of defeat, struggle, splits, polemics, etc., played a not insignificant role in the process which allowed Stalin to use the old Bolsheviks against Trotsky in order to strengthen the growing power of the bureaucracy in the Soviet Union. One can fairly speculate that had Trotsky joined the Bolsheviks a decade or even five years before he did, the situation could well have been different. While it would be facile to argue that there exist groups in Britain who can be compared to the Bolsheviks, this does not invalidate the general thesis that from now on the struggle for theoretical advance will become increasingly intertwined with the struggle to build an international revolutionary party.

8 The Revolution in Britain: The Leninist Party and the International

The tragedy of the bourgeoisie is reflected historically in the fact that even before it had defeated its predecessor, feudalism, its new enemy, the proletariat, had appeared on the scene. Politically, it became evident when at the moment of victory, the 'freedom' in whose name the bourgeoisie had joined battle with feudalism, was transformed into a new repressiveness. Sociologically, the bourgeoisie did everything in its power to eradicate the fact of class conflict from the consciousness of society, even though class conflict had only emerged in its purity and became established as an historical fact with the advent of capitalism. Ideologically, we see the same contradiction in the fact that the bourgeoisie endowed the individual with an unprecedented importance, but at the same time that same individuality was annihilated by the economic conditions to which it was subjected, by the reification created by commodity production.

GEORG LUKÁCS,
History and Class Consciousness (1919–22)

The world political situation as a whole is chiefly characterised by a historical crisis of the leadership of the proletariat.

Transitional Programme of the Fourth International (1938)

I

In previous chapters we have attempted to delineate the development of an awakened political consciousness which was the result of the decline of British capitalism, the death agony of left social democracy, the belated realization of the significance of the colonial revolution and the evolution of the left since the Second World War. The conclusion is inescapable: despite all the problems which exist for the left, a socialist revolution is possible in Britain. Whether or not it takes place depends on certain subjective factors, but we can be confident that the coming decade will see the beginning of social upheavals and explosions which will totally shatter the complacency of the British bourgeoisie as it tries to adjust to the changed situation.

Who will make this social revolution? What is the main agency for social change in Britain? On these questions our answer has always been clear, despite the distortions of the mass media: the working class is the only social class capable of overthrowing the existing property relations and abolishing capitalism in Britain, thus taking it out of the capitalist world market. One can almost imagine this answer provoking cynical and self-satisfied smiles on the face of any supporter of the bourgeois system or, for that matter, a bourgeois himself. One can even hear him say to himself, 'I know the British workers better than these dreadful revolutionaries because I deal with them every day and I know that they will never be attracted by any of the Marxist rubbish.' How often have we heard the argument that the British workers are only interested in more money, that they support Enoch Powell, that they are very backward, that even if they pulled out of line, the 'sensible' T.U.C. is there to drag them back in, etc., etc., etc. Much of this, of course, has a certain element of truth in it and that is why we will discuss in some detail how a change in the objective conditions of capitalism affects the thinking and the ideas of the working-class movement.

14

To understand the optimism of revolutionary Marxism, which survives periods of capitalist stability, of economic boom, one has to accept that the essence of the proletarian condition is rooted deep in the existence of capitalist society. The fact that a worker has no access to the means of production forces him to sell his labour-power, as a commodity, to the highest bidder in a system based on generalized commodity production. In exchange for the sale of his labour-power, the worker receives a wage which is sufficient to satisfy his immediate needs and those of his family.[1] From this position there develops a certain relationship to his work and to the society in which he lives which can be summarized in the words exploitation and alienation. His position as a wage earner, regardless of the level of wages or of the amount of money he spends on consumption, whether he be a worker in New Delhi, London or New York, ties him to the necessity of selling his labour power — this is a social and economic necessity from which a worker cannot withdraw. However, this structural stability in the position of a worker under capitalism would be a gross oversimplification in getting a picture of the working class if it was considered on its own; few Marxists peg their case on this fact alone, unlike their opponents, who point to the conjunctural changes in the working class as a sign of the fact that everything has changed. They thus completely ignore the fundamental contradiction of capitalist society.

Capitalism itself is not a static system and it is therefore essential to understand that certain changes have taken place inside capitalism which force one to differentiate it from previous phases of its development. Many Marxist economists have argued that capitalism has entered a third stage of development; the third industrial revolution which has produced neo-capitalism, which while it has *all* the basic *elements* of classical capitalism has nevertheless discarded some of its

---

[1] 'Sufficient' is used in a very strict sense and is not to be confused with 'just' or 'deserved'.

basic *characteristics*. Thus Ernest Mandel, one of the leading Marxist economists today, has written:

We shall define neo-capitalism as this latest stage in the development of monopoly capitalism in which a combination of factors—accelerated technological innovation, permanent war economy, expanding colonial revolution— have transferred the main source of monopoly surplus profits from the colonial countries to the imperialist countries themselves and made the giant corporations both more independent and more vulnerable.

More independent, because the enormous accumulation of monopoly surplus profits enables these corporations, through the mechanisms of price-investment and self-financing, and with the help of a constant build-up of sales costs, distribution costs and research and development expenses, to free themselves from that strict control by banks and finance capital which characterized the trusts and monopolies of Hilferding's and Lenin's epoch. More vulnerable, because the shortening of the life cycle of fixed capital, the growing phenomena of surplus capacity, the relative decline of customers in non-capitalist milieus and, last but not least, the growing challenge of the non-capitalist forces in the world (the so-called socialist countries, the colonial revolution and, potentially, at least, the working class in the metropolis) have implanted even in minor fluctuations and crises the seeds of dangerous explosions and total collapse.[2]

But despite the technological innovations and the comparative prosperity which the capitalist system projected, none of the fundamental contradictions of capitalism have been overcome and to protect itself from its own myths and propaganda, the bourgeoisie is forced to use its state power more and more openly. Thus we see that incomes policies, wage-stops,

[2] Cf. Ernest Mandel, 'Workers Under Capitalism', *International Socialist Review*, vol. 29, no. 6 (December 1968).

state subsidies to big business and guarantees of surplus profit have become a way of life in the neo-capitalist world. At the same time there are forces which are at work today and which will play havoc with the capitalist system. There are the growing problems of the international monetary system and a trend towards a generalized economic recession in the entire capitalist world. Then there is the whole process of gradually restricting the rights of the trade unions with the purpose of finally suppressing them altogether. Coupled with this is the growing alienation of the producers and the consumers from the products of commodity production, which go nowhere near satisfying the needs or aspirations of the people; the contradiction between the potential of these societies and the grim actualities, epitomized by the growing misery of the countries of the 'Third World' which are still under the domination of Wall Street, and the wealth which is wasted on weapons of destruction.

The last few years have come as both a blow and a shock to the 'theoreticians' of the periphery, who argued that the metropolitan working class had been totally integrated into the structures of the bourgeois state through high wages and ideological control and that the real hope lay in the groups, either nationally oppressed or aware of their alienation and largely on the periphery of the working-class movement. The international implications of this theory were expressed in a very striking way by the Chinese leader, Lin Piao, who transferred the Chinese experience into a world-wide scale and argued that the 'countryside of the world' (i.e. Latin America, Asia and Africa) would encircle the metropolis like a massive red flame and thus bring about revolutions in the advanced capitalist world. Modified and sophisticated variations on this theme had become fairly current when the massive working-class upsurge in France in May 1968 shattered this pessimism. The social and political upheavals in Italy in 1969 and 1970 further showed the real potential of the working class and in every single Western European country the working class acquired a new dynamism. Even the social-democratic paradise, Sweden, caught the infection and there were important working-class struggles in 1970, some of which continue even today. It can be argued that the working class is experiencing a change in its composition, with the increase of technology, automation and the rapid pace of innovation, but this strengthens the revolutionary potential of the working class rather than the reverse. More and more workers are striking not merely for higher wages, but against working conditions which make them mere cogs in a wheel owned and manipulated by a tiny percentage of capitalists. Today the workers realize that the old paternalistic argument of the old bosses (namely, that bosses were essential because someone had to direct the ignorant and unskilled workers) is simply a load of crap; workers have, much more than before, a better understanding of the work processes than the bosses. Thus the realization that the boss is unnecessary begins to develop, particularly during factory occupations. Because of their crucial role in the productive processes, symbolized by their capacity to end production at a stroke, the workers are the only force capable of overthrowing capitalism. Can they do this on their own, without any intervention by revolutionary currents from the outside? Can they develop a spontaneously generated socialist consciousness? Can they overthrow the existing social structure via their organizations, the trade unions? The answer to all these questions is a firm and clearcut *no*. That is why we have to discuss the whole concept of working-class consciousness and ways in which this can be harnessed to destroy the capitalist state.

II

How do Marxists begin to challenge the effect and influence of bourgeois and petty-bourgeois ideology inside the working-class movement? It is clear that this will not happen on its own. Lenin's most important contribution to and elaboration of the Marxist method lay precisely in his concept of the party and its relation to class consciousness. The Leninist organization is the dialectical intertwining of three basic elements: the actuality of the revolution in both the semi-colonial world *and* the capitalist world in an epoch of declining capitalism; the uneven development of working-class consciousness and its different stages; and the key role and importance of Marxist theory and its relationship both to science and the class struggle. Thus the Leninist theory of the party is a complex *political* totality which emerged out of the concrete needs of the class struggle on a global scale and whose importance has been stressed time and time again by the many defeats suffered by the revolutionary movement. The administrative aspects of the Leninist party depended on the political conditions which prevailed in any given country; Czarist Russia was a tyranny and quite clearly the organizational discipline and centralism had to be of a very high order simply to survive. The Stalinists of course completely distorted and inverted this fact to suit their own purposes. For Stalin and the epigones, 'democratic centralism' became the axe with which the Leninist leadership could be executed after the death of Lenin. For many others, 'democratic centralism' is a purely practical question and can be explained in a few pet formulae. What all these explanations completely ignore is that 'democratic centralism' as understood by Lenin was very clearly a political concept, dictated by the necessity to combat capitalism and to impart a very high level of theoretical practice to *all* the cadres of the party. In fact any meaningful democratic centralism can be applied effectively only when the revolutionary organization or nucleus has passed beyond a certain stage in the primitive accumulation of cadres. A distorted democratic centralism not only leads to bureaucratization, even inside the most revolutionary of organizations, but has a logic of its own: it leads to the accumulation of primitive 'cadres' who are trained not to understand the theory and practice of Marxism, but in repulsive concepts such as 'party pride', 'party loyalty' and unquestioning obedience to the dictates of the 'leadership'. To say that this is what Comrade Lenin had in mind is a gross distortion, but the very fact that it can be presented in this light only by appeal to quotations taken out of context from the works of Lenin says more than enough about the nature of the organization itself.

When we talk about the working class and its consciousness there is often a tendency to generalize, and while this is correct within certain limits it can often lead to over-simplifications and therefore must be combated vigorously. Because the working class is certainly not homogenous as far as its ideas are concerned. There are many different reasons for this and it is not within the scope of this book to discuss the different levels of working-class consciousness on a national and an international scale, and explain the different factors which led to this state of affairs. Suffice it to say that the different social backgrounds from which proletarians emerge (some are descended from generations of urban workers, others from agricultural labourers, some indeed from the lower ranks of the petty-bourgeoisie), the different environment in which they work (small plant, medium-sized factories, the service industries or large industrial combines), the political and educational differences (in Scotland there were Labour Colleges run by socialists which played a significant role coupled with the high level of militancy) and differences in nationality, etc., play a vital role in determining the class consciousness of different layers of the working-class movement. To imagine that Marxist theory will emerge spontaneously from the shop floor or the computer-room is not to understand Marxism. It can be assimilated *completely* only in an individual and not in a collective fashion.[3] In *What Is To Be Done?* Lenin speaks of the ability of intellectuals to understand Marxism and take it to the working-class movement. The conclusion to be drawn is

[3] Ernest Mandel, 'Class Consciousness and the Leninist Party' (I.M.G. Publications, London, 1971). This article should be compared to the centrist hotchpotch of Lucio Magri in *N.L.R.*, no. 60 (March–April 1970); the difference will be quite illuminating.

that only the best, most class-conscious, self-confident, intelligent proletarians are able to acquire a Marxist consciousness directly and, in fact, *independently* of their class position as proletarians. The same holds true for individuals belonging to other layers of society. From this we learn that it helps no one to idealize the working class blindly and worship its behind, because this could lead, in certain circumstances, to an adaptation to the backwardness of this class and hence a capitulation to reformism. On the other hand it is equally clear that Marxism as a theory could only develop out of the development of the class struggle in bourgeois society:

> There is an inextricable tie between the collective, historical experience of the working class in struggle and its scientific working out of Marxism as collective, historical class consciousness in its most potent form. But to maintain that scientific socialism is an historical product of the proletarian class struggle is not to say that all or even most members of this class can, with greater or lesser ease, reproduce this knowledge. Marxism is not an automatic product of the class struggle and class experience but a result of scientific, theoretical production. Such an assimilation is made possible only through participation in that process of production; and this process is by definition an *individual* one, even though it is only made possible through the development of the social forces of production and class contradictions under capitalism.[4]

However, theoretical production only acquires a positive role if the theoreticians are also professional revolutionaries and aware of the historic tasks which have to be confronted. The most important of these tasks is to create and build a revolutionary organization *based* on the vanguard layers of the working-class movement, which can extend its tentacles deep into the proletariat and strangle the reformism which has for so long characterized the movement in Britain. The most

[4] Ibid.

urgent task confronting revolutionists today is that of uniting the revolutionary nuclei with the vanguard layers of the proletariat. Because while it is plain that the consciousness of the working class as a whole develops only through concrete actions and struggles, it is even clearer that unless a vanguard exists to mature this consciousness and lead it to the question of state power, there will once again be a downturn and a return to the old pattern of 'business as usual'. Because working-class consciousness is not static, nor does it develop in stages any more than a socialist revolution. If the latter were the case there would be no serious problems confronting revolutionaries in Britain. We could all sit down and wait for the automatic progression of working-class consciousness till it reached an understanding of scientific socialism and seized power. If that were so then the task would not be to build a revolutionary party, but to retreat into an epicurean shell and encourage research on drugs which lengthen the lifespan, so that one could be alive when the big upheaval took place. Unfortunately things are not as simple as that and a study of the French general strikes of 1936 and 1968 and the struggles in Germany (1918–23) and Italy (1920, 1948 and 1969) gives one a fairly good indication of the limits of working-class spontaneity. Certainly the consciousness of the workers advances by leaps and bounds during struggles, but unless there exists a Leninist combat party to develop and co-ordinate these struggles politically, there will always be a downturn of consciousness when the struggle is defeated. Thus many French workers could vote for de Gaulle soon after the May 1968 upsurge, a fact which demonstrated the need for a strong revolutionary organization with cells inside every French factory much more than it did the 'inherent conservativeness of the European working class in general'.

Another important aspect which necessitates political, and hence organizational, centralism is the capitalist system itself. Any theory based on the understanding that we are living in a period of revolutionary upheavals must of necessity confront the problem of state power and the centralizing influence of the bourgeois state. To think that the power of this state can be dismantled brick by brick is completely to abandon revolution for reform. The organized might of the bourgeois state therefore is another key factor which explains the necessity for a powerful and organized anti-capitalist force. In this the example of the Russian Revolution is still perfectly valid and Trotsky, who had not understood the importance of Lenin's concept of the party, was the first to realize his mistake and write much later:

> A colossal factor in the maturity of the Russian proletariat in February or March 1917 was Lenin. He did not fall from the skies. He personified the revolutionary tradition of the working class. For Lenin's slogans to find their way to the masses, there had to exist cadres, even though numerically small in the beginning; there had to exist the confidence of the cadre in the leadership, a confidence based upon the entire experience of the past. To cancel these elements from one's calculations is simply to ignore the living revolution, to substitute for it an abstraction, the 'relationship of forces', because the development of the revolution precisely consists of this, that the relationship of forces keeps incessantly and rapidly changing under the impact of the changes in consciousness of the proletariat, the attraction of backward layers to the advanced, the growing assurance of the class in its own strength. The vital mainspring in this process is the party, just as the vital mainspring in the mechanism of the party is its leadership.[5]

An understanding of the uneven nature of the development of class consciousness is not sufficient on its own. It has to be accompanied by a struggle to transform trade-union consciousness to a political and revolutionary class consciousness, and

[5] Trotsky, quoted in ibid.

this can only be done by the interaction of a revolutionary cadre, advanced workers and the bulk of the working class. The question of how small groups of revolutionaries largely on the periphery of the working-class movement in Britain can begin to develop an implantation in the vanguard layers of the class is therefore posed rather sharply at the present moment. For unless a base is gained inside the working-class movement and, let us add for the sake of clarification, this must be a *political* base, no group or organization can refer to itself as a party. A revolutionary party can exist *only* with the winning over of vanguard militants of the working class to a revolutionary Marxist position. A correct programme does not give any tendency the right to arrogate to itself the position of *the* Party. A party can only be built when part of that programme mediated through a programme of transitional demands filters through to sections of the working class and is tested in struggle. The entire process of constructing a revolutionary organization acquires its unity only through a process of learning through the action of the masses, the learning of the advanced workers in their daily confrontations with reality, the education of the revolutionary cadre by the dialectical inter-relationship of theory and practice. In brief, there are no short cuts to the building of a revolutionary party as opportunists and sectarians seem to imply.[6]

Does a revolutionary party exist in Britain? The answer is no. Can it be developed, and if so, how? These are the questions which the revolutionary movement must answer if it is to move forward. As we saw in Chapter 5, the implementation of differing strategies and tactics is one of the reasons for the divisions inside the revolutionary movement.

---

[6] Opportunists, by adapting to the backwardness of the class and idealizing it till they begin to capitulate politically (for instance preparing a minimum programme within the framework of bourgeois democracy), and sectarians, by denying the existence of the class and claiming it has been integrated into capitalism because it does not follow the policies laid down by the sectarians.

III

The new rise of *political* consciousness in the proletariat throughout Western Europe has not left Britain unmarked. The reason
is simple. The oft-mentioned crisis of capitalism is today really
upon us; it might not affect every country at the same time
(though soon it will do precisely that), but it certainly does so
at different periods. We discussed in the first two chapters the
reasons for this in Britain in order to explain the intensification
of the struggle at this particular moment. It is necessary now to
elaborate on this process and to attempt to project not only
how revolutionaries can intervene in this situation, but what
the logic of the situation as it develops could turn out for the
working-class movement itself. The viciousness with which the
Tory Party continues the policies of Labour are one indication
of the critical position of British capitalism. The unemployment
levels had in the summer of 1971 reached the highest peak for
thirty years. If anything, the revolutionary left tended to
underestimate the real crisis of British capitalism. A striking
symbol of this crisis was the collapse of the firm of Rolls-Royce
—the aristocracy of British capitalism—and the amusing sight
of the Tory government being forced to nationalize its more
profitable sectors.[7] A further sign of how far are the days of
empire was the servility with which Mr Henry Ford, a leading
representative of American capital, was greeted by a Tory
Prime Minister, Edward Heath, when he visited Britain to try
and pressure the Ford workers into submission during the 1971
Ford strike.[8] A sharpening of the crisis could well present us
with an old variant of the British ruling class: a National
Government. However, in the present circumstances, when
there is nothing but contempt for the House of Commons, a
feeling which is today becoming more generalized amongst

[7] Cf. Dave Bailey, 'Whatever Happened to Rolls-Royce', *The Red Mole*, vol. 2,
no. 4, for a useful analysis of the Rolls-Royce fiasco.

[8] The only two groups which defended British prestige were the C.P. and the
Labour left.

politically advanced sections of the working class, this would lead to an even greater stress on extra-parliamentary action and could also lead to a withdrawal of the trade unions from the Labour Party with a small rump of the Parliamentary Labour Party. Precisely for these reasons the Wilson leadership might try to prevent an old-style National Government and devise a new formula which would amount to the same thing. For revolutionary militants the task of multiplying their forces thus becomes all the more urgent, and we mention briefly in what areas the initial forces for revolutionary organizations can be won:

1. *The Radicalized Youth*

We have discussed this in great detail in previous chapters. It is necessary to stress, however, that the youth, and student youth in particular, remain the most vulnerable to revolutionary ideas; this is partly because of the crisis of bourgeois ideology, and increasingly because of the failure of the capitalist system to service even their material needs efficiently. Thus the polytechnics and teachers' training colleges could become more and more explosive as the crisis of capitalism continues. A special strategy has also to be worked out to win young workers to the revolutionary movement, but this would be done best by a vigorous schools' movement. As the nurseries of bourgeois ideology the schools have to be attacked and a concerted effort made to develop a revolutionary tradition inside them. In this sense the schools' movement is a hundred times more advanced in France, Italy and Scandinavia than in Britain. It has also to be noted that there has been a marked levelling of cultural barriers between working-class youth and the student movement, largely through the influence of pop music and such groups as the Beatles (and now more specifically John Lennon),[9] the Rolling Stones, The Who, etc. This influence has also affected the life-style of large numbers of young workers and

[9] Cf. John Lennon's interview with Robin Blackburn, 'Power to the People', *The Red Mole*, vol. 2, no. 5.

at many gatherings it isn't all that easy to distinguish between petty-bourgeois and working-class youth. Young workers could be decisive in challenging the reformist and bureaucratic structures of the trade-union movement within the next few years, provided they are in a revolutionary youth organization and have worked out a strategy. The shifting of the centre of the struggle to the industrial sector (i.e. to the heart of the capitalist system) undoubtedly overshadows every other struggle, and correctly so. But to draw the conclusion from this that revolutionary groups can now win over large numbers of older workers directly to the revolutionary movement could have serious and demoralizing repercussions. We will discuss below the perspectives for revolutionaries in this milieu, but it remains obvious that as long as the process of the primitive accumulation of cadres is not completed the youth milieu provides the best field of work for the making of professional revolutionaries.

2. *Black Workers*

The existence of racism in Britain is not a new phenomenon. It is vital that the roots of racism are recognized as being part of the capitalist mode of production, which has an inner logic of its own and creates divisions inside the working-class movement, particularly in times of crisis. The strength of the anti-Irish immigrant feeling was at certain points much higher than any white racist manifestation today. The Jews who fled from persecution were, during the early years of the twentieth century, victimized by fascist thugs and government alike (i.e. the Aliens Act). It was inevitable that black people coming to this country would be prey to similar tendencies and pressures, with one difference: because of the colour of their skins they become easily identifiable targets and thus racism becomes institutionalized, extending deep into different layers of bourgeois society. Whether racism becomes a major factor dividing the working class depends largely on the degree of class consciousness and the levels of unemployment, and also, of course, on exactly to what extent bourgeois ideologists use racist ideology. Many on the 'left' who would accept this would also draw from it a wrong conclusion: if racism is one of the by-products of the capitalist system, then clearly it will be abolished only with the overthrow of existing society. From this our sectarians conclude that there is no need for a specific anti-racist campaign and the struggle of the black people against white racism is diversionary. 'Let's leave everything till the revolution' is not an attitude which helps the black people in this country. It is therefore worth pointing out that since the ending of the economic boom, there has been a growing racism in this country (the Notting Hill Gate anti-black riots in the late 'fifties were an image of the future) encouraged by the policies of successive capitalist governments. The Immigrants Acts of 1962 (Tories), 1965 and 1968 (Labour) and 1971 (Tory) are in fact blatantly racist acts which discriminate against black people and therefore encourage the practice of racism, not least in the police force whose task it is to see that these racist laws are observed.

The British working class which has been saturated historically with British imperialist ideology (one of the most racist ideologies in history) still bears the traces, and a minimum amount of sustained effort by fascists in periods of passivity and demoralization in *certain* sections of the working class could find a response. The phenomenon of Powellism is slightly different, as Powell's ambitions transcend the issue of race; he is generally concerned with the creation of a British nationalism which recovers some of the lost potency of British capitalism. Powell seeks a key place in British political history, but within the framework of the Conservative right. He uses racism quite blatantly to challenge the complacence of his own party leadership and though he is an absurd figure in British politics his political importance cannot be underestimated, because

Powellism is a symptom: the true threat lies in the developing disease of which it is a symptom. Powell has emerged apparently as an active challenge to the existing political consensus from the Right. In fact, he and his repercussions are symptomatic of the growing paralysis and deterioration of the consensus itself. There *is* a national insanity in the air, but it did not originate in Powell's second-rate ruminations. It is located squarely in the mainstream of English politics and — beyond that — in the harsh contradictions of English capitalism which the political consensus has been struggling with in vain for a quarter of a century.[10]

The differences inside the black community itself, and this is a community which consists largely of black proletarians, make it difficult to project a common political strategy. The differences in this case are cultural, linguistic, religious, etc. Many of them will be overcome in the present generation of black youth, but till then one can talk only in terms of a militant struggle against racism rather than a single and unified independent black party. Also because of the small number of black people and their dispersion, it is not realistic to project the slogan of 'Black control of the black communities' or talk in terms of self-determination, as is the case in the United States.

The fact that blacks have become the scapegoat for the failures of capitalism and are blamed for all the social problems which neo-capitalism is unable to solve (Mr Crosland, where is your 'threshold of abundance'?) calls for the most vigorous solidarity from white revolutionaries. So far this has not materialized except in the embryonic shape of the Black Defence Committee, which has been sponsored mainly by the Spartacus League and has not attracted the support of other revolutionary tendencies. Unless white revolutionary organizations are capable of performing this elementary task, they will make it more and more difficult for black militants to work within revolutionary groups. For black militants the question

[10] See Tom Nairn, 'Enoch Powell: the New Right', *N.L.R.*, no. 61 (May–June 1970), for the best *Marxist* analysis of Powellism.

is also organizational: while the Indian and Pakistani Workers' Associations in many cases provide an excellent platform for radicalizing black workers from those two countries (as do many black groups with other black workers), the question of a united organization to defend black people of different backgrounds against white racism and police brutality is posed very clearly. With an increase in racism we will see an increase in the number of attacks on black people (as, for instance, after utterances by Powell). To expect the police to take serious action against racism is a joke which never fails to stir a ripple of laughter inside the black communities. Ask any black worker what he thinks of the nice, kind, 'impartial police'. He will tell you in no uncertain terms. He knows because he cannot afford to be ignorant. The number of carefully documented cases of police brutality is mounting rapidly, but both white liberals and black Uncle Toms prefer to ignore the facts. Instead, many of them concentrate their wrath on black militants who suggest ways of defending black people. Hence there is a burning need for co-ordinated action to set up Committees of Self-Defence in black ghettoes, which can defend black people against all racist brutality. In some areas in London this has been tried with limited success, but it is vital to generalize this experience. The young black proletarians are in the forefront of the struggle (particularly those from Indo-Pak backgrounds) as much against racism as against the mentality of their families who are scared of any involvement with 'trouble'. They represent the layers which can be won over to the revolutionary movement, provided the latter shows itself capable of *action*.

3. *Women's Liberation*

The women's revolt in Britain was started, significantly, by the strike of the Ford's women sewing-machinists in May–June 1968, which led directly to the formation of N.J.A.C.C.W.E.R. (National Joint Action Campaign Committee for Women's

Equal Rights), but the dominance of the C.P. in the organization almost predetermined its future and after organizing a demonstration on equal pay in May 1969 it frittered away, till today it exists only on paper.[11] At the same time the interest in women's liberation by non-working-class women led to a conference on the subject in Oxford in February 1970 and certainly revealed the potentialities of the movement. Five hundred women from different parts of the country turned up. They were unable to set up a unified movement because of differences of opinion not only on political questions (feminism or a Marxist approach) but also because many of the participants came from a petty-bourgeois milieu. These women were hostile to organizing effectively on principle, and viewed with suspicion and hostility the women who belonged to revolutionary socialist groups.

The oppression of women in capitalist society takes place on different levels. Economically they provide unpaid labour in their role as 'housewives', which involves them in the production and care of the next labour-power-producing generation and also in providing facilities and advantages for male workers which increases the latter's productivity. The institution of the family therefore acts as a powerful superstructural prop to capitalism and is an important anchor of bourgeois ideology. In addition many married women provide cheap labour and accept bad working conditions. Although this is beginning to be challenged, one can in no way talk in terms of a *mass* movement of working-class women. It is extremely important that it develops because it could herald an important beginning where the real roots of the oppression are both visible and recognized. The economic oppression which women suffer only pinpoints their biological, sexual and ideological oppression. The fact that most men view women as sexual objects, regard them as inferior in many ways,

[11] The only organization which reacted politically was the I.M.G., which organized a paper in Nottingham, *Socialist Woman*, which has since been moved to London and has become the paper of all the Socialist Women's groups. From the very beginning, I.M.G. women members have been extremely active in the movement.

have double standards of sexual behaviour (a man who remarks on the attractiveness of a woman is accepted, a woman who does the same to a man is automatically classed as 'loose', to give just one example), expect women to do certain types of work at home (work which men would either have to do themselves or would have to pay for!) and behave in a certain way (i.e. as women are expected to behave), makes them guilty of what women militants very aptly and correctly describe as male chauvinism. This is a disease which flows from bourgeois ideology and which has also infected many male revolutionaries. The growth of the women's liberation movement has forced socialist men to reconsider or, in many cases, to consider for the first time the position of women. Some extremely backward groups, which consider themselves revolutionary, continue to pour scorn on the movement, forgetting Lenin's important dictum that the revolutionary party must make the cause of *all* the oppressed sections of society its own cause or else it remains partially oppressed itself. This has yet to be understood by sections of the revolutionary movement in Britain. However, for the women's movement, too, all the questions have not been solved. There is a continuous debate between the socialist women, who argue that working-class women are the most oppressed and that the movement should take an anti-capitalist direction, and the feminists, some of whom regard women as a class, and others, who talk in terms of 'male-dominated politics' rather than base themselves on a class analysis.[12]

For male revolutionaries, however, it is important to give unconditional support (this does not mean that it should be uncritical, but revolutionaries who don't support unconditionally have no right to criticize!) to the struggle being waged by women for equality and for liberation. Apart from all else it provides an invaluable reservoir of experience for the revolution itself.

[12] Cf. Margaret Coulson, 'Women's Liberation: Potentialities and Perspectives', *International*, vol. 1, no. 4 (March–April 1971). Also Branka Magas, 'Liberation of Women is a Revolutionary Task', *The Red Mole*, vol. 2, no. 5.

4. Ireland

Just over a hundred years ago Karl Marx was writing vigorously on the Irish question and putting forward the view that
unless the British workers' movement understood what the
Irish were fighting for and supported them, it would not be
able to free itself. Marx did not mean this in a moral sense, to
show his outrage at the lack of any meaningful solidarity with
the Irish people in England. He meant that quite literally: a
working class which never developed the consciousness to
support an oppressed people would not be able to grasp the
necessity of emancipating itself from the grip of capitalism.
Today, despite the changes that have taken place, the Irish
question still troubles the British bourgeoisie. The first country
to be dominated by British imperialism, Ireland is the last which
struggles to free itself from British imperialism. It threatens to
create a situation which could easily overflow into Britain,
where there are two million Irish workers, many of whom still
retain links with their country of origin and frequently travel
to and fro.

It would be futile, and indeed impossible, to try and sum-
marize Irish history in a few paragraphs. It is sufficient to say
that the statelet of Ulster, created by British imperialism to
serve its economic interests, has grown to be a Frankenstein's
monster which threatens the British ruling class. It serves no
real economic purpose and has outlived its usefulness. British
imperialism would much prefer a united Ireland with which
it had extremely close links, but its past sins determine the
present; the ideology which imperialism nurtured and sustained—Orangeism—still exists as strongly as ever before and
the people who believe in it, the Protestant workers (the poor
whites of the British 'Empire') and the landed gentry, are still
prepared to fight and die for it. Thus the oppressed Catholics
(the 'whites with black skins'), who were smashed in every
possible way by the thuggery of the Orange police state, have
emerged as a force once again. Their consciousness awakened

by the Civil Rights marchers in 1969–70, they turn towards Republicanism to free them from the straitjacket of Ulster. Thus British troops are seen once again in action, this time not killing wogs in Aden, but brutalizing Catholics in Ulster. The immediate prospect remains one of continuous urban guerrilla warfare, which could spread into the South where the Green Tories maintain their hegemony. For them, as for their friends in Westminster, this new upsurge of Republicanism is a curse which cannot be exorcized. It sparks off a historical re-awakening which can only draw attention to the aborted struggle which produced Eire. Moreover, if there is an attempt to pogromize the Catholics in the Six Counties, the wave of anti-imperialist sentiment in the twenty-six counties will not be held back by the Fianna Fáil fakers. Ireland could thus turn out to be the Achilles heel of European capitalism, a Cuba in Europe! This is the prospect which worries the Orangemen, the Green Tories and British capitalism. In a distorted way it unites them, but it is a unity which cannot prevent a massive explosion of discontent leading to social upheavals in the near future. We can predict with certainty that despite the fluctuations normal in any struggle, the Irish question will rapidly become a spectre to haunt the British bourgeoisie—hopefully, to its grave.

The need for British revolutionists to solidarize with the Irish struggle is therefore paramount. They must support the armed action of Irish republicanism against British imperialism in public. They must attempt to build a solidarity campaign which can win over Irish workers in large numbers and radicalize them. While the Irish Solidarity Campaign exists and does a fair amount of limited propaganda work, they are hampered by the fact that the British left is reluctant to commit itself to something more than mere paper support—and not all of them can do even that. The methods which are being used in Ireland are not new to that country, where guerrilla warfare was born, but they have succeeded in shaking the complacency of many in Britain who have been a bit taken aback that an armed struggle involving thousands of British troops can take place just across the water. The Irish workers, who in this respect have a memory which the British working-class lacks, could be decisive in bringing these traditions into the heart of industrial Britain. One can visualize a situation within the next few years where a city like Liverpool could witness an armed insurrection by sections of the proletariat.

5. On revolutionary violence

Whenever revolution is discussed the question is raised, will it be violent? Will blood be spilled on the clean streets of London? It is not surprising that in Britain this question has greater weight than it would in any Continental country. For hundreds of years British imperialism spilled innumerable gallons of blood in the colonies it occupied and plundered and whose citizens it dragged under its heels. The reason it did this was precisely to avoid *its* blood from soiling the streets of *its* cities as a result of class confrontations. For many years it bought social peace at home with the skins of the peoples of Asia, Africa and Latin America. Today it is no longer able to do this for reasons we have detailed in this book. We have therefore to ask ourselves quite frankly how the British bourgeoisie would deal with a situation which threatened its very existence as a class by seeking to destroy its ownership of the means of production. The answer is to be found both in history and in the way the British bourgeoisie has dealt with rebellions abroad. It is doubtful whether the British bourgeoisie will become the first social class to give up its power voluntarily. On the contrary it will attempt to crush any attempt to do so *by force*. The only option open to the workers will then be to arm themselves and fight back. Of course the scale and degree of the violence depends on the balance of forces, the strength of revolutionary organizations, the degree of disintegration of the ruling class and its repressive apparatus, etc., but that a certain amount of violence will take place is inevitable and unavoidable.

IV

Dual power

The above sectors of intervention we have discussed are largely on the periphery of the working-class movement or represent certain specific sections which are more oppressed or/and more open to revolutionary ideas. These peripheral areas are not decisive as far as the social revolution is concerned; their importance lies in another direction. For various reasons they are not as susceptible to the reformist ideology which dominates the organized working class as are the adult workers themselves. This makes it possible for revolutionaries to intervene directly *as revolutionaries* and win large numbers of people active in these layers to revolutionary Marxism, to the concept of the Leninist party, and thus acquire a firm theoretical base as well as the quantitative strength with which to start the process of modifying the balance of forces between revolutionaries and reformists inside the centre of the capitalist system, the factory.

As we have stated before, even the British C.P., which is insignificant when compared to its European counterparts, has in its ranks the most class-conscious workers, many of whom are shop stewards. Many of these militants are totally opposed to the C.P.'s industrial policy, but they will not leave the party unless they can see a meaningful alternative, which has not only the correct political perspectives, but also the necessary organizational strength to service the needs of industrial militants. Those worker militants not in the C.P. are either active trade unionists, and wary of all political organizations because of their experiences with both the Labour Party and the C.P., or else are ideologically still tied to Labourism. Hence the revolutionary organization has to build its forces on the periphery and start the move towards the centre, but twin mistakes have to be avoided. First, it is extremely mechanistic to interpret this periphery/centre relationship as a static concept. In other words, to imagine that once the periphery has been won and an organizational base prepared, the vanguard layers of the working class will automatically move towards the organization in large numbers. That assessment would amount to accepting the theory of the spontaneous development of socialist consciousness, which we have attempted to rebut. The lesson to be drawn from all this is that even when working largely on the periphery, the centre *cannot* be ignored. This does not mean that a revolutionary organization dilutes its politics or anything of the sort; it simply implies that political propaganda must be directed at vanguard layers of the working class (specifically the shop stewards). As part of this a thorough analysis must be made of specific situations which affect the workers' movement. In particular, during strikes the revolutionary organization must produce propaganda material both for the shop stewards and to educate its own cadres. Unless this activity is carried out and a nexus of *contacts* established in key sectors of industry, the revolutionary organization will suffer politically.

The other error is that once a revolutionary organization moves to the centre there is a tendency to forget the peripheral sectors and their organization. This has to be combated firmly and a dialectic of the sectors of intervention established. Also it should be remembered that in the initial stages many of the more political workers will get involved in the campaigns organized on the periphery. These must be won over to revolutionary Marxist positions immediately, as quite clearly they develop an individual semi-revolutionary consciousness. For instance many militant and political trade unionists used to turn up at V.S.C. demonstrations and meetings quite regularly, and similar situations could occur in other fields in the not too distant future.

However, even when revolutionary organizations are weak inside industry, in their propaganda they must adopt a transitional approach based on a series of transitional demands. These demands must have as their object both the increased awareness of workers and the projection of a series of requirements which in their entirety challenge the status quo and cannot be accepted by the capitalists. This does not mean that individual transitional demands cannot at certain stages be accepted (when capitalism feels strong), but this in itself leads to an escalation of demands by workers. The Transitional Programme of the Fourth International, which was written by Trotsky, explains very clearly what this approach entails:

> Classical Social Democracy, functioning in an epoch of progressive capitalism, divided its program into two parts independent of each other: the *minimum program* which limited itself to reforms within the framework of bourgeois society, and the *maximum program* which promised substitution of socialism for capitalism in the indefinite future. Between the minimum and the maximum program no bridge existed. And indeed Social Democracy has no need of such a bridge, since the word *socialism* is used only for holiday speechifying. The Comintern has set out to follow the path of Social Democracy in an epoch of decaying capitalism: when, in general, there can be no discussion of systematic social reforms and the raising of the masses' living standards; when every serious demand of the proletariat and even every serious demand of the petty bourgeoisie inevitably reaches beyond the limits of capitalist property relations and of the bourgeois state.[13]

The transitional demand par excellence is the demand for workers' control, which history has shown to be valid, and which has awakened a certain response inside the workers' movement itself. This explains partially why the bourgeoisie has tried to deflect this demand by talk of workers' participation and by even offering workers seats on boards of directors, etc. The early response to the Institute for Workers' Control revealed very clearly the interest of shop stewards in this concept. But the Institute failed to deliver the goods; by restricting the concept to industry, failing to provide a political lead, and by trying to

---

[13] *The Death Agony of Capitalism and the Tasks of the Fourth International* — 'the *Transitional Programme*', first published in New York, 1938.

provide a left cover for the left-wing social-democratic trade-union leaders Jack Jones, Lawrence Daly and, notably, Hugh Scanlon, they brought about an impasse. The need to build a workers' control movement, therefore, still remains an important priority because apart from the obvious reasons it would provide the ideal base for the interaction of the different sectors in which revolutionaries are engaged today. When workers' control and the shop stewards who support it develop to such an extent that in certain conjunctural situations factory occupations begin to take place, then a real challenge to capitalist property relations takes place and dual power becomes a reality. However, the institutionalization of workers' control can only take place after a revolution when workers' self-management becomes or should become the norm not only in industry but in society as a whole. In the conditions of neo-capitalist Western Europe this is a very real possibility after a revolutionary seizure of power.[14]

V

The controversy regarding the Common Market negotiations, whether it involves the C.P., Enoch Powell, the Tories or the Labour Party, is today couched in the gentlest of terms. This condition will harm British agriculture, that condition will create venereal disease in New Zealand, etc. The reason why Britain is being forced into the Common Market is totally ignored—because few of the parties involved in the debate would like to admit that British capitalism is really crumbling and desperately needs support. The Common Market offers a better choice than a take-over by the multinational corporations of the U.S.A. For the revolutionary movement the antics of the British bourgeoisie are of interest only insofar as they affect the working-class movement. Because the Common Market would

[14] Cf. the excellent article by R. Davies, entitled 'Theories of Workers' Control', *International*, vol. 1, no. 2 (September–October 1970). See also Ernest Mandel, ed., *Controle Ouvrier, Conseils Ouvriers, Autogestion* (Maspero, Paris, 1971).

cut the living standards of the workers we are totally opposed to it as we are to monopoly capitalism nationally. We have nothing in common with the chauvinistic opposition of the C.P. which calls on all 'patriots' to oppose the entry into the Common Market. When the bourgeoisie is being forced to acknowledge that national boundaries, established in the epoch of the national bourgeois state, are outdated, the C.P. is trying to pull capitalism backwards. What a bizarre situation for a party which still has the gall to quote Marx and Lenin!

What the Common Market of the capitalists stresses is the need for the revolutionary movement to transcend national frontiers and to organize themselves internationally. This is not a new discovery. As long ago as 1902, while commenting on Plekhanov's first Draft Programme for the Russian Social Democracy, Lenin wrote:

> But the development of international exchange and the world market has established such close ties among all the nations of the world, that this great goal can be attained only through the united efforts of the proletarians of all countries. Hence the present-day working-class movement had to become, and has long become, an international movement. Russian Social-Democracy regards itself as one of the detachments of the world army of the proletariat, as part of international social democracy.[15]

A far cry from the philistines of today who, nearly seventy years later, still mock at the task of building an international movement. Today the Fourth International is attempting to do precisely that; that is why four thousand cadres assembled in Brussels in November 1970 under the banners of the F.I. to proclaim the strategy for a Red Europe; that is why the French Section of the F.I. organized an international rally to mark the centenary of the Paris Commune some months later. Why do we need to organize internationally? Because it sounds more

[15] V. I. Lenin, *Collected Works*, 45 vols. (Progress Publishers, Moscow, 1964), vol. 6, p. 24.

romantic, or because it is morally necessary? Not a bit of it. An international organization is necessitated by the law of uneven and combined development, which implies that the battle lines of the struggle between the proletariat and the bourgeoisie are not uniform and do not reproduce the international contradictions of these two forces in simple subdivisions. The front is diverse, but this diversity does not imply a geographical juxtaposition of fronts foreign to each other. On the contrary, it indicates a complex interaction between the different fronts, which are interdependent. The most elementary example is the Indo-Chinese Revolution, which has repercussions that completely transcend the geographical boundaries of Indo-China. More important, it occupies a large part of the imperialist war machine and thus prevents its efficient use elsewhere on the same scale, and in addition it weakens U.S. imperialism internally. But it is not enough merely to *affirm* the interdependence of the different sectors of struggle internationally, and say that everything influences everything else. The maximum utilization of this independence demands an international strategy which can analyse the contradictions and consciously deploy its forces accordingly. The failure of both the Soviet and the Chinese leaderships to do this demonstrates their bankruptcy better than anything else, at a time when the Vietnamese revolutionaries are being forced to bear the brunt of the burden. That is why the Vietnamese lay such stress even on simple demonstrations of solidarity, which have been organized *internationally* only by the Fourth International and its supporters. The Vietnamese understand this fact well, which is why they appeared publicly on the platform of the Fourth International in Paris in March 1971 despite the fact that this would annoy both Moscow and Peking.[16]

[16] Thus both Moscow and Peking accuse each other of being under the influence of the Fourth International. In his report to the C.P.S.U. Central Committee (April 1964), the leading Stalinist hack Suslov maintained that it was in the theses of the Fourth International that 'the source of the political wisdom of the Chinese leadership must be sought'. The Chinese, for their part, accused the Russians of the same criminality in their text 'On the Question of Stalin'.

The rapid growth in the internationalization of capital is even forcing the trade-union bureaucrats to talk in terms of internationalizing their efforts. It is a long overdue and extremely logical move, for, to give one instance, if Fords have plants all over the world, a strike in country A can be really successful if there are solidarity actions in countries B, C and D and if there is a ban on all components coming from country A in addition to a ban on overtime. The reformist C.P.s have not been capable of doing this on a European scale, the centrists don't understand the importance of it and in the face of the growing organization of capital it would seem to be the ABC of revolutionary politics today, because the 'specific national characteristics' of any revolution are only relative and not absolute. Otherwise it would be impossible to formulate any strategic rule or historical law and Marxism would be totally irrelevant. Every revolution today has international repercussions, which is one of the reasons why the United States is trying desperately to delay the victory of the Indo-Chinese people. They understand full well the effect this would have all over the world. The Indo-Chinese struggle is no more Indo-Chinese than the May events in 1968 in France were French. Can anyone deny that the seizure of power in France by the working class and the overthrow of capital would have had phenomenal repercussions throughout Western Europe: the rhythm of the revolution would have spread to the United States itself. Hence unless one is preparing to build a revolutionary International in the same way as one is struggling to build a revolutionary party nationally, by organizing revolutionary nuclei *internationally* on the basis of a common programme, one's efforts are foredoomed, particularly in the context of Western Europe today.

VI

And after the revolution? How will things be different? What guarantees do we have that it will not degenerate like the Russian one into rule by bureaucracy? The answers to these questions lie in the changed objective conditions. Western Europe today is not the same as Czarist Russia. In Britain the working class is the largest social class, there is universal literacy, etc. To imagine that a working class which made the revolution in Britain (which would require a revolutionary change in its consciousness) led by a revolutionary party would allow anyone to take away its rights and give it fewer rights than it enjoyed under capitalism, is to have a contempt for the masses in general. It is to imply they can always be manipulated. With this view we Marxists disagree. Only in exceptional conditions can the workers' rights be taken away, and the situation in Russia was exceptional in the highest degree.

A revolutionary society in Western Europe today would in reality be a society where the overthrow of capitalism would liberate the creative energies of millions of workers and other layers of society and lay the basis for the rapid achievement of socialism. But a real classless and communist society cannot be achieved while the power of United States capitalism goes unchallenged. This classless society would mean a system of government based on workers' self-management, where the workers have the right both to elect and to *recall* their representatives, where real democracy can flourish by the election of representatives on every level to local, regional and national councils in which all revolutionary parties and tendencies fight and argue for their political positions and where there is a free and uninhibited interplay of ideas on questions affecting the life of the revolution. This situation could not remain within a national boundary. It would have a lightning effect on the consciousness of millions of people in the Soviet Union and Eastern Europe and would hasten the political revolution which would establish similar norms based on a return to Leninism.

To those who demand detailed blueprints of the future society we can only say: We are not utopians who spend our time preparing blueprints while history passes us by; many new institutional forms develop in the process of struggle itself which in many cases are far more advanced than the thinking of the greatest of revolutionaries, and we have no desire to enter into a competition with the historical process. Of one thing, however, we are sure: no revolutionary society created on the ruins of neo-capitalism will be 'less free'. We have too much confidence in the masses to believe that the lessons of the degeneration of the Russian Revolution have not been learnt. It is our enemies who fear the spontaneity of the masses and will do all that is in their power to stop or damp down or deflect the mobilization of the masses. They are right, because these mobilizations are the small beginnings which could lead to major repercussions for the capitalists in the not too distant future. Capitalism has dug its own grave. Now we need a force strong enough to bury it and seal the tomb.

Postscript

The sharp turn which events have taken since this book was completed, both in Britain and on a world scale, has tended to bear out the general line of our theses. While it would be frivolous to argue that the socialist revolution in Britain is just round the corner, nevertheless it cannot be denied that recent events have served to emphasize the extremely shaky position of British capital.

The recent dollar crisis, which forced Nixon to embark on an economic war against West Germany and Japan, marks an extremely significant divide. United States capitalism has discovered that it cannot police the world, conduct counter-revolutionary wars and compete favourably with German and Japanese capital at the same time. The American bourgeoisie, like any other, defends its own class interests above all else and its blows are directed against its most formidable enemy — the American proletariat. Thus a more intensified inter-imperialist competition and the further rise of class struggles in the United States will open up new roads for the world revolution. That is why Nixon has moved to try and heal the breach with the Maoist leadership so that the latter can help preserve the status quo in the semi-colonial world as the Soviet bureaucracy has done in Western Europe. The attitude of the Chinese bureaucrats to the events in Bengal, Ceylon and the Sudan indicates that they would be prepared to play this role. The 'new Czars' are today joined by the 'new Mandarins'.

The collapse of the dollar coincides with a generalized deterioration of the international capitalist economy. This can be measured by the growing unemployment in most of the major capitalist countries. The total number of unemployed in the seven leading imperialist countries is reaching ten million. This is the highest figure since the Second World War: 5 million unemployed in the United States, 1·5 million in Italy,

1 million in Japan, over 1 million in Britain, 700,000 in Canada and 600,000 in France (only West Germany has so far managed to avoid similar levels of unemployment). In the 'depressed areas' of most of these countries, the unemployment levels are considerably higher than the national average, and in Britain this could lead to devastating effects on the political consciousness of the working class.

Thus in Scotland the average rate of unemployment is 6 per cent of the total work-force, and in the Clyde Valley area nearly half the working population is unemployed. This is the result of a deliberate running-down of certain industries in Scotland, as part of a process intended to rationalize British capital before the entry into the Common Market. While the collapse of Upper Clyde Shipbuilders (U.C.S.) has been the most dramatic, Rolls-Royce, Burrough Machines, Singers and Plessey Electronics have all made thousands of workers redundant. In this situation the example of the U.C.S. occupation could have played an extremely vital role, but the struggle was from the very start hampered by the reformist limitations of the C.P. The leading shop stewards—long-established members of the C.P.—were obsessed by the question of 'appearing respectable'. Thus the occupation became a 'work-in' resulting in increased productivity in the yards and increased profits. The shop-stewards committee was congratulated by the Tory-appointed Liquidator for their 'hard work'. Given the situation in the west of Scotland as a whole, the strategy of the C.P. should have been to extend the struggle beyond the Clyde, to involve the local population by a series of rent, rate and hire-purchase strikes, to set up Citizens' Committees composed of workers and other layers active in the localities and to prepare a General Strike in Scotland against the Tory government. This would have sharpened the tempo of the class struggle in Scotland and resulted in a big increase in the level of the political consciousness of the working class. Instead the C.P.'s reformist outlook forced it to appeal both to British capitalism and to individual capitalists in order to get them to understand the predicament of the Clydeside workers; the latter were encouraged to work harder in order to impress the capitalists.

This reactionary utopianism of the C.P. is bound to have

disastrous consequences in the coming period. It stresses once more the need for constructing a revolutionary alternative: the impotence of *all* the revolutionary groupings was only too visible as their members stood outside the yard gates attempting to sell their newspapers. They could analyse the situation, but were unable to intervene and influence its direction. Despite all the drawbacks, however, there can be no doubt that factory occupations are on the increase. This indicates that a demoralization has not set in despite the Tory onslaught. While the occupation of unprofitable factories scheduled to be closed down does not affect capitalism adversely, it is nevertheless vital for the development of workers' consciousness and will lead, in due course, to the occupation of factories more strategic to the interests of British capitalism. Clearly this development could open up vital new opportunities for the revolutionary left.

A fascinating aspect of the present conjuncture in Britain is the coming together of all the contradictions of British imperialism. The total failure of the British Army to make internment effective has led to a new phase in the development of the struggle in Ireland. The increasing number of British casualties points to an interesting fact: the Irish Republican Army (I.R.A.) — both wings — enjoys more support from the Catholic population in Northern Ireland today than it has done since the 'twenties and its popularity inside the oppressed ghettoes in the six-county Orange statelet shows no sign of diminishing. The political differentiation which is taking place inside the Republican movement could well lead to the development of a political force, which in association with revolutionary Marxist currents could pave the way for exploiting the objective situation in Southern Ireland, where a decaying Green Tory order will not be able to maintain its hegemony for much longer. The uncompleted tasks of the bourgeois-democratic revolution in Ireland — notably the question of national re-unification — can be accomplished only after a successful armed class-struggle throughout the country.

As the struggle in Ireland develops, we can be sure that it will have an impact in Britain, not least because of the large concentrations of Irish workers here who still maintain links with their native country. Thus the most urgent task confronting the revolutionary movement in Britain is to aid in the defeat of its own bourgeois class by vigorously and unconditionally defending the armed vanguard of the Irish people against British imperialism. The struggle in Ireland demands from the British revolutionary movement a display of exemplary class solidarity. Those who failed in this task nearly a century ago were denounced by Lenin, never one to mince words, as 'scoundrels and imperialists'. The same holds true today.

The crisis at present confronting the British bourgeoisie extends to all layers of society. The vicious wave of repression symbolized by the imprisonment of Purdie and Prescott on charges of 'conspiracy' for ten months (at the time of writing) without trial, the sentences inflicted on the editors of *Oz* magazine, the banning of the *Little Red Schoolbook*—all provide an interesting indicator to the thought-processes of a section of the British ruling class. The old subtlety and complacency for which the British bourgeoisie was so well known is fast disappearing. The reasons are understandable. Large numbers of students, intellectuals *and* workers are rapidly losing their faith in the old-established parliamentary institutions of British capitalism. The bourgeoisie is trying to hold back this process—this explains its paranoia with regard to 'subversive' literature directed at school students—and is bringing its repressive machinery into action. What we have seen is only the beginning. The repression will increase as working-class militancy increases and as more and more social layers begin to challenge the legitimacy of the system. Given the developments throughout Western Europe and the turn of events in the United States, coupled with the favourable balance of forces in Asia and Latin America, one can say that we shall once again see soviets in Europe in the 'seventies. Whether they lead to defeat or victory will depend on a very concrete fact: the strength of the revolutionary vanguard and the level of its organization.

October 1971   T.A.

Appendix I · The End of the Long Imperialist Boom*

In the United States since the beginning of the second world war, and in Western Europe and Japan since the postwar reconversion period, the imperialist countries have undergone a long-term economic expansion comparable to, if not exceeding, capitalism's best periods in the past.

Of course, the world context in which this expansion occurred was different from that of former times. This time, it did not go hand in hand with an extension but rather with a shrinkage of the area in which capital could freely exploit labor power. It was not an uninterrupted boom. During this period, except in West Germany, the imperialist economy experienced multiple recessions, all reminders of capitalism's inability to resolve its underlying economic contradictions. Moreover, parallel to this expanding imperialist economy was a still more rapidly growing economy in the workers states and a stagnating one in the colonial and semicolonial countries, both highlighting the crisis of the world capitalist system.

Finally, it must be remembered that the expansion in the imperialist economy, above all in Western Europe, was not automatically generated by spontaneous economic forces. To the contrary, it was a result on the one hand of the reformist and Stalinist leaderships betraying the European working class's revolutionary opportunities after the war; and, on the other hand, of massive aid from American imperialism, which

* Ninth World Congress Documents. Published as a special edition of Intercontinental Press, 1969. This is an extract from the main document entitled 'The New Rise of World Revolution'.

245

in the immediate post-war period concentrated all its energies on consolidating and reviving capitalism in Western Europe.

However, these reservations in no way detract from the scope and importance of this long-term period of expansion for the imperialist economy. The fact that the imperialist economies could enjoy such a boom even though fourteen countries had freed themselves from capitalist exploitation, that the disintegration of the colonial empires and declining colonial superprofits for the economies of the imperialist countries could go hand in hand with an exceptional expansion in these economies, must be recognized and explained.

To deny such obvious facts would not mean 'maintaining unshakable faith in the revolutionary potentialities of the working class'; it would mean transforming the grounds for such confidence—a rigorously scientific grasp of reality—into dogmatic, religious humbug unworthy of Marxism. However, to limit analysis to the *current* facts, without indicating the deep-going, long-term trends, without clarifying the basic contradictions and thus disclosing their historically limited and passing character would obviously mean falling victim to vulgar empiricism. It would mean becoming a prisoner of bourgeois and petty-bourgeois ideology which has been proclaiming in all keys that capitalism has found out how to 'stabilize' continued expansion and guarantee full employment.

In general, revolutionary Marxists have succeeded in avoiding these twin evils. They have provided an overall analysis of the causes of the long period of imperialist expansion consistent with general Marxist theory.

This expansion was generated by accelerated technological renovation spurred by an exceptionally high level of arms spending maintained continuously over two decades (three decades in the United States)—an unprecedented phenomenon in the history of capitalism. This resulted in a more thoroughgoing industrialization of most of the imperialist countries themselves, involving a veritable revolution in the social structure of countries like France, Italy, Japan and Spain, with a rapid decline in the importance of the peasantry in the population and the economy. This expansion was protected against a recurrence of grave periodic crises of overproduction through the systematic and deliberate institution of a permanent credit and monetary inflation. The boom was sustained by an enormous, unprecedented volume of debt. Overproduction was not eliminated. It was concealed, on the one hand, by buying power generated through inflation; and it was 'frozen', on the other hand, by the emergence of greater and greater excess capacity in a number of industries (coal, shipbuilding, steel, textiles, petrochemicals, and tomorrow, no doubt, automobiles).

This Marxist analysis reached three conclusions: first, that the essential motor forces of this long-term expansion would progressively exhaust themselves, in this way setting off a more and more marked intensification of interimperialist competition; secondly, that the deliberate application of Keynesian antirecessionary techniques would step up the worldwide inflation and constant erosion of the buying power of currencies, finally producing a very grave crisis in the international monetary system; thirdly, that these two factors in conjunction would give rise to increasing limited recessions, inclining the course of economic development toward a general recession of the imperialist economy. This general recession would certainly differ from the great depression of 1929 32 both in extent and duration. Nonetheless, it would strike all the imperialist countries and considerably exceed the recessions of the last twenty years. Two of these predictions have come true. The third promises to do so in the seventies.

West Germany's first real recession, in 1966 67, strikingly confirmed the inevitability of cyclical fluctuations in the capitalist economy. This recession, coinciding with Great Britain's fifth postwar recession, affected almost every country in capitalist Europe. Only Italy managed to escape because it had already had a serious cyclical downturn in 1964. This recession, the most serious in Europe since the second world war, brought the unemployed figure up to three million.

However, since it paralleled a boom in Japan and a period in
the American economy characterized by an initial boom followed by a mild short-term downturn ('an inventory-liquidation
downturn'), a general recession throughout the imperialist
world was narrowly averted.

Nonetheless, though still limited to the major countries of
capitalist Europe, this recession has already seriously sharpened
interimperialist rivalry. The devaluation of the pound sterling;
the measures taken by the Johnson administration to 'defend
the dollar'; the masked devaluation of the French franc in
November 1968; the Japanese automobile manufacturers'
invasion of the European and North American markets; the
competition between the American and European trusts within
the Common Market; capitalist Europe's own crisis of economic
integration (ostensibly provoked by the Gaullist rejection of
British membership in the Common Market, but in reality
spurred primarily by the fears and hesitations of the principal
bourgeoisies facing a general slowdown in the expansion of
the international imperialist economy)—these are the chief
manifestations of this interimperialist competition. It is heading
inevitably toward a new and more advanced phase of capital
concentration—in many instances international concentration
of capital—and thus generally tending to exacerbate excess
productive capacity, mounting debt, and declining profit rates
for the monopolistic trusts. The products of a first slowdown in
the growth rate, this competition and stepped-up capital
concentration must in turn produce a further decline in this
rate.

All these factors, therefore, are combining to erode the
foundation on which for thirty years it was possible to erect a
colossal pyramid of debt and inflation. Confidence in the international capitalist economy's two so-called 'reserve' currencies
—the dollar and the pound sterling—has been profoundly
shaken. This has tended to inhibit the expansion of international
capitalist trade and impede the expansion of the means of
international payment. Return to the gold standard is im-

possible in a declining imperialist world at grips with powerful anticapitalist forces. It would risk provoking an economic crisis too great for the system to bear.

But at the same time, continuing international inflation collides more and more sharply with the interests of a growing section of the international bourgeoisie. Growing lack of confidence in the dollar tends increasingly to cut back the expansion of international liquidity at a time when such expansion is urgently needed to revive the boom. This contradiction is pointed up by the failure of the New Delhi Conference and the imperialist countries' inability to increase their 'aid' to the semicolonial countries (which is primarily aid to their own export industries), coming in conjunction as it does with the first signs that the expansion of trade among the imperialist countries is running out of steam.

Doubtless, American imperialism still commands sufficient reserves and resources to continue using Keynesian techniques in the United States for some time without mounting a direct assault on the living standards of the American working class. But the pressures on it to put an end to its chronic balance-of-payments deficit are becoming so great that an important restraint has been put on the inflationary expansion of the world monetary system. This increasingly general deflationary pressure is imposing a common monetary and financial discipline on a growing number of imperialist countries, which is to a large extent independent of the economic policies their changing governments select. Thus, they are being drawn one after the other into a general current which will carry them toward a general recession in a few years.

One of the imperialist economy's most striking features since the second world war has been the absence of an international synchronization of recessions. The American recessions of 1949, 1953, 1957, and 1960, which had more or less immediate repercussions for the British economy and the economies of a whole series of lesser imperialist countries, coincided with a sustained boom in West Germany. The Japanese recession did not come until 1965, when the French and Italian economies were already on the upturn. And the German and British recessions of 1966–67 were accompanied by a boom in Italy and Japan and at least partial maintenance of the high economic cycle in the United States.

This diffusion of recessions in time and space has clearly tended to moderate the extent and duration of business downturns, an increase in exports compensating in every instance for drop in sales on the domestic market. The causes of this situation lay in the fact that while in the last analysis recessions follow from a decline in productive investment, that is, the emergence of excess capacity or 'frozen' overproduction, their immediate causes lie in governmental measures — credit restrictions and deflationary policies aimed either at balancing international payments or 'dampening an overheated economy', or both at once. It was the general expansionist tendency and international inflation together that made possible this widespread monetary and financial manipulation in the imperialist world.

These two stimuli have already begun to weaken, considerably reducing every imperialist government's margin for maneuver. The Wilson government learned this to its cost when international finance virtually rammed down its throat a devaluation insufficient to enable the British bourgeoisie to win back their lost international markets. Because of the close international collaboration among central banks, the decline in these two stimuli is tending to result in the imposition of increasingly rigid monetary discipline. This is producing a tightening coordination of the monetary policies of the principal imperialist countries, which will sooner or later make inevitable a synchronization of economic recessions.

The synchronization of economic recessions is rooted in the productive process itself. It reflects, in the last analysis, the growing internationalization of capital, the levels of productivity and competitiveness among the different imperialist economies becoming evened out. In these conditions margins for monetary and financial maneuvers shrink considerably.

Every maneuver, whether deflation, monetary devaluation, or protectionism, immediately brings on negative consequences for the economies of the other imperialist countries and prompts them to take a similar course. In fact, the close collaboration among the central banks expresses on a conscious level the objective inability of the imperialist countries, even the strongest of them, to escape simultaneously the imperatives of inter-imperialist competition and the monetary retaliation inevitably provoked by any attempt to improve their own competitive position with the aid of financial expedients.

Historically there are more profound causes for the approaching end of the long-range expansion in the international imperialist economy from 1940 to 1965 than monetary problems, credit systems, or the interventionist policies of bourgeois states. It signifies that the contradiction between the expansion of the productive forces and the braking role of private appropriation, which capitalism was able to repress for a whole period with the help of temporary expedients, is emerging to the surface again in a powerful way. The efficacy of these expedients is waning. The stimulus of permanent inflation is being neutralized by the negative effects of this inflation on world trade. The stimulating effects of arms production are declining at a time when it has reached colossal proportions. Reviving the boom would require a new hike in military spending which even the American economy can no longer sustain. The more and more pronounced relative impoverishment of the semicolonial countries constantly reduces the fraction of the total industrial production of the imperialist countries which they can absorb. However, trade between the imperialist countries, which grew enormously during the long period of expansion, is increasingly restricted by interimperialist competition and by progressive equalization of the technical level among all the imperialist countries.

To sum up, the enormous productive capacity built up in these countries is coming into conflict more and more with the needs of capital realization. Only the expanding economy of the workers states might offer a temporary safety valve. But, although rising constantly, their trade with the imperialist countries is still too small to put the brakes on a general recession. The limitations on this trade, due to both the workers states' very meagre export potential and the general international context which makes long-term credits very risky, will not be overcome to any great extent in the near future.

Appendix II · Lenin on the Labour Party

(*Speech on the Labour Party at the Second Comintern Congress,* 1920)

Comrade Gallacher began his speech by expressing regret that we were compelled for the hundredth and thousandth time to listen to phrases that Comrade McLaine, and other English comrades have repeated a thousand times in their speeches and articles. I do not think we need regret this. The method of the old International was to leave such questions to be decided by the separate parties in the countries interested. This was fundamentally wrong. It is quite possible that we do not always clearly understand the mutual relationships prevailing in this or that country, but what we are discussing here is the formulation of the tactics of the Communist Party. This is very important and we, in the name of the Third International, must expound here the genuine Communist point of view.

First of all I want to observe that Comrade McLaine was guilty of a slight inaccuracy with which it is impossible to agree. He calls the Labour Party the political organization of the trade-union movement. Later on he repeated this when he said: the Labour Party 'is the political expression of the trade-union movement'. I have read the same expression of opinion in the organ of the British Socialist Party. It is not true and partly is the cause of the opposition, to a certain degree justified, of the British revolutionary workers. Indeed, the concept: 'the political organization of the trade-union movement', or the 'political expression' of this movement, is mistaken. Of course, for the most part the Labour Party consists of workers, but it does not follow logically from this that every workers' party which consists of workers is at the same time a 'political workers' party'; that depends upon who leads it, upon the content of its activities and of its political tactics. Only the latter determines whether it is really a political proletarian party. From this point of view, which is the only correct point of view, the Labour Party is not a political workers' party but a thoroughly bourgeois party, because, although it consists of workers, it is led by reactionaries, and the worst reactionaries at that, who lead it in the spirit of the bourgeoisie and with the aid of the British Noskes and Scheidemans they systematically deceive the workers.

But we have heard another point of view expressed by Comrade Sylvia Pankhurst and Comrade Gallacher. What was the substance of the speech delivered by Comrade Gallacher and those of many of his friends? They told us that we were not sufficiently connected with the masses. Take the British Socialist Party, for example, it is still very badly connected with the masses and very weak. Comrade Gallacher told us here how he and his comrades have organized a very successful movement in Scotland and how during the war they manœuvred very successfully, supported the petty-bourgeois pacifists Ramsay MacDonald and Snowden, and with their aid organized a mass movement against the war in Glasgow.

Our aim is precisely to lead this successful, new, revolutionary movement represented here by Comrade Gallacher and his friends into a Communist Party with real, i.e. Marxian tactics. That is our task at the present time. On the one hand, we see that the British Socialist Party is weak and is not very well adapted for carrying on agitation among the masses; on the other hand, we see the younger revolutionary elements so well represented here by Comrade Gallacher, who, although in close contact with the masses, are not very experienced in organizing political work and do not represent a political party, and in this sense they are even weaker than the British Socialist

Party. Under these circumstances we must quite frankly express
our point of view regarding the correct tactics to be pursued.
When in speaking of the British Socialist Party, Comrade
Gallacher said that it is 'hopelessly reformist', he undoubtedly
exaggerated. But the general sense and content of the resolutions
we have adopted here absolutely definitely show that we
demand a change in the tactics of the British Socialist Party in
this spirit, and the only correct tactics of the friends of Gallacher
would be to join the Communist Party without delay for the
purpose of straightening out its tactics in the spirit of the resolutions that have been adopted here. If you have so many adher-
ents in Glasgow that you are able to organize mass meetings,
it will not be difficult for you to increase the influx of new
members into the party by more than ten thousand. The last
Congress of the British Socialist Party which took place in
London three or four days ago decided to change the party into
a Communist Party and adopted points in its programme about
participating in parliamentary elections and about affiliating
to the Labour Party. At the Congress ten thousand organized
members were represented. Therefore, it would not be difficult
for the Scottish comrades to recruit for this 'Communist Party
of Great Britain' another ten thousand revolutionary workers
who would be better able to carry work on among the masses
and who, instead of the old tactics of the British Socialist Party,
would advance more certain methods of agitation in the sense
of more revolutionary action. Comrade Sylvia Pankhurst,
several times in the commission, said that England required
'lefts'. Of course, I replied that this was absolutely true, but
that one must take care not to be too 'left'. Furthermore she
said that 'We are good pioneers, but for the moment we are
making more noise than anything else'. I interpret this in a
good sense; I think they mean that they are able to carry on
good revolutionary agitation. We prize this and should prize it.
We expressed this in all our resolutions and emphasized that
we shall be a recognized party, and particularly recognized as a
workers' party, only if we are really connected with the masses

and will fight against the old, thoroughly decayed leaders, against the right-wing chauvinists, as well as those who take up a centrist position like the Right Independents in Germany. In all our revolutions we repeated this ten times and more, and by that we emphasized that when we say reforming the old party we mean establishing closer contacts with the masses.

Sylvia Pankhurst also asked: 'Is it permissible for a Communist Party to join a political party that is affiliated to the Second International?' I replied that it was not. It must be borne in mind that the British Labour Party finds itself in particularly peculiar conditions: It is a very peculiar party, or more correctly, it is not a party in the ordinary sense of the word. It is made up of all the trade unions, which now have a membership of about four million, and allows sufficient liberty to all the political parties affiliated to it. The majority of British workers who still follow the lead of bourgeois elements, of social-traitors who are worse than Scheideman and Noske and gentlemen of that ilk, belong to the Labour Party. But at the same time the Labour Party allows the British Socialist Party to remain in its ranks, allows it to have its own organ of the press in which the members of this very Labour Party can freely and openly declare that the leaders of the party are social-traitors. Comrade McLaine gave exact quotation from such declarations made by the British Socialist Party. I too can certify that in *The Call*, the organ of the British Socialist Party, I have read statements to the effect that the leaders of the Labour Party are social-patriots and social-traitors. This shows that a party affiliated to the Labour Party is not only able to criticize sharply, but is able openly and definitely to name the old leaders and to call them social-traitors. This is a very peculiar situation in which a party which unites an enormous mass of workers, and which is a political party, is nevertheless obliged to allow its members complete liberty. Comrade McLaine has stated here that at the Labour Party Conference the British Scheidemans were obliged to openly raise the question of affiliation to the Third International and that all

the local organizations and sections were obliged to discuss this
question. Under such circumstances it would be a mistake not
to affiliate to this party.

In private conversation with me, Comrade Pankhurst said:
'If we remain real revolutionaries and affiliate to the Labour
Party these gentlemen will expel us.' But this would not be a
bad thing at all. In our resolution we say that we are in favour
of affiliation in so far as the Labour Party allows sufficient
freedom of criticism. In that point we are absolutely consistent.
Comrade McLaine has already emphasized that such peculiar
conditions prevail in England at the present time that a political
party, if it wishes to, may remain a revolutionary workers'
party, notwithstanding the fact that it is connected with a
labour organization of four million which is half trade union
and half political party and which is led by bourgeois leaders.
Under such circumstances it would be a great mistake if the
revolutionary elements did not do all that was possible to
remain in such a party. Let Messrs Thomas and the other
social-traitors, whom you call social-traitors, expel you. This
will have an excellent effect upon the masses of the British
workers.

The comrades also say the aristocracy of labour in England
is stronger than in any other country. That is really so. Why,
in England it has existed not for decades, but for a century!
In England, the bourgeoisie, which has had experience, managed to bribe the workers and to create among them a wide
stratum, wider in England than in any other country, but which
is not so wide after all when compared with the broad mass of
the workers. This stratum is thoroughly imbued with bourgeois
prejudices and pursues a definitely bourgeois, reformist policy.
Thus, in Ireland, we see two hundred thousand English soldiers
who by frightful terror are suppressing the Irish. The English
Socialists are not carrying on any revolutionary propaganda
among them. But in our resolutions we say that we permit the
affiliation to the Communist International only to those parties
which conduct real revolutionary propaganda among the

British workers and soldiers. I emphasize that neither here nor in the commissions have we heard any objection to this.

Comrade Gallacher and Sylvia Pankhurst cannot deny this. They cannot deny the fact that while remaining in the ranks of the Labour Party the British Socialist Party enjoys sufficient liberty to write that such and such leaders of the Labour Party are traitors, champions of the interests of the bourgeoisie and their agents in the labour movement; this is absolutely true. When Communists enjoy such liberty, then, taking into account the experience of the revolution in all countries, and not only Russia (for we here are not at a Russian, but at an international congress), it is their duty to affiliate to the Labour Party. Comrade Gallacher ironically said that we were under the influence of the British Socialist Party. That is not true; we became convinced of this by the experience of all revolutions in all countries. We think that we must tell this to the masses. The British Communist Party must preserve for itself sufficient liberty to expose and criticize before the workers the traitors who are more powerful in England than in any other country. This is not difficult to understand. Comrade Gallacher is wrong when he says that by advocating affiliation to the Labour Party we will repel the best elements of the British workers. We must test this by experience.

We are convinced that all the resolutions and decisions that will be adopted by this Congress will be published in all the British revolutionary socialist newspapers and that all the local organizations and sections will be given the opportunity to discuss them. The general content of our resolutions quite clearly shows that we are the representatives of revolutionary tactics in all countries and that our aim is to fight the old reformism and opportunism. Events are showing that our tactics are indeed defeating the old reformism. And then all the best revolutionary elements in the working class who are dissatisfied with the slow progress of development which in England, perhaps, will be slower than in other countries, will come over to us. Development is slow because the British bourgeoisie is in a position to create better conditions for the aristocracy of labour and by that retard the progress of the revolution. That is why the British comrades should strive not only to revolutionize the masses, which they are doing excellently (Comrade Gallacher has proved that), but must simultaneously also strive to create a real working-class political party. Neither Comrade Gallacher nor Comrade Sylvia Pankhurst, who have both spoken here, belong to a revolutionary communist party yet. That excellent proletarian organization, Shop Stewards' Committees, does not yet belong to a political party. If you organize politically you will find that our tactics are based on the properly understood political development of the past ten years, that a real revolutionary party can be created only when it absorbs the best elements of the revolutionary class and takes advantage of every opportunity to fight against the reactionary leaders wherever they reveal themselves.

If the British Communist Party starts out by acting in a revolutionary manner in the Labour Party and if Messrs Henderson are obliged to expel this Party, it will be a great victory for the Communist and labour movement in England.